THE
Hot Dog
COMPANION

❧

THE Hot Dog COMPANION

A Connoisseur's Guide
to the Food We Love

DAVID GRAULICH

LEBHAR-FRIEDMAN BOOKS
NEW YORK

Lebhar-Friedman Books
A company of Lebhar-Friedman Inc.
425 Park Avenue
New York, New York 10022

Library of Congress Cataloging-in-Publication data
Graulich, David J.
The hot dog companion : a connoisseur's guide to the food we love / David Graulich.
   p.   cm.
ISBN 0-86730-761-7 (cloth : hc.)
1. Cookery (Frankfurters). 2. Cookery, American.
3. Frankfurters—Anecdotes. I. Title.
TX749.G78   1999
641.6'62—dc21   98-55742
CIP

BOOK DESIGN BY KEVIN HANEK
COMPOSITION BY MILLER-WILLIAMS
SET IN ADOBE MINION

Manufactured in the United States of America on acid-free paper
99   00   01   02   10   9   8   7   6   5   4   3   2   1

In memory of my mother,

Estelle Graulich, who loved music,

laughter, and good food

CONTENTS

THE
Hot Dog
COMPANION

Chapter One

HOT DOG AMERICA

The hot dog is a twin pillar of democracy along with Mom's apple pie.
– WILLIAM ZINSSER

ITHIN THE AMERICAN collective memory is a prototypical urban scene, which looks like something out of a Fox Movietone newsreel or the Depression-era photographs of Berenice Abbott. This dreamlike scene is populated by a repertory cast of characters: the wise-cracking cab driver, the imperious hotel doorman, the screeching newsboy. The produce merchant fusses over his sidewalk stands of melons and tomatoes. . . . a broad-shouldered, nightstick-twirling cop walks the beat, whistling.

Over at the intersection of Grand Avenue and Main Street, at the southwest corner a few strides from the bus stop, is a hot-dog vendor with a pushcart. The vendor is shielded from the wind and sun by an umbrella that's a shade of red, yellow, or orange that once was vivid and jaunty, but now, after a decade or so of accumulated dirt and smoke, is the color of flat soda pop. A sign under the umbrella proclaims the brand of hot dog that the vendor sells—great names with local appeal, like Sabrett in New York or Vienna in Chicago. The

Real hot dogs do dance: A sign photographed near Hatteras, North Carolina

A classic part of the urban American landscape is the hot-dog vendor,
selling local brands, such as New York's Sabrett

man at the cart, who has the
earnest, harried manner of any
small entrepreneur, banters with
patrons while juggling an intricate
assemblage of dogs and coins and
soda and sauerkraut and relish and

napkins. In the cold weather the
vendor is barely visible behind the
haze of steam rising from the cart.

There's a stream of customers
from all niches and rhythms of the
city's life. Stockbrokers wolf down

their franks and chatter about the day's market action. Office workers flirt and gossip while waiting for their orders, which they affectionately refer to as "dirty water dogs." A short, muscular guy with *The Daily Racing Form* under his arm—an ex- stretched hand as they scurry to beat the traffic light. A bus driver yells out the window for a dog with relish and kraut. The ex-jockey finishes his hot dog and gets on the bus. Boys and girls in their parochial-school uniforms march

Salesmen demand a dog, hurriedly pay, and run off, grabbing the frankfurter like a baton.

jockey?—eats his dog in silence at the bus stop. Shoppers laden with bags from the big downtown department stores are pausing for refreshments. A bicycle messenger pedals away with his lunch. Salesmen racing between appointments demand a dog, hurriedly pay, and run off, grabbing the frankfurter like a baton from the vendor's out- up and buy hot dogs in waves of crimson and green and gray.

That's the magic of the hot dog. It plays on memories and nostalgic cravings so subtly that we hardly realize how hard it is tugging at our heart strings. Baseball games, Fourth of July picnics, Cub Scout camp fires, lifeguards' lunches at the suburban swim club, late-night chow runs from the frosh dorm—all have the hot dog in common. The dog will not be denied.

"I'll be driving, and I'll pass the Berkeley exit where the university is," says my friend Steve, a pension consultant who lives near San Francisco. "Suddenly, my mouth is watering, because I start thinking about Top Dog, the hot-dog stand near campus where I used to go all the time in grad school. I'm on the freeway, and I'm not even hungry, and all of a sudden I can just taste that wonderful hot dog." GraceAnn

The bemused, behatted frankfurter in Top Dog's logo is an eagerly sought icon for hungry students at the University of California, Berkeley

Walden, a writer who grew up in the New York City area, recalls that Northern New Jersey has a delicacy called "an Italian hot-dog sandwich": half a pita bread is stuffed with two griddled dogs, fried potatoes, mustard, ketchup, peppers, and onions. "Oh my youth! Oh the heartburn!" she says.

"My husband and I are from Rochester, New York," says Lynn Pribus, who now lives in Fair Oaks, California. "When I was growing up, and you asked for a hot dog, you were asked, 'Red or white?' The reds were the 'normal' hot dogs. The whites were some sort of bratwurst. If you had a cookout, you always had a package of 'white hots.' It was a regional habit you hate to let go of—like dark-brewed Genesee beer, available only in October. My sister-in-law, who still lives in Rochester, says that white hots are also called zwiegle hots, and that a summer is not complete without them."

and his wife, Debbie, are parents of twins Ethan and Benjamin. "There is no greater joy for a father than taking your children to the ball park and having your kids eat hot dogs, while you reminisce about how you did exactly the same thing with

> *"There is no greater joy for a father than taking your children to the ball park and having your kids eat hot dogs, exactly as you did with your dad and grandfather."*
>
> – SCOTT DAVIS

Scott Davis is president of a Chicago management consulting firm, and his hot-dog affinity began as a teenager, when he had a part-time job with a Chicago chain called Irving's for Red Hot Lovers. Today, Davis views the hot dog through a different perspective—he

your dad and grandfather," Davis says. "I took my boys to Wrigley Field to watch the Chicago Cubs. All they could talk about afterwards was how they wanted to go back to see Sammy Sosa and eat hot dogs."

There's a Web site where Internet-savvy hot-dog aficionados

"The World Famous Hot Dog Page" Internet web site

nominate the world's best hot dogs (www.xroadsmall.com/tcs/hot-dog/best.html). Resonating through all of the impassioned opinions are currents of discovery, estrangement, and redemption, such as this post from Mark D.:

> Arnie's Hot Dog House in Whiting, Indiana, has the best dogs I have ever had. They are one mile from Chicago on Route 41. I now live in Portland, Oregon, and there are not any hot dogs even close to those I grew up with. I go home once or twice a year, and I always stop at Arnie's. I have not had one bad meal there in 20 years. I cannot wait to go back home to have another. I better go now; my mouth is watering.

There was this plaintive request from John D.:

> I moved to Virginia 10 years ago and miss Shickhaus Hot Dogs from New

Jersey. Can you send me the address of the Shickhaus Company in New Jersey? Thank you.

Another contributor, going by the handle "littlefarm," made this suggestion:

I grew up in Reno, Nevada. The best hot dog, along with the best pastrami sandwich, was at the Sierra Turf Club. This was a racehorse bookie joint across the alley from a casino and next door to a pawn shop. The floors were littered with betting slips, newspapers, etc., and I would sneak in the back door and order a hot dog to go—heavy on the mustard, extra kraut and pickle relish. I'm sure that by today's standards, my best hot dog wasn't any better than your best hot dog because, you see, it wasn't the hot dog. It was the atmosphere, or as they say, the ambience. Remember when you eat the best hot dog to take a minute to look around, where you are and who you're

with—that's the best hot dog, so enjoy it.

In an era when food drifts relentlessly upscale, the hot dog is a refusenik. It refuses to be yuppiefied, prettified, or gentrified. If the hot dog were played by an actor, I'd cast Dennis Franz, who plays the gruff, no-nonsense detective Andy Sipowicz on the television series *NYPD Blue*. "The hot dog is a twin pillar of democracy along with Mom's apple pie," says essayist William Zinsser. "In fact, now that Mom's apple pie comes frozen and baked by somebody who isn't Mom, the hot dog stands alone." Kelly Alexander, writing in the magazine *Food & Wine*, admires the craftsmanship of hot dogs, especially among smaller, local producers: "It's reassuring to know that small family-run companies are quietly producing items of quality. . . . there's no need to look beyond that humblest of foods, the hot dog."

Jeff Smith, host of a public television cooking series, professed his hot-dog enthusiasm in his book *The Frugal Gourmet Cooks American*:

I have had parties at my home in which I serve nothing but Chicago hot dogs with all the condiments. People on the West Coast are surprised by such a wonderful meal.

Junk food this is not. It is a hot dog and fine salad on a bun.

Burt Wolf, the New York food writer and restaurateur, adds: "It has been said that the most loyal and most noble dog of all is the hot dog—it feeds the hand that bites it."

This book is a celebration, consideration, and appreciation of the hot dog. From a personal point of

No American childhood is complete without a day at the ball park, including a between-innings break for hot dogs

view, writing this book has sparked a rediscovery of the pleasures of eating hot dogs. I enjoyed them as a child in New Jersey, often sliced into wedges and mixed with baked beans, with thick slices of rye bread and a bottle of Canada Dry ginger ale. In the summer a day at the Jersey shore, in towns like Long Branch and Belmar, would conclude with char-broiled hot dogs from The Windmill, Max's, or The Flame. As a stalwart saxophonist in the Marlboro High School Mustang Marching Band, I gleefully ate rubbery, lukewarm franks sold by the Spirit Club at football games, usually managing to get a nice mustard stain on my band uniform.

In college hot dogs were an inexpensive and fast meal at the snack bar, particularly in those vast and hungry hours of the late afternoon, after classes ended but before the student cafeteria served dinner. If I scooped enough relish and mustard on top of the boiled hot dog, I felt tolerably full. In my 20s, as a bachelor, hot dogs were a typical repast while I was watching Monday Night Football or a typical meal after coming home from a business trip and bleakly looking into a vacant refrigerator before seeing, with delight, the resilient package of hot dogs in the freezer.

Then came a parting of the ways. I got married, and my wife, a native Californian, is more likely to eat a veggie burrito with rice and a mango for dessert than any kind of meat. My curiosity led me to more adventurous foods and exotic cuisines. As my career developed, business meals revolved around pasta and sushi and blackened swordfish. I'd encounter the occasional miniature cocktail frank— confusingly called pig-in-a-blanket—at a wedding reception, and I'd eat one or two to stave off my appetite while I was waiting impatiently for the bridal party to finish taking pictures (some people cry at weddings; I get hungry). Other times, while racing to catch a flight

Hot Dog Terms...

"Dirty water" method—Hot dogs are heated in water and replaced by unheated ones when served. Soon the water is permeated with concentrated hot dog flavoring, and becomes "dirty" with flavor.

"Drag through the garden"—To top a hot dog with relish and vegetables.

"Dress the dog, not the bun" —Toppings should be placed on the hot dog already in the bun, not on the bun beneath the hot dog.

Frankfurters—A sausage made of beef and pork, all beef, or poultry, which is cured, smoked, and fully cooked.

To Hot-Dog—To go very fast, show off, or perform fancy feats. A surfing term.

Ketchup (or catsup)—A condiment that is used on hot dogs only by the unenlightened.

connection or waiting out a delay in the arid stretches of an airport, I would devour a frankfurter, usually eating it too hurriedly and regretting it later. Overall, however, the hot dog disappeared from my culinary life.

My work on *The Hot Dog Companion* has reintroduced the dog and me, and a reconciliation has flowered. I'm enjoying hot dogs again, not only as a snack or as a meal of last resort but also on their own merits as tempting, rich, and satisfying food. There's a nostalgia factor in all this, to be sure, but there's also the sheer pleasure of savoring the basic hot dog as a delicious, honest food.

Before going any further, let's establish some ground rules. Most of us use the phrases "hot dogs" and "frankfurters" interchangeably, but there is a difference. A hot dog is a frankfurter on a bun. Sharon Tyler Herbst delineates the specifics in her book, *The Food Lover's Companion*:

hot dog—The term for one of America's favorite sandwiches, which consists of a frankfurter in an oblong-shaped bun with any of various toppings, including mustard, ketchup, pickle relish, cheese, sauerkraut and beans. Regular hot dogs are about six inches long, while they are also available in foot-long versions. Among the many aliases for hot dogs are *wiener dog, frankfurter, frank* and *tube steak*.

By the power vested in me as author (one of the few perks of the job), I'll confine this expedition to hot dogs that are made from beef, pork, or a combination of the two. True, a plethora of other main ingredients are available: chicken dogs, sometimes called barking birds; turkey dogs; veggie dogs; tofu dogs; and other variations that fall under the general rubric of "Not Dogs." With all due respect to the chemical engineering and good intentions behind these pseudo-franks, I'm sticking with the genuine items.

Night has fallen over our prototypical city scene. The crush of homebound commuters is easing—seats actually are available now on the bus. The schoolchildren are home, eating dinner. The produce stand is closed, and a different cop walks the night beat. The hot-dog vendor takes down the umbrella, packs up the inventory, and rolls the pushcart back to a warehouse, which could be either an industrial storage area or the garage of his apartment building. In the morning it will be back to the corner of Grand and Main for a new day of work in Hot Dog America.

Chapter Two

FRANK FACTS & HOT DOG DATA

OTHER THAN WITH MUSTARD and relish, hot dogs seem happiest when they are accompanied by an assortment of data, facts, and trivia. Let's start with a look at the consumption statistics:

- Americans consume an average of 60 hot dogs per person annually.

- People who cook hot dogs at home tend to be women, 25 to 44 years old, married with school-age children, and concentrated in the Southeastern region of the country and in small towns and rural areas.

- Hot dogs are eaten most frequently between Memorial Day and Labor Day.

- Larger families, with five or more members, eat larger numbers of hot dogs, as do younger families, where heads of households are younger than 35 years old.

- The total of all hot-dog production in the United States is

A classic rainy day lunch—a hot dog served with macaroni and cheese and pickles

HOT DOG PRODUCTION
(2 BILLION POUNDS PER YEAR)

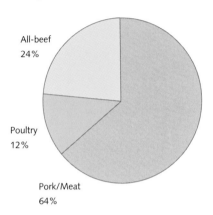

All-beef
24%

Poultry
12%

Pork/Meat
64%

snack bar/hot dog stand, park, and beach.

🖎 Every second of every day of every year, 450 hot dogs are eaten in the United States.

🖎 In 1997 the average household spent about $12.55 to purchase 7.65 pounds of hot dogs.

approximately 2 billion pounds a year. Of that total, 64 percent are pork/meat combinations, 24 percent are all-beef, and 12 percent are poultry.

🖎 The dollar value of all retail hot-dog sales is about $1.5 billion a year.

🖎 The majority of hot dogs are eaten in the home, followed, in descending order of frequency, at a barbecue, baseball game,

Now let's look at those famous side dishes that provide the individualistic signature on top of the hot dog:

🖎 Mustard is the most popular topping, followed by ketchup, chili, and sauerkraut.

🖎 Preference in toppings appears to follow demographic lines, according to a survey commissioned by Hebrew National. Older wiener lovers—55 to 64 years old—prefer mustard, while young hot dog eaters—18 to 34—designate ketchup as their topping of choice. Almost two-thirds of hot-dog eaters surveyed like two or more toppings. Of the favorites, sauerkraut is declining in popularity, while ketchup, onions, relish, mustard, and chili top the list (as well as the dog).

Mustard is the most popular topping for hot dogs

❧ Regional variations on the basic hot dog are the Chicago dog—poppyseed bun, relish, onions, and tomatoes; Kansas Dogs—melted cheese; and Baltimore Dogs—split and deep-fried.

Baseball and hot dogs are two American classics that have a shared history as well as a joint affinity for statistics:

❧ During baseball season, four out of every 10 fans will buy a hot dog. That results in more than 26 million hot dogs consumed at baseball games. If those hot dogs were laid end to end, they could reach from Yankee Stadium in New York to Dodger Stadium in Los Angeles.

❧ More than 2.2 million Dodger Dogs are sold each year at Los Angeles Dodger baseball games. The Dodgers lead the major leagues in hot-dog sales, followed by the Cleveland Indians at Jacobs Field, who sell just over 2 million.

Their team may not always win the pennant, but Los Angeles baseball fans at Dodger Stadium lead the major leagues in consumption of hot dogs, known as Dodger Dogs

Like other major industries, the hot-dog business has its own jargon, statistics, research reports, and analysis:

　According to All American Hotdog Carts of Miami Beach, Florida, it takes from $2,000 to $5,000 of start-up capital for someone to enter the hot-dog business. The typical person buying a pushcart is in the 45-to-55 age bracket, and either is tired of working for someone else, has been fired from another job, or is taking early retirement. A hot-dog vendor in a good location earns $30,000 to $35,000 a year, while the busiest vendors earn $65,000 annually.

The cost per hot dog to the vendor is about 25 cents. The typical retail price of a hot dog is $1.25 although it can reach $2 in major cities.

Dressing a hot dog with relish and vegetables is known as "dragging it through the garden."

In the convenience-store industry, the most popular day of the year for hot-dog sales is Christmas.

The most popular hot dog size in the United States is 6 inches long.

About 10 percent of hot dogs have casings (skins). The remainder are skinless.

O'Hare International Airport, Chicago, is the record-holder for most hot dogs sold at a single location. In a typical year 1.5 million hot dogs are sold at O'Hare.

The composition of a standard hot dog is 85-percent meat, 10-percent water, 2.5-percent salt, and 2.5-percent spices and curing agents.

After bewildering several generations of Americans by selling hot dogs 10 to a pack—a mismatch with buns, which are usually sold eight to the pack—manufacturers now are selling hot dogs in packages of four, six, eight, and 10.

In 1998 Sara Lee introduced single franks, each sold in its own airtight plastic wrap and ready for 20 seconds of microwaving, wrapper and all. The *Wall Street Journal* said the new product was intended "for people too busy to boil water."

- The motto of the Star Manufacturing Company of St. Louis, which makes a leading line of steamers, broilers, bun warmers, and grills, is: "When it comes to dogs we're the masters."

Lodge Farms of Norval, Canada. In 1978 David Berg of Chicago made a 6-foot, 681-pound hot dog in a 100-pound poppy-seed bun covered with two gallons of mustard.

- The town of Frankfort, Indiana, celebrates a Hot Dog Festival every summer on the last Saturday in July. The celebra-

Corn dogs were invented by Neil Fletcher at the 1942 Texas State Fair.

Finally, here's an anything-goes grab bag of hot dog trivia and esoterica:

- Contenders for the title "World's Largest Hot Dog" are a 1,983-footer made by Bil-Mar Foods of Zeeland, Wisconsin, in 1983 and a 2,377-foot chicken dog made in 1985 by Maple

tion features a Hot Dog Golf tournament, a 4-mile Bun Run and Walk, and a Stray Dog Street Dance, with music by Duke Tumatoe and the Power Trio. The cartoon festival's mascot is Frankie, a very large, smiling hot dog wearing a baseball cap emblazoned with the letter "F."

The Russian fondness for hot dogs predates the collapse of the
Soviet Union. Former Soviet Premier Nikita Khruschev lustily enjoyed
a hot dog in Des Moines, Iowa, during his 1959 tour of the U.S.

Regional Hot Dog Variations...

Baltimore Dog—Hot dogs that are split and deep fried.

Boston Bull Dog—A hot dog topped with baked beans and BBQ sauce.

Chicago Style—A hot dog served with mustard, green relish, raw onions, tomatoes, a kosher dill pickle wedge, peppers, topped with celery salt, served on a steamed poppy seed bun.

Coney Island Dogs—A hot dog topped with chili, onions, and cheese.

Junk Yard Dog—A hot dog with mustard, coleslaw, sweet relish, hot relish, and chopped tomatoes.

Kansas City Dog—A hot dog served with sauerkraut and melted cheese.

New York City Dog—A hot dog topped with steamed onions and a pale yellow mustard sauce.

The Rabbit Hound—A hot dog wrapped in bacon, topped with sauerkraut, mustard, coleslaw, and chili.

A packaged hot dog already has been cooked, so it can be eaten right from the package without further cooking, as if it were a slice of bologna.

Corn dogs—hot dogs in a fried cornmeal batter—were invented by Neil Fletcher at the 1942 Texas State Fair. They usually are served on a stick.

Russia is a big importer of American hot dogs. Russians eat about $70 million worth of imported franks, and hot-dog vendors are increasingly common in the streets of Moscow. Unlike Americans, who eat more hot dogs in the summer, Russians eat more hot dogs during the winter.

The primary difference between kosher and nonkosher hot dogs is that kosher hot dogs do not contain pork. Kosher dogs are made from beef or poultry that has been slaughtered according to Jewish law and tradition. Of people who eat kosher hot dogs, only about one-quarter are Jewish.

In England frankfurters are called "bangers."

The upset winner of the 1997 Nathan's Hot Dog Eating Contest in Coney Island was Hirofumi Nakajima, a 5-foot-6- inch noodle-eating champion from Japan. He defeated the reigning champ, Ed Krachie, a 6-foot-7-inch resident of Maspeth, New York, who weighs 360 pounds. Nakajima set a world's record by eating 24.5 hot dogs in 12 minutes, thus winning the Coveted Mustard Yellow International Belt.

A national survey by the Yankelovich research firm revealed that 42.4 percent of Americans believe that summer is the best time for eating a hot dog. However, 34 percent of our fellow citizens hold a

Competitors go for the gold in a 1993 Coney Island hot-dog eating contest.

Hot Dog Davy—National Hot Dog Month mascot created by cartoonist Al Capp

different point of view. They think that any time of the year is a good time for eating a hot dog.

In a bipartisan show of support, 4,300 hot dogs were eaten by congressional staff, lawmakers, and federal officials in a 1998 ceremony on Capitol Hill honoring National Hot Dog Month. Along with the hot dogs, the celebrants also consumed 800 bags of potato chips, 275 pounds of baked beans, and 600 Hostess Twinkies.

A combination of fireworks and frankfurters makes for a spectacular duo in Buenos Aires, Argentina

Chapter Three

HOT DOG HISTORY

A good sausage doesn't need any mustard.
– AN OLD SWISS SAYING

HE HISTORY OF HOT dogs is closely linked—pardon the pun—with that of the sausage, one of the earliest and most essential foods known to mankind.

The Oxford English Dictionary defines "sausage" as "a quantity of finely chopped pork, beef, or other meat, spiced and flavored, enclosed in a short length of the intestines of some animal, so as to form a cylindrical roll."

Homer had references to sausage in the *Odyssey*, which was written around 850 B.C. According to James Trager in his authoritative book, *The Food Chronology*, Julius Caesar introduced the Gallic art of making sausages into Rome around 48 B.C. During the reign of Nero, sausages were associated closely with the lusty Lupercalian and Floralian festivals, which were early versions of Mardi Gras during which the Romans got to act wild and crazy. The word "sausage" derives from the Latin *salsus*, meaning salted or preserved. *Salsus* has the same root that our contemporary words "salt" and "salary" have: *sal*, meaning salt.

During the Middle Ages,

A pretty smile, a cool drink, and a hot dog make for a classic publicity shot, circa 1955

Although it has been a commercial hub for centuries, the ancient city of Frankfurt, Germany, is best known in the United States for its eponymous sausage

sausages became identified with their cities of origin: Bologna, from Bologna, Italy; Gothaer, from Gotha, Germany; and Romano, from Rome. In Scotland a mutton sausage known as *haggis* became a national dish. The Irish favored *Drisheen*, a black sausage made with sheep or pig's blood and flavored with herbs. In England, where sausages are referred to as pud-

dings, batches of Savory Duck or Poor Man's Goose sausages that caught fire in a shop on Pudding Lane were believed to have ignited the Great Fire of London in 1666.

The city of Frankfurt am Main, in what is now western Germany, was a hub of commerce and transportation during the Middle Ages. The city held its first trade fair in the year 1240, and an international stock exchange opened in 1585. The Rothschild banking family launched their empire from Frankfurt. A butcher named Johann Georghehner brought his custommade sausages from the smaller town of Coburg to seek his fortune in the bustling Frankfurt of the 1600s, and his work became the signature dish of his adopted home. As a cosmopolitan business center of taste and affluence, Frankfurt became widely known for its delicious sausages, or frankfurters.

Even today, sausages are serious business in Europe. More than a food, they are a cultural bedrock. Sausage making is a source of local identity and pride as well as an art form. Jim Mosle, owner of Saags Products, Inc. of San Leandro, California, trained with *wurstmachers*, or sausage makers, in Europe and learned the Old World philosophies and craftsmanship from those masters. Different villages are proud of the distinct taste of their sausages, Mosle says, and the competition at

festivals for the honor of "best sausage" is fierce. "The butcher is *the man* in those villages," Mosle says. "He is highly respected for his skill at making sausages. The sausage itself is usually eaten plain,

Jim Mosle, of Saags Products, learned his craft from European *wurstmachers*

without a topping, so as not to dilute its flavor. There's an old saying in Switzerland: A good sausage doesn't need any mustard."

"Most people, unfortunately, still look upon the sausage as the cheapest form of meat," says British food writer Antony Coxe in *The Great Book of Sausages*, which he wrote with his wife, Araminta Hippisley Coxe. "They do not realize that much more care and hard work goes into making a sausage than into the preparation of, say, a fillet steak. There is chopping, blending, and seasoning, and preparing the casing, which is itself a complicated and delicate operation. . . . Then there may be salting and smoking. And all this happens before it gets anywhere near the kitchen stove." Coxe continues:

Sausages were believed to have ignited the Great Fire of London in 1666.

As a student in London [in the 1920s], dwindling funds at the end of every month forced me to patronize S.P.Os, which—as some readers may remember—stood for Sausage, Potato, and Onion, and was the name given to cheap eating houses where, if one peered through the steamy window, one could see three big enameled pans sizzling away behind the glass. Then, in the 1930s, I was asked to design the sets for a theatrical company, led by Lionel Birch and Alistair Cooke, which went from Cambridge University to Munich. Here, I first sampled Münchener weisswurst [a popular white sausage], washed down with steins of Löwenbrau. My German was so bad that when I asked for sausages and beer, they brought me wild strawberries (Erdbeere) and milk.

Immigrants brought their foods with them during the great waves of migration to the United States throughout the 19th and early 20th centuries. In 1894 the newspaper *San Francisco Midwinter Appeal* complained that "four bits for a Frankfurter seems rather steep." In 1899 an advertisement in the *Chicago Daily News* offered "Frankfurt Sausage per lb 7c."

In 1893 a St. Louis bar owner named Chris Von de Ahe, who also owned the St. Louis Browns baseball team, began selling sausages at ball games, launching the intimate baseball-hot-dog relationship.

Sausage also may have played an indirect role in the invention of the hamburger in 1892. According to that theory, a food vendor in Akron, Ohio, named Frank Menches was selling sausages at a county fair. His supply was running low, because his butcher had been unable to provide the regular shipment that morning. Out of desperation, Menches started grinding up the sausages, seasoning them, putting them on a grill, and selling them as cooked meat patties.

At the 1904 Louisiana Purchase Exposition in St. Louis, a sausage vendor named Anton Ludwig

1908

Vienna Beef has been a favorite of Chicago's hot-dog aficionados for generations

Feuchtwanger tried selling frank-furters along with white gloves, so that patrons could stroll around the fair, eating his product while keeping their hands clean. Sales went up, but so did costs, as patrons failed to return the white gloves. Feucht-wanger asked his brother-in-law, a baker, to devise a soft roll that could hold the sausages, and the hot-dog bun was born.

Another man at the St. Louis fair, a mustard salesman from Rochester, New York, took note of Feucht-wanger's experiments. The man's name was George T. French. His product was milder than competing brands, and French's mustard soon rose in tandem with the hot dog and the hot-dog bun until French's became the country's largest-selling prepared mustard.

Some immigrants from Middle Europe referred to a sausage that had origins in the Austrian city of Wien (pronounced "veen"), or Vi-enna. In America the "v" sound softened into a "wuh," and the sausage became known as a wiener, weener, or weenie.

The Europeans brought their Old World respect for and devotion to the sausage to their new homes in America. Russians liked to cook their *saussikas* in tomato sauce and eat them as a snack between shots of vodka. Polish immigrants called their varieties *kielbasa*, while Hun-garians called theirs *kishka*. Immi-grants from Latin countries brought a pork sausage known as *chorizo*, such as *Chorizo de Sala-manca*, a pork, paprika, and garlic sausage from Spain, and *Chorizo Picuante*, made with pork, cumin, and hot red peppers, from Mexico. In his 1969 history *The Sausage Book*, Richard Gehman affection-ately recalled an Italian sausage artist on the streets of lower New York:

In Greenwich Village, many years ago, I used to know a man named Charles Caruso, a hard-working man with a bearish, brusque voice

Hot Dog Etiquette...

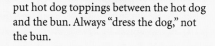

Do...

serve sesame seed, poppy seed, and plain buns with hot dogs. Sun-dried tomato buns or basil buns are considered gauche.

eat hot dogs on buns with your hands. Utensils should not touch hot dogs on buns.

use paper plates to serve hot dogs. Every day dishes are acceptable; china is a no-no.

Condiments remaining on the fingers after eating a hot dog should be licked away, not washed.

Don't...

put hot dog toppings between the hot dog and the bun. Always "dress the dog," not the bun.

use a cloth napkin to wipe your mouth when eating a hot dog. Paper is always preferable.

take more than five bites to finish a hot dog. For foot-long wiener, seven bites are OK.

bring wine to a hot dog barbecue. Beer, soda, and iced tea are preferable.

that in no way resembled that of the great Italian tenor of the same last name. Nevertheless, Charles was every inch the artist that Enrico Caruso was. Nearly every day around noon, Charles would go into his studio on Carmine Street and grind up pork butts and scraps, season the grindings with salt and strong black pepper and a couple of herbs—the names of which he would never divulge—and stuff the resulting redolent mixture into an animal casing to make *salsiccia dolce*, or sweet sausage.

By the time he made about 50 pounds of short, fat sausages, it would be nearly dusk. Charles carried his sausages, plus several gallons of stewed peppers, previously prepared by his wife, out to a large iron-roofed pushcart parked near the curb. This cart, constructed of sheet metal to his own specifications, was Charles' pride and joy. It was equipped with a grill, compartments to keep the peppers warm, and a small stove. . . . He trundled the cart a couple of blocks north to the busy subway-stop corner of West Third Street and Sixth Avenue. There he climbed into the cart, lighted a fire under his grill, and placed on it a succulent coil of *salsiccia dolce.*

Within a few seconds, the sausages began to snarl, spit, and buzz, sending out a wonderfully magnetic odor. A customer would step up and demand one. Charles would cut a single sausage from the coil, split it neatly in half and press it down on the grill, browning its insides before placing it on a soft fresh roll. He added a large spoonful of the simmering peppers, sprinkled the sausage with dried red pepper seeds, wrapped neatly in a paper napkin, handed it to the customer, and collected 35 cents. Meanwhile, the mingled smell of sausages and peppers attracted more people. It even drew some of Charles' neighbors from Carmine Street. It drew me, too.

THE CONEY ISLAND CONNECTION

In 1990 three public television stations in New York, Boston, and Los Angeles created a documentary called *Coney Island.* In the production notes that accompanied the documentary was this evocative description of an urban beach resort that was "the unofficial capital of the new mass culture:"

Variously called "Sodom by the sea" and "The Electric Eden," Coney Island was a vast playground of light and color that delighted, and sometimes appalled, its throngs of visitors. In 1895, a spit of land at the foot of Brooklyn was miraculously metamorphosed into an extravagant world of amusement—a safety valve for the teaming metropolis and an experiment in egalitarian enjoyment that would transport America

A Riviera for the working class, New York's Coney Island was a vibrant beach resort as well as a real-life laboratory for hot-dog innovators.

With Prohibition a fading memory, copious amounts of "five-cent beer" were enjoyed along with Coney Island hot dogs during the Depression. On the day this photo was taken in July, 1936, the temperature soared to 102 degrees.

from the Victorian Age into the modern world. The hot dog and the roller coaster were invented here. Three extraordinary amusement parks, Luna Park, Steeplechase Park, and Dreamland, featured mechanical horses, an Infant Incubator for premature babies, a Trip to the Moon, the largest herd of show elephants in the world, and Lilliputia, a miniature town inhabited by three hundred little people.

In the midst of this colorful scene, a German immigrant named Charles Feltman operated a popular beer garden and dinner house, Feltman's German Gardens, on West 10th Street and Surf Avenue. Feltman, who had grown up in Frankfurt, started his business in the 1870s by driving a meat-pie wagon along the Coney Island beach. Around 1901 he began putting boiled tubes of spiced meat on a roll and selling them for 10 cents. He also employed a youngster named Nathan Handwerker as a roll-cutter and delivery boy.

Two of Handwerker's friends—one a singing waiter, the other a musician—complained that Feltman's franks were too expensive and that what Coney Island really needed was a five-cent hot-dog stand. The friends' names were Eddie Cantor and Jimmy Durante.

According to 1968 memoirs written by Nathan's son, Murray, the elder Handwerker scraped together savings of $300 and, in 1916, opened his own 8-foot-by-25-foot stand at Surf and Stillwell avenues, competing against his former boss, Feltman. The house specialty was a five-cent frankfurter known as a "red hot." The spiciness came from a secret recipe devised by his fiancée, Ida, who soon became his wife and business partner.

When Handwerker suspected that the public was wary of a five-cent hot dog, because the meat content might be unwholesome, he devised a creative marketing tactic to convey a healthful image. He hired medical students from a nearby

Their music and comedy would enchant America, but Jimmy Durante (with cigar) and Eddie Cantor made their first impact on pop culture when they sought a five-cent hot-dog on Coney Island.

hospital and had them eat the franks while they were standing in front of his stand, wearing their white doctor's coats and stethoscopes.

According to Murray Handwerker, the business's name came after a customer complained that the five-cent stand was lost amidst the general hubbub of Coney Island. At that point all the stand had was an oilcloth sign that said "Hot Dogs." The owner considered calling it

The crew at Nathan's posed for this photo in 1922, when the
original hot dog stand was 6 years old

"Handwerker's Hot Dogs," but that
didn't fit on the sign. Murray
Handwerker explains:

Providence in the form of Tin Pan
Alley provided a bright idea. At that
time, a song called "Nathan, Nathan,
Why Are You Waitin'?" was enor-
mously popular. Handwerker decided that since Nathan was his real
first name and the song was popularizing that name, he would call his

place "Nathan's." The "Famous" bit
came a bit later.

When the New York City subway
system was extended to Coney Island in 1923, the hot-dog stand's
Surf Avenue location was precisely
at the entrance and exit to one of
the busiest subway stations in the
entire city, bringing thousands of
hungry consumers to Nathan's
doorstep. In the following years

Nathan's became as much a New York landmark as the Statue of Liberty and the Brooklyn Bridge. In 1939 a public-relations coup was achieved when President Franklin D. Roosevelt served Nathan's hot

Nathan's Famous."

"Hot dogs may be boiled, of course, as well as grilled and boiled," wrote Murray Handwerker. "Nathan's never boils frankfurters. The tastiest hot dog is one that is

> *"In the offbeat section of cities. . . would be a store called the Coney Island Red Hot with a great steaming frankfurter dripping with chili painted on the window."*
>
> *– JAMES BEARD*

dogs at a picnic honoring the king and queen of England (there's no historical evidence that Roosevelt took this action on the advice of one of his Supreme Court appointees, Felix Frankfurter). The late Nelson Rockefeller, while governor of New York, quipped that "no man can hope to get elected in New York State without being photographed eating hot dogs at

grilled and then put on a toasted roll."

Nathan Handwerker died in 1972, and his wife, Ida, passed away shortly afterwards. Murray Handwerker succeeded his father as president. Nathan's Famous is currently a publicly owned corporation traded on the NASDAQ exchange, with some 200 units around the New York City region. The original restaurant at

Coney Island remains in business; it now encompasses an entire block. Many Nathan's Famous fans swear that, to really enjoy a genuine Nathan's hot dog, you *have* to eat one at the original site.

The fame of the Coney Island hot dog, or red hot, spread so far that it influenced millions of people who had never set foot in Brooklyn. "Coney Island" became a generic description, as the late James Beard reminisced in his book, *James Beard's Simple Foods*:

A classic of American eating, according to the late James Beard

with a great steaming frankfurter dripping with chili painted on the window. . . . The store was not, as a rule, decorated with any sense or style; it had just stools, chairs, and a few tables, and usually you would order one or two redhots per person and carry them home in a sack or eat them on the street, unless you decided to sit there and have just one Coney Island red hot with a glass of beer.

I remember when I was a child in Portland, Oregon, there were two Coney Island red hot joints in my particular bailiwick, one right next to the streetcar I would take home at night and another a couple of streets away. At one-thirty or two in the morning, you'd find there a mixture of what were then called hoboes,

Let us not forget a classic of American eating that goes back as long as I can remember—the Coney Island red hot. . . . In the more offbeat section of cities, almost in the tenderloin section, there would be a store called the Coney Island Red Hot

fashionable people in evening clothes, and just plain lovers of Coney Island red hots, all indulging in their consuming passion. It was great fun.

TALE OF THE DOG

That brings us to the origins of the phrase "hot dog." First, the story, as it is widely told:

Thomas Aloysius "Tad" Dorgan was a young sportswriter and cartoonist for the *New York Evening Journal*, who had come to New York from San Francisco. One cold day in 1901 (or 1902 or 1906) Dorgan was at the Polo Grounds, home field of baseball's New York Giants. Dorgan was doodling on his sketch pad and was stumped for a topic for that day's cartoon. He heard food vendors calling out, "Get your red hots! Get your dachshund sausages while they're red hot!" Dorgan sketched the picture of a dachshund inside a roll and started writing a caption. He couldn't remember how to spell "dachshund," so he wrote the words "hot dog."

New York's Polo Grounds no longer stands. As former home for the New York Giants and New York Mets baseball teams, it is associated by legend with the creation of the phrase "hot dog."

It's a great story, resplendent with ingenuity and resonating with the tight bonds between baseball and hot dogs. The only problem, according to one expert, is that it isn't true.

"The Dorgan story is an absolute myth," says Gerald Cohen, a language professor at the University of Missouri, Rolla, and a researcher of American and British slang. "The idea that Dorgan, a writer, didn't know how to spell dachshund or was too lazy to consult a dictionary strains credulity. Furthermore, the cartoon itself doesn't exist. The newspaper files from those years have been thoroughly searched, and it hasn't surfaced. I'll pay $200 to anyone who can produce the Dorgan hot-dog cartoon from the Polo Grounds."

Cohen says that Dorgan didn't arrive in New York from San Francisco until 1903. There is a Dorgan hot-dog cartoon that appeared on December 12, 1906, but it had to do with an indoor bicycle-racing marathon, not a baseball game.

So where did "hot dog" come from? Cohen traces the usage to Yale University in New Haven, Connecticut, around the year 1898. He cites his own etymological research along with that of David Shulman, a consultant to the *Oxford English Dictionary*, and Barry A. Popik, a New York City judge who is also a word-origin sleuth. According to Cohen's theory, Yale students ate at a food cart near campus that they dubbed "the dog cart." In Professor

"I'll pay $200 to anyone who can produce the Dorgan hot-dog cartoon from the Polo Grounds."

– GERALD COHEN

Cohen's words the students "combined keen wit with very bad taste" and joked that sausages sold at the cart contained dog meat. That led to references that those who ate at the cart were members of a "kennel club," and that those going for lunch were about to eat some "hot dog."

"It was a standard joke in America during the 19th century that sausages contained dog meat," Professor Cohen says. "There has always been a trend toward irreverent humor in American culture." The *Yale Humor* magazine of March 5, 1904, had this bit of poetry:

Mary had a little dog.
It played a naughty trick;
Just think—it bit poor Mary so,
The mustard was too thick.

Another blow to the Dorgan legend comes from Dennis R. Means, a local historian in Hull, Massachusetts. Means discovered an issue of *The Hull Beacon*, July 3, 1898, with an advertisement for a business on the Nantasket Pier, a beachfront resort:

NO FOOLING!
Don't Fail to See
Bartlett's Hot Dog Factory
The Finest Ice Cream in the World
Peanut Row
Head Nantasket Pier

Means points out that in the summer of 1898 young American soldiers were returning from Cuba and the brief Spanish-American War. In high spirits and with their military wages in hand, they flocked to beach resorts, such as Nantasket. "Perhaps it was the soliders, more than the wiseacres in college, who gave the real impetus to the widening acceptance of the term *hot dog* across the land."

Meat vendors of that era were horrified by the jocular canine references to their products and embraced the Dorgan legend as a more palatable and folksy alternative.

Professor Cohen credits a sports stadium vendor named Harry Mozely Stevens with popularizing the term "hot dog," first at the Polo Grounds, then in other baseball stadiums, and later throughout a network of sports and entertainment one day arrived at a minor-league baseball game in Columbus, Ohio. He heard fans complaining that players' uniforms had only numbers without names, which made it difficult to tell who was who. Stevens persuaded the Columbus

While walking through the stands selling his new product, Harry M. Stevens used the line, "You can't tell the players without a scorecard."

venues, such as Madison Square Garden, where Harry M. Stevens Inc. dominated the concession industry.

Stevens was an English immigrant who began working in a steel mill in Niles, Ohio, in 1882. When the mill workers went on strike, he became a traveling salesman and team's owner to sell him exclusive rights, for $500, to the production and sale of a program and scorecard that would match the player's names and numbers. Stevens then sold advertising space alongside the information about the players. While walking through the stands, selling his new product—actually, a new medium—Stevens used the line, "You can't tell the players without a scorecard."

As he expanded to major-league cities, Stevens added soda, peanuts, and popcorn to his lines and in 1893 snagged a contract to be the official concessionaire at the Polo Grounds. According to Professor Cohen, Stevens popularized the Dorgan association with "hot dog" because it was a harmless story that didn't hurt anyone and diverted negative connotations away from frankfurters. Stevens died in 1934, and his highly successful company later became part of Aramark, a Philadelphia-based institutional foodservice company.

By the 1920s the phrase "hot dog" had entered mainstream usage, both to describe a frankfurter and as a hip way, during the Flapper era, to express joy and enthusiasm, for example, *hot diggity dog*. In the 1960s, hot dog would take on a different meaning, to describe a form of surfing that was spectacular and flamboyant. Later the expression was applied to a style of downhill skiing that is acrobatic and exhibitionist.

Another stream of hot-dog history began in 1873 when a 14-year-old German immigrant responded to a "Help Wanted" poster for an apprentice, or "butcher's boy," at George Weber's retail meat market in Detroit. The youngster, whose name was Oscar F. Mayer, was restless and ambitious. He moved to Chicago in 1876 to take a job with Kohlhammer's market and then worked for six years in the giant stockyard of Armour & Co.

Mayer saw a business opportunity and sent for his two brothers, who were back in Bavaria: Gottfried Mayer, a *wurstmacher* who had studied traditional methods of sausage making, and Max, a bookkeeper. In 1883 the three brothers leased the Kolling Meat Market, a small store in a German neighborhood on Sedgewick Street in Chicago's Near North Side, and began selling fresh and cured meats. After a dispute with the landlord, the Mayer brothers moved their market to a new location two blocks away and lived in apartments over the store.

The business thrived, as Oscar F. Mayer displayed a flair for marketing and showmanship. He sponsored German polka bands and a German exhibit at the 1893 Chicago World's Fair and began making de-

It wouldn't qualify for the Daytona 500, but Oscar Mayer's Weinermobile
has been an effective vehicle for hot dog promotion

liveries from horse-drawn carriages around the city and suburbs. By 1904 eight salesman were selling Oscar Mayer sausages in northern Illinois and southern Wisconsin. In 1944 the company invented a machine that could put a yellow paper ring on every fourth wiener in a package to differentiate its products from the anonymity of most meat products.

Oscar F. Mayer's son, Oscar G. Mayer, joined the company in 1904 after graduating from Harvard and became president in 1929. Two great publicity stunts were devised in 1936: Little Oscar and the Wienermobile. Little Oscar, a diminutive person dressed as a chef, was a sort of spiritual ancestor of Ronald McDonald. Little Oscar would drive the sausage-shaped vehicle, the Wienermobile, to store openings, hospitals, and other locations around Chicago, where he would sign autographs, giving away samples and handing out Wiener-whistles. In 1955, following the death of Oscar F. Mayer at the age of 95, the company moved from Chicago to Madison, Wisconsin, where it had a major processing plant. Oscar G. Mayer became chairman of the board, and his son—Oscar G. Mayer Jr.—was elected president.

Today Oscar Mayer & Co. is part of Kraft Foods, which in turn is owned by Philip Morris. The Wienermobile lives on, usually sans Little Oscar, as does the Oscar Mayer jingle: "I wish I were an Oscar Mayer wiener. . . ." The ditty first was introduced in 1963 and has become one of the longest-running commercial songs in advertising history.

An overlap between the histories of the hot dog and the hamburger occurred in Southern California as America entered World War II. Carl Karcher, a native of Upper San-

Former truck driver Carl Karcher (holding his daughter, Anne Marie, with an employee on the right) went from a single hot-dog cart to a tiny stand, The Blimp. He later switched to hamburgers and built the Carl's Jr. empire.

dusky, Ohio, quit school after the seventh grade and moved to Orange County, California, to work at his uncle's feed store. While driving a truck to deliver bread to customers, Karcher saw opportunity in the hot-dog stands he supplied. In 1941 he bought a hot-dog cart in Los Angeles for $326 and entered the food-service business—his wife, Margaret, operated hot-dog cart number two. In 1945 Karcher opened his first full-service restaurant, Carl's Drive-in Barbecue, in Anaheim, introducing the yellow star logo that is still used. The first Carl's Jr. was opened in 1956 by Karcher and his brother, Donald, and the company gradually switched to an emphasis on the burger and salad bar, rather than the hot dog.

As part of the post-war Southern California architectural and design boom, the Los Angeles area also was the spawning ground for stands that actually looked like hot dogs. In 1946 the Blake family opened Tail o' the Pup on North Vicente Avenue in West Hollywood, in a specially designed stand that is a 17-foot-long stucco hot dog. The Blake family still operates the stand, which is located near the fashionable Beverly Center mall.

A classic example of surrealistic Los Angeles architecture, Tail o' the Pup in West Hollywood leaves little doubt about what its signature item is

Chapter Four

LOCAL LEGENDS

When you are eating a hot dog, you are laughing. It's a good time.
– BRUCE BUNCH, THE WEENIE WANDERERS

BOUT 10 YEARS AGO three friends who worked for the same company in Connecticut got to talking about where they liked to eat lunch. It turned out they shared a passion for hot dogs although each one was wary about confessing to this affection. "We were embarrassed to admit that, instead of going to a 'nice' restaurant or, say, a steak house, we preferred going to a hot-dog stand," says Bruce A. Bunch, one of the three friends.

As the trio traded notes about favorite hot-dog haunts, they started an informal custom of traipsing out together to various stands and critiquing them. "We tried to find the best hot dog and apply the same standards as one might to a fine restaurant—ambience, bun preparation, mouth feel," Bunch explains.

Soon other friends expressed an interest in joining the endeavor, and the three devised "a silly little initiation ritual" in which candidates

The sentimental logo of Nu-Way Weiners of Macon, Georgia, was inspired in 1939 by a real stray dog, "Sam," who was known as "The Mystery Dog of Cotton Avenue." Sam had a talent for appearing at the hot-dog stand around 4 P.M. and begging—quite effectively—for food from Nu-Way customers.

would be quizzed on hot-dog knowledge, appropriate times to eat a hot dog, and personal choices for toppings. "Mustard, pickles, and relish are acceptable answers," Bunch says. "If a person says, 'ketchup,' we try to find a polite way not to admit him or her."

It was apparent that a name was needed for this rapidly growing group. After some consideration The Weenie Wanderers were born. The group now has about two dozen members. A membership certificate, written with impressive black-ink calligraphy, proclaims:

The Fairfield County Chapter of THE WEENIE WANDERERS hereby bestows membership status upon (name) and certifies him/her to be a relentless seeker of all that is winsome in wieners. As a dedicated W2, the above-named promises to place above all else the search for the most wonderful wiener, wandering wherever the quest for the quintessential tube steak may lead.

In addition to their field research, the Weenie Wanderers began collecting hot-dog memorabilia. Today, the collection is housed in The Weenie Museum, which is located inside an out-of-the-way bookcase at their company. The collection includes a hot-dog teapot, hot-dog memo paper, hot-dog erasers, a ski cap stuffed with a hot dog, and other classic items.

Bunch says that the Weenie Wanderers have a genuine and deep-felt devotion to their favorite food. "When you are eating a hot dog, you are laughing, the atmosphere is informal. It's a good time. It's just about impossible to have an argument while you are eating a hot dog."

These days the Weenie Wanderers usually are found in booth number two at their favorite hot-dog stand, Rawley's, whose food and atmosphere Bunch describes as "perfection." We'll learn more about Rawley's later in this chapter.

The Weenie Wanderers' dedication is inspirational. More than

A shared, secret passion for hot dogs motivated Bruce Bunch and friends to form The Weenie Wanderers, a society whose members search for excellence in their favorite food. Bunch also maintains a small museum of hot-dog memorabilia.

The Fairfield County Chapter
of

THE WEENIE WANDERERS

hereby bestows membership status upon

Bruce A. Bunch

and certifies him/her to be a relentless seeker of all that is winsome in weiners. As a dedicated W² the above-named promises to place above all else the search for the most wonderful weiner, wandering wherever the quest for the quintessential tube steak may lead.

John H. Hollenback
Navigator

Bruce A. Bunch
Publicity Chairman

James Abraham
Treasurer

hamburgers or pizza, hot dogs remain a localized product that can be interpreted in a distinctive way by a small entrepreneur. In that questing, quixotic spirit, *Hot Dog Companion* sought local legends

homage, by proxy, to the thousands of restaurants serving up great hot dogs in cities, hamlets, bus terminals, baseball stadiums, strip malls, and highway exit ramps all over America.

> *"Mustard, pickles, and relish are acceptable answers. If a person says 'ketchup,' we try to find a polite way not to admit him or her."*
>
> *– BRUCE BUNCH, PRESIDENT OF THE WEENIE WANDERERS*

whose frankfurters merit inclusion inside an elite circle of renown. Nominations came from restaurant critics and food writers as well as from enthusiasts who posted their opinions on Internet forums.

We salute a few of these local legends here—starting in the Northeast and moving through the Midwest, South, and West. We pay

THE NORTHEAST

Ted's

Buffalo, New York

David Shribman is Washington bureau chief for *The Boston Globe* and has won a Pulitzer Prize for his political coverage. As he travels throughout the United States reporting on elections and campaigns, he is also a fond patron and ardent chronicler of great local food.

Asked to nominate his choice for favorite frankfurter, Shribman gave an enthusiastic and spontaneous endorsement. "Easily the best hot dogs in the United States are from a chain called Ted's, headquartered in the Buffalo area," he says. "They get their dogs from a local producer named Sahlen's. The hot dogs are cooked on open grills all year round. I call them tube steaks, and I would rather have a foot-long from Ted's than any entrée from any restaurant in any city at any time." Many patrons like to wash down their Ted's tube steak with a glass of loganberry juice.

Gary Sable uses his extensive foodservice experience and entrepreneurial flair to make That Hot Dog Place a success in Red Bank, New Jersey

That Hot Dog Place
Red Bank, New Jersey

Gary Sable, the owner of this small establishment, found the location for his restaurant when he was walking around the central Jersey town of Red Bank and got lost. He found a little place in an alley, next to some shops and a restaurant, and decided that this was where hot dogs should be cooked and sold.

After working 23 years in the full-service restaurant business, Sable decided to open That Hot

Dog Place for the independence of working for himself. The house special is a quarter-pound hot dog on an Italian bun. The dogs are both grilled and boiled in the traditional "dirty water" pushcart technique. Popular toppings are sauerkraut and a chili made with "secret" ingredients. Another favorite is the "Junkyard Dog"—a hot dog with mustard, coleslaw, sweet relish, hot relish, and chopped tomato.

Flo's
Cape Neddick, Maine
Wasses Hot Dogs
Rockland, Maine
Miller's General Store
Holden, Maine

The cuisine of Maine is associated with clam chowder, lobster, and other seafood, accompanied by a side dish of boiled Maine-grown potatoes. It's surprising that this New England state is also fertile territory for hot dogs.

Flo's, located in the southwestern tip of Maine near the New Hampshire border, is a discovery of Jane and Michael Stern, a husband-and-wife team who write a delightful road food column for *Gourmet* magazine. Gail Stacy, daughter-in-law of the original Flo, is the cook and proprietor of what the Sterns describe as a "tiny roadside shack." The house specialty is a sweet-and-sour onion relish called hot sauce, a potent concoction that is flavorful but not overly hot.

"Ladled on plump Schultz-brand steamed wieners in soft buns," say the Sterns, "and then sprinkled with a dash of black peppers (Gail does that for you), the hot sauce is one part of a transcendent combo—the finest little dog on the East Coast. Hot dogs are the only thing on Flo's menu, and six or eight is not an unreasonable number to satisfy a good appetite." Look for Flo's along Route 1 but don't bother calling; there's no telephone.

According to Liz M., a contributor to the "World's Best Hot Dog" Internet site mentioned in Chapter One, hot-dog lovers should journey to Rockland, a coastal town in southern Maine, about midway between Bangor and Portland. "I live two blocks from the original Wasses, at the junction of Route 1 and Route 17 in Rockland's North End. When the wind is right, the aroma of the grill fills the air, and the scent alone is almost enough to satisfy your hunger. You can get 'em straight, with mustard, relish, grilled onions, with Maine-made Morse's sauerkraut, with chili, or with cheese."

Miller's General Store maintains a small-town tradition, in which the place where you buy nails and aspirin and shampoo is also where you buy your lunch. "Miller's is a perfect example of a one-store operator that has had an extensive track record of success with its steamed hot dogs," says Heather Reese Grimshaw, who writes for a convenience-store trade magazine. Lynne Miller Saucier, the store's general manager, says Miller's sells about 150 of its "Famous Steamed Hot Dogs" on a *slow* day. On a busy summer day during tourist season, the dog tally can jump as high as 350. The red-colored, all-beef dogs sometimes snap when broken, because of the amount of juice inside. "People come in and say, 'Oh, I just couldn't pass your store without coming in for one of those hot dogs," Saucier says. "And they just keep coming back."

Gray's Papaya
Papaya King
New York, New York

These two establishments are under separate ownership, but they both are outposts of a bizarre but effective pairing of hot dogs with papaya juice. The magazine *Eat Out* recommends Papaya King, which is located on East 86th Street and Third

Papaya King is one of two establishments whose unlikely pairing of frankfurters and papaya juice has captured the fancy of New York hot-dog lovers

Avenue, an affluent, fashionable area known as the Upper East Side: "The neighborhood with possibly the highest concentration of lap dogs is also home to the city's best hot dog. Papaya King's dense, 100-percent beef links (which New Yorkers have been lining up for search of food. Says New York food writer Steven Shaw: "I am constantly amazed at how good the hot dogs are at Gray's—crispy on the outside (I always ask for mine well done) and spicy/juicy on the inside. They are truly remarkable." At the end of 1998 a customer could buy two

> *"The sweet-and-cool aspects of papaya juice marry perfectly with the hot-and-spicy characteristics of hot dog, sauerkraut, and mustard."*
>
> *– STEVEN SHAW*

since the shop opened in 1934) have a great charred flavor and an important German casing that gives a proper snap when you bite down."

Gray's Papaya, on the corner of Broadway and 72nd Street, is open 24 hours and is particularly interesting around 4 A.M. when taxi-loads of inebriated celebrants from bachelor parties arrive in urgent

grilled hot dogs with fixings and a 14-ounce papaya juice for $1.95.

Regarding the implausible duo of hot dogs and papaya juice, Shaw says, "I have no idea why these two food products from opposite ends of the planet can work so well together, but they do. It is the ultimate in fusion cuisine. The sensation is similar to the interplay of those Indian yogurt-and-fruit lassi drinks when paired with spicy Indian food. The sweet-and-cool aspects of the drink marry perfectly with the hot-and-spicy characteristics of the hot dog, sauerkraut, and mustard."

Rutt's Hut

Clifton, New Jersey

Steve Rushmore is president of HVS International, a consulting firm in Mineola, New York, that appraises hotel and resort properties. A constant business traveler, Steve writes an informal newsletter for friends and clients that describes his "road food" finds in unusual and delectable locations.

Asked to nominate his favorite hot-dog places, Rushmore salutes Ted's of Buffalo, New York, mentioned earlier in this chapter, and Rutt's Hut in northeastern New Jersey. "Rutt's is a 60-year-old, greatly expanded hot-dog stand serving some of the best tube steaks in the world," Rushmore says. "What makes its creations unique is a special cooking method. Unlike most hot-dog purveyors, who either grill or boil their dogs, Rutt's deep-fries them in fat that reaches 310 degrees. The result is a hot dog whose skin literally crackles on the outside, thus comes it nickname, 'rippers.' Be sure to top this delicacy with Rutt's special relish, which has a unique sweet-and-sour taste and the consistency of oatmeal."

Rushmore says that the allure of this New Jersey landmark is so strong that the chairman of a multi-billion-dollar hotel corporation once invited him to get together for a few "rippers at Rutt's."

Rawley's

Fairfield, Connecticut

Located near Long Island Sound between Westport and New Haven, Rawley's is the venue of choice for the estimable Weenie Wanderers mentioned at the beginning of this chapter. The owner is Richard "Chico" Bielik, a former Fairfield High School football star who bought the establishment from Richard Rawley in 1971, after having worked there in the 1950s and 1960s. "People want a fun place where they can still get a good, 100-percent-meat hot dog with the works," says Bielik, who sells 2,000 hot dogs a week. Rawley's is a small but democratic place; everybody has to stand in line for a turn. When local resident David Letterman came in for a hot dog, Bielik didn't know who he was.

Bruce Bunch, a founder of the Weenie Wanderers, suggests sitting in one of the four booths or eight stools and watching Chico prepare your meal: "Chico fries Roessler hot dogs in fat and brings them out on the grill with one flick of his spatula. He scores them on the edges with the spatula. The toasted buns are happily resting to the right of the dogs under a modified metal shelf from a refrigerator. There's mustard, relish, and real bacon bits. Hot dogs just don't get any better than Rawley's."

Even David Letterman had to wait his turn at the hugely popular Rawley's in Fairfield, Connecticut

The tempting atmosphere of Ben's Deli can lure even the most die-hard hot-dog aficionado through its doors

Ben's Deli

Katz's Deli

New York, New York

Steven Silk has to be cautious about displaying frankfurter favoritism. As president of the company that makes Hebrew National franks, he attempts to be evenhanded toward all hot-dog venues as long as the dog being served there has the Hebrew National brand.

Nevertheless, when asked to name an especially desirable place

A New York food critic hails the hot dogs at Katz's Deli in lower Manhattan as the best in the city. Katz's also got a second recommendation from an unimpeachable source, shown with owner Fred Austin.

to enjoy a hot dog, Silk mentions Ben's Deli, located in midtown Manhattan at Seventh Avenue and 37th Street. "As I'm walking by Ben's, I look through the window and see a Hebrew National hot dog sitting there on the grill, and I can't resist. I could be on my way somewhere else for lunch; it doesn't matter. I *have* to go into Ben's Deli and have one of those hot dogs."

Food writer Steven Shaw, who hosts an on-line guide to New York restaurants and food, salutes Katz's Deli on Houston Street near Ludlow in lower Manhattan. "I think the best hot dogs in New York are at Katz's Deli on the Lower East Side. . . . they are the best I have ever tasted." However, Shaw qualifies his praise by pointing out that Katz's also has excellent pastrami, and that if you are quite hungry and have schlepped to Katz's off-the-beaten-path location, it would not be an egregious mistake if you ordered a pastrami sandwich instead of a hot dog.

Nick's Nest

Northampton, Massachusetts

Nick's Nest is a local institution in this area of western Massachusetts, having been established in 1948 by a Greek immigrant, Nicholas Malfas. Malfas started selling popcorn out of a pushcart in 1921. He pushed his cart all over town, but his favorite corner was at Northampton and Dwight streets, because of the traffic pouring off Route 5, the main north-south artery in New England.

In 1927 Malfas built a small store on Northampton Street about 50 feet south of the current location. His 1920's recipe for hot dogs, fresh ground from beef and pork, still is used. Malfas's grandson Constantine "Charlie" Malfas Jr. now runs the business, having taken it over from his father in 1989. Besides hot dogs, the restaurant is known for doors that open "automatically" when the counter person activates them by means of a rope and pulley

The late Nick Malfas, Sr., began his foodservice career selling popcorn and then switched to hot dogs. Here he poses at his first hotdog stand, located about 100 yards south of the present location of Nick's Nest, circa 1940.

It was a big day in Northampton, Massachusetts, when Nick's Nest celebrated its 50th anniversary in 1971

rigged along the ceiling. A small-scale merry-go-round is above the counter, and the restaurant still sells popcorn, too.

THE MIDWEST

O.K. Market
Wahoo, Nebraska

The O.K Market is another discovery of Jane and Michael Stern. "The old sign outside says MEAT, but the one kind of meat you want at the O.K. Market is a wiener, a Wahoo wiener, to be exact. Invented in 1919, a Wahoo wiener is something special: peppery, coarse-ground beef in a taut natural casing. The only way to eat one is inside a fresh bun

The Wahoo Wieners at the O.K. Market, Wahoo, Nebraska, have been hailed as "Little Rolls Royces of the frankfurter world."

heaped with fried onions and some zesty mustard," the Sterns explain. Texan food writers Bill and Cheryl Alters Jamison refer to Wahoo Wieners as "Little Rolls Royces of the frankfurter world. Wahoo Wieners combine beef chuck, pork picnic, and a secret spice blend, all wrapped in sheep's casings and smoked twice over hickory chips, with a stint of steam-cooking between visits to the smokehouse."

Hefty's—the Coney Islander
Redford, Michigan

This family-owned stand in a blue-collar Detroit neighborhood is praised as having "some of the most imaginative and tasty variations of hot dogs that you could ever believe," by an enthusiast at the "Best Hot Dog" Internet site. The Rabbit Hound is a wrapped in bacon and dressed with sauerkraut, mustard, coleslaw, and chili. The Beeney Wienie comes with pork and beans.

A jumbo-sized hot dog takes a commanding position amid the downtown Chicago skyline in this postcard from Vienna Sausage Manufacturing Co.

(Various Locations)

Chicago, Illinois

Chicago has an estimated 2,000 hot dog stands, more than all of the city's McDonald's, Wendy's, and Burger Kings combined. It is the only serious challenger to New York City as America's hot-dog capital, and the hot-dog lover cannot go wrong in sampling the Windy City's abundance of outlets: Portillo's, Poochie's, Wolfie's, Demon Dogs, SuperDawg, Byron's, The Wiener's Circle, Gold Coast, and Fluky's. In addition, a locally made brand, Vienna Beef, dominates the city's hot-dog trade and has a loyal following of its own although there are also fierce adherents of Slotkowski

Sausage Co. and the wieners of Leonard Slotkowski.

Chicagoans tend to boil, not grill, their hot dogs and to dress them with relish and tomatoes and serve them on a poppyseed roll. Ketchup is frowned upon, and the meat of choice is beef, not pork.

Jeff Smith, writing in *The Frugal Gourmet Cooks American*, makes clear his preference: "Don't talk to me about hot dogs in other cities. I have tasted them. The best ones in the country (oh, New York, forgive me!) are in Chicago." Writing for the magazine *New City* in 1994, Liz Stevens offered this memorable description of Jim's Hot Dog Stand, located at the corners of Maxwell Street and Halstead:

Half-a-block away, I smell it: the sweet, oily odor that seeps between wool threads and permeates thermal underwear to settle quasi-permanently onto the body itself. It's a scent that clings relentlessly to hair—even paper, pens, rubber soles. And with each trip I make to the corner of Maxwell and Halstead, I'm increasingly conscious of its potency. Grilled onions.

Most conversations about Chicago hot dogs begin with Portillo's. Dick Portillo started the chain in 1963 as The Dog House, a tiny trailer without running water that cost him $1,100. He and his wife, Sharon, took pots and pans home every night to wash them in their apartment bathtub. Today, his company, Portillo Restaurant Group, has revenues of $110 million and operates more than 30 Portillo's Hot Dog Restaurants as well as several restaurants based on other themes.

Portillo's is a favorite of columnist Ann Landers, who told *Chicago* magazine, "The buns are always fresh and warm, and the hot dogs are always juicy and delicious." Robb Walsh, writing in the flight magazine *American Way*, described what happened after he entered

Chicago's Dick Portillo started his restaurant career in 1963, selling hot dogs from a trailer called "The Dog House." Today, Portillo's Restaurant Group employs more than 2,000 people and is the largest privately owned restaurant company in the Midwest.

Portillo's and asked, "Make me one with everything":

With astonishing speed, the guy behind the counter slathers mustard and green relish on a poppyseed bun, inserts a steaming wiener, puts a spear of half-sour pickle along one side, chopped onions on the other, then tops it with three tomato slices dusted with celery salt from a plastic shaker. Finally, he sticks two skinny sport peppers into the tomato slices on each end so that the peppers protrude at jaunty angles.

These tiniest of nuances make it one of the best Chicago hot dogs I have ever eaten. The crunchy, natural casing on the sausage squeaks just right when I bite in, and the soft, oversize, steamed poppyseed bun folds perfectly around the entire sandwich so that the tomatoes can't get away.

Fluky's, another acclaimed Chicago landmark, was described this way by Renee Enna, food writer for *The Chicago Tribune*:

Fluky's has made its mark in the wiener world, and indeed its dog proved to be the best part of its menu: a flavorful Vienna beef frank in the uniform of Chicago's finest bright green relish, fresh onions, ripe tomato, sport peppers, and plenty of mustard on a fresh poppyseed bun.

Fresh tomatoes, green relish, and a fresh poppyseed bun are de rigeur when ordering a frank at Fluky's in Chicago

Ed Vohasek, a businessman who grew up on Chicago's South Side in a neighborhood called Canaryville, remembers that in the summer the streets would be full of hot-dog vendors, many of them men who worked a second job operating mostly tomato—slices of fresh tomato and a little bit of celery salt on top of that. When I was in a deli in Hartford, Connecticut, a few years ago, they thought I was nuts. They couldn't fathom how I could put tomatoes on a hot dog. I

> *"When I was in a deli in Hartford, they thought I was nuts. They couldn't fathom how I could put tomatoes on a hot dog."*
>
> – ED VOHASEK

pushcarts on warm nights. People would gather on front porches to chat, listen to baseball games on the radio, and eat hot dogs. "For some reason the hot dogs always came in poppyseed buns. If I get a hot dog without a poppyseed bun, it is not complete, even today," Vohasek says. "People in Chicago put a lot of stuff on top of the hot dog. For me it was reached over the counter and showed the lady how to do it. I guess it is a Chicago thing."

Dog n Suds Drive In
Plainfield, Indiana

This Midwestern chain was one of the original drive-in restaurant

New management at Dogs n Suds is attempting a revival of the chain's
drive-through concept and sudsy root beer

concepts in the fast-food industry, featuring carhops who served Coney Island hot dogs and root beer in frosted mugs. At its peak in 1969, Dog n Suds had about 700 units in 32 states and was a popular destination for families and office workers on lunch breaks. After suffering a decline in popularity in the 1980s, the company is under new management and is expanding again, helped by a nostalgia wave among baby boomers who are taking their own kids there for a hot dog and a sudsy cold root beer.

THE SOUTH

The Varsity
Atlanta, Georgia

Founded in 1928, The Varsity has drawn generations of students from nearby Georgia Tech. The Varsity sells more gallons of another Atlanta institution—Coca-Cola—than any other single outlet in the world. The drive-in format can accommodate 600 cars and more than 800 people inside; on football days some 30,000 people are served.

Fortune Magazine, in a roundup of hot-dog places called "When Only a Wiener Will Do," recommended the Varsity to business travelers: "If you're waylaid in Atlanta, a chili dog at The Varsity is a great change of pace."

Pete's Famous
Birmingham, Alabama

This small establishment is located in Birmingham's downtown business district and is known for its "cheese beef" hot dogs. A man named Gus and his wife run the place, which looks like a long hallway with a counter. "No frills, just the best hot dogs I've ever eaten," exclaims a Pete's devotee named Donald on the Internet. "If you don't love them, I'll personally pay for your lunch."

Warren's Hot Dogs
Greenville, North Carolina

The "hot" at Warren's comes from a pepper-based, spicy gravy that drenches the "Ole Tar Heel" franks, which are fried and served with mustard and hot onions.

Nu-Way number two in downtown Macon, circa 1948

Nu-Way

Macon, Georgia

The little boy on the sign is accompanied by a motto: "I'd go a Long Way for A Nu-Way." The original store opened in downtown Macon at 430 Cotton Avenue in 1916. Nu-Way features a grilled hot dog that is stuffed into a steamed bun with mustard, onions, chili sauce, and a mild barbecue sauce made with chopped pork. Southern-style coleslaw is also available, and packages of Nu-Way private-label red wieners can be bought to take home.

A contributor to the Internet's hot-dog page has this endorsement: "Nu-Way is not a johnny-come-lately enterprise. Its formula hasn't changed in my 54 years. Just the best hot dogs anywhere in the world. As a well-traveled hot-dog gourmand, I know firsthand!"

Lucky Dog

New Orleans, Louisiana

Located in the heart of the city's party-hearty French Quarter, Lucky Dog is sold by street vendors and consists of a large hot dog on an equally large steamed roll. A frequent combination of Mardi Gras revelers is a Lucky Dog with a cocktail known as a Hurricane from Pat O'Brien's, also in the French Quarter. "After one Lucky Dog and one Hurricane, you are full, intoxicated, and the happiest person in the world!" exults a contributor to the "Best Hot Dog" Web page.

Lucky Dog is a staple of New Orleans' party-hearty French Quarter

The Purple Turtle

Pleasant Grove, Utah

Since opening in 1968 in this town about halfway between Provo and Salt Lake City, the Purple Turtle has developed a loyal following among Utahans, including foot-bought it from the founder. Evans says his work has brought him fame of sorts: "Every time I go to church somewhere else, and I say that I'm from Pleasant Grove, do you know what people always ask me? They ask, 'Do you know the Purple Turtle?' "

The foot-long hot dogs are a particular favorite of parents with their

> *"Every time I go to church somewhere else, and I say that I'm from Pleasant Grove, do you know what people always ask me? They ask, 'Do you know the Purple Turtle?' "*
>
> – *CLARK EVANS*

ball players from nearby Brigham Young University, the Osmond entertainment family, and officials from the Latter Day Saints church. The current owner, Clark Evans, began working at the Purple Turtle as a youth and ultimately kids, since the Moms and Dads remember eating them with *their* parents. The atmosphere is usually described as "stuck in the '60s," with the predominant color being purple—the tables, decor, and the purple turtle sign outside.

Top Dog

Berkeley, California

Located on Durant Avenue just a few blocks from the University of California campus, Top Dog has attracted a loyal following among students and faculty. The setting is modest—a few stools, an ancient television, and lots of newspaper clips on the walls espousing various causes. Generations of Berkeley students have eaten grilled hot dogs here, during both the turbulent student protests of the 1960s and 1970s as well as the more placid yuppie era. Local corporations with a high density of Cal alumni among their employees have social events catered by Top Dog.

Richard Riemann, the proprietor, is a transplanted New Yorker who has fond memories of the classic German butcher shops and sausage makers of his youth. Riemann is also a social philosopher and hot-dog historian and loves to talk about the lore and legend of his favorite food. Speaking of his career in the hot-dog business, Riemann says: "I wear the mantle proudly. I'm very proud of what I do. I have pleased and fed and satisfied millions of people."

Shotwell 59

San Francisco, California

This local watering hole is located in San Francisco's multicultural, blue-collar Mission District. On Wednesday night patrons enjoy Hot Dogs For a Buck—smoked dogs, polish sausage or hot links that are served up at 5 P.M. for a dollar each and are generally gone by 9 P.M.

Caitlin Boyle, writing in the *San Francisco Chronicle*, says that each hot dog at Shotwell 59 "is cooked in Guinness Stout (a definite bonus) and is accompanied by a full array of toppings, including warm sauerkraut and homemade hot mustard. The jukebox belts out a little of everything, from Johnny Cash to Sinatra to the Violent Femmes."

Surf Dog

Carpinteria, California

Surf Dog consists of a man named Bill Connell, standing at his push-cart on Highway 101 at the Bailard exit in Southern California. You'll notice his car with a huge hot dog on top of it and an American flag. Surf Dog is a favorite stop for people caught in freeway traffic while they are driving home from the beach in Santa Barbara or from visiting the nearby Seal Rookery. "You'll leave Surf Dog with a full stomach and a big smile," Connell says. In addition to its franks, Surf Dog offers marinated onions and homemade lemonade.

Wienerschnitzel

Newport Beach, California

This chain was launched in Southern California by a 23-year-old entrepreneur named John Galardi in 1961. Galardi sold 15-cent hot dogs

and was among the pioneers of the fast-food industry. His first job, at age 19, was working for Glenn Bell, founder of Taco Bell.

Today, Wienerschnitzel calls itself the world's largest hot-dog chain. It is part of the privately held Galardi Group and sells some 60 million hot dogs from more than 300 restaurants in 10 states. The company's distinctive orange, A-frame stands still feature hot dogs as their signature item, with chili dogs the most popular item. Indoor seating has been added to the original drive-in and walk-up windows.

John Galardi founded the Wienerschnitzel chain in 1961. Today, it is the centerpiece of the Galardi Group and sells some 60 million hot dogs annually.

Hot Dog on a Stick

Solana Beach, California

"It's a hot dog. It's on a stick. It's fried in a sweetish corn batter and served by pretty college girls who wear tall, multicolored caps that look like something that might have been worn by a Pan Am stewardess Ocean Park, where you probably ate your skewered weenie while waiting in line for the Bob-o-Sled with Mom and Dad."

Hot Dog on a Stick was founded by the late Dave Barham, a Missouri native who opened his first store on a Santa Monica beach. Barham combined a corn dog on a stick and

> *"A mere whiff of a hot dog on a stick transports you back to the old Pacific Ocean Park, where you ate your skewered weenie while waiting in line for the Bob-o-Sled with Mom and Dad."*
>
> *– LOS ANGELES MAGAZINE*

on *The Jetsons*," says *Los Angeles* magazine of this chain, which is located in some 90 shopping-mall food courts. The magazine continues: "If you are an Angeleno of a certain age, a mere whiff of a hot dog on a stick is enough to transport you back to the old Pacific attention-getting employee uniforms with fresh lemonade. The company now is expanding beyond its California base into the Midwest and Rocky Mountain states.

Hot Dog on a Stick is expanding into the Midwest and Rocky Mountain states

✳ *Chapter Five* ✳

THE MAKING OF A HOT DOG

HERE'S AN OLD SAYING that a person is better off *not* seeing how two things are made: laws and hot dogs. Philosophically, I suppose I can understand how some people might agree with that statement regarding laws. But frankfurter makers have nothing to hide.

I also recognize that many readers like to know the behind-the-scenes, nuts-and-bolts, how-did-they-do-that of everything they deal with, particularly the foods they eat. In appreciation of those individuals, I am including this background on how hot dogs are made.

This information on how hot dogs are made was provided by a trade group, The National Hot Dog & Sausage Council. The Council is based in Arlington, Virginia, just outside of Washington, D.C., where it gets to witness the making of both laws *and* hot dogs.

The hot dog plays on memories and nostalgic cravings so subtly that we hardly realize how hard it is tugging at our heart strings

National Hot Dog & Sausage Council Internet web page

(1) Special selected trimmings are cut and ground into small pieces and put into a mixer. Formulas are continuously weighed to ensure proper balance of all ingredients.

(2) A high-speed, stainless-steel chopper blends meat, spices, and curing ingredients into an emulsion or batter.

(3) The emulsion is pumped and fed into a stuffer. Strands of cellulose casings are mechanically positioned on the stuffing horn. As the emulsion flows through the horn into the casing, the filled strands are linked into hot dogs of exact size. The strand is then put on the smokehouse conveyor system.

At Saags Products, San Leandro, California, hot dogs are made in the tradition of European sausage masters

(4) In smokehouses, under controlled temperature and humidity, the hot dog is fully cooked and hardwood smoked for texture, color, and flavor.

(5) After passing through the smoke and cook cycle and being showered in cool water, the hot dog goes into the peeler. Here the protective, air-and-smoke permeable cellulose casing "skin" is stripped away and individual links are conveyed to the packaging line.

(6) Finally, the hot dog is conveyed to the scales—which divert off-weight franks—and fed into the vacuum packaging equipment. Individual packages of exact number and precise weight are wrapped and vacuum-sealed in plastic film to protect the freshness and flavor of the hot dog.

(7) Once packaged and boxed, hot dogs are moved to storage coolers and loaded on refrigerated trucks for delivery. The entire process, from cut trimmings to the consumer's table, is often measured in a matter of hours.

A Vienna Beef smokehouse early in the century

Chapter Six

SECRETS OF THE HOT DOG MASTERS

ANY VARIABLES GO into achieving the quintessential, definitive hot dog: choice of meat, type of cooking, length of time, and selection of toppings and bun, among other critical factors. Here are some insights, tips, and general wisdom from the experts:

James Beard

House & Garden, July 1956

The late James Beard was no snob when it came to popular American foods. He had an unabashed enthusiasm for the hot dog, as we learned in Chapter Three. Writing during the Eisenhower years—before Americans became concerned about fat and cholesterol—Beard presented his high-calorie frankfurter advice:

Many people think all frankfurters are the same. Nothing could be more wrong. Too often the frankfurter in the market display case is a dreary hunk of pressed meat. There is not much you can do to give it flavor. Hunt out German shops, Greek

A trio of frankfurters, as presented by Nathan's Famous

The late James Beard was fond of preparing hot dogs with garlic butter, chopped chives, and bacon strips

or Kosher delicatessens for the well-seasoned franks.

(1) Cut a gash in the side of each frankfurter. Spread prepared mustard inside; add a strip of cheese and push the frankfurter back into shape. Wrap a strip of bacon around it. Fasten with a toothpick. Grill until cheese melts and bacon is crisp.

(2) Cut gashes in the frankfurters and spread the inside with garlic butter to which you have added chopped chives and parsley. Wrap with bacon strips and grill.

(3) Mash blue cheese with a little grated onion and blend in chopped chives and parsley. Gash the frankfurters and stuff

them with this mixture. Wrap the bacon strips and grill.

(4) Cut frankfurters in 1-inch pieces. Alternate these on skewers with tiny whole tomatoes and strips of green pepper. Grill. Serve with a good hot Mexican chili.

Steven Shaw

Steven Shaw's New York Restaurant Review and Food Guide

"When I evaluate a hot dog," says Shaw in his Internet food site, "the first thing I look for is a crispy exterior and a juicy interior. For me, part of the pleasure of eating a hot dog is

The versatile hot dog lends itself to any number of presentations

feeling the resistance of the casing or skin, and, after my teeth break through the exterior, tasting the soft juicy interior. Thus, I am opposed in principle to boiled hot dogs because they can never provide the same textural experience. I also think that boiled hot dogs lose a lot of their flavor to the water. . . . I also think that these desirable textural qualities are most likely to appear in a modestly sized hot dog. Those big, thick, foot-long monsters rarely contain a good ratio of casing to meat.

"The next thing I notice," Shaw continues, "is the flavor of the hot dog itself, which is a combination of the meat, the spices, and the smoking process. . . . I do not necessarily think that better meat makes a better hot dog. As peasants have known for generations, there tends to be more flavor in the undesirable parts of the animal. Anyway, the meat in hot dogs is primarily a vehicle for the smoky, spiced flavors.

"Just as important as the hot dog itself are the condiments. In New York the vast majority of people seem to prefer sauerkraut and mustard. I like just a little of each—too much and you may as well not even have the hot dog in there. Try that experiment at home and you will be surprised at how little you notice the lack of a hot dog.

"Finally, there is the bun. I prefer the traditional, soft, white hot dog bun. I like it best when it has been allowed to sit on the griddle for a while next to the hot dogs so that it both gets toasted and absorbs some of the flavors of the nearby meat."

The Brake Light Special
Geno Peegoo

This contribution to the Internet's "World Famous Hot Dog Page," by the presumably pseudonymous Geno Peegoo, offers a mouthwatering approach to a vehicular hot dog:

Although the hot dog is a culinary superstar, it is unselfish and generous in sharing the spotlight. Here the hot dog poses with a variety of side dishes, toppings, relishes, and supporting players.

In a car with disc brakes, set the parking brake. Now, go for a ride around the neighborhood. Keep going until you smell hot metal. When that happens, zoom home, jack up the car, and remove one of the rear wheels, using pot holders.

and laying them face-down on the exhaust pipe.

Serve with cheap yellow mustard to hide the carbon flavor. Note: We aren't sure if this recipe would be a good idea if you have asbestos brake pads.

> *"Toast the buns by opening them up and laying them face-down on the exhaust pipe. Serve with cheap, yellow mustard to hide the carbon flavor."*
>
> – *GENO PEEGOO*

Carefully remove the brake disc (it's hot) and lay it flat on the garage floor. You can get about four or five hot dogs on one brake disc.

The hot dogs will start sizzling and cook up real fast, so pay attention. Toast the buns by opening them up

Hot Dog Soup

FamilyFun magazine, 1997

This recipe asserts that kids will skip using ketchup and/or mustard on their hot dogs if given a chance, instead, to use lentil beans. "The dogs will help them down the pro-

Hot dogs and sausages prepared outdoors on a grill are an American tradition

tein-loaded beans," advises *Family-Fun*. Using plastic knives, children cut hot dogs into one-inch pieces and sauté them in oil until browned. Later, the dogs are added to a chunky, stewlike soup that contains lentils, onion, celery, basil, and pepper. "A small bowl makes a filling lunch," concludes *FamilyFun*.

Born to Grill

Bill Jamison and Cheryl Alters Jamison

This Texan husband-and-wife team, in their 1998 compendium of grilling techniques and recipes, describe some interesting historical approaches to cooking hot dogs.

When you grill a precooked sausage like a hot dog, the goal is to crust the skin and create a bold, contrasting texture between the seared surface and the juicy interior. You don't need to worry about the doneness or exact timing, but you do want to roll the doggie around for a thor-

> *"You do want to roll the doggie around for a thorough crisping that stops well short of the incineration once popular at wiener roasts."*
>
> – BILL AND CHERYL JAMISON

For example, the Jamisons note that in 1959, *Better Homes and Gardens* proposed "a new favorite for all ages called Nutty Pups," which advocated spreading a hot dog with chunky peanut butter and pickle relish.

More in the here-and-now of hot dogs, the Jamisons offer this technique tip:

ough crisping that stops well short of the incineration once popular at wiener roasts. Because of the frequent turning and short cooking time, the process works much better on an open rather than covered grill.

Woman's Day Encyclopedia of Cookery

"Frankfurter," Volume 9

The 1979 edition of this classic cookbook has 59 different recipes for frankfurters, covering the culinary range of appetizers, snacks, soups, casseroles, salads, and main dishes. Although several of these recipes could give pause to the most ardent hot-dog maven (for example, "Frankfurter Eggs Fu Yung"), the most alarming is "Frankfurter, Prune, and Onion Kabobs," which involves skewering an ensemble of diagonally cut franks, green-pepper squares, canned white onions, and pitted prunes.

Samba Dogs

Steven Raichlen, *The Barbecue Bible*

Raichlen includes this exotic Latin interpretation of a grilled dog in his 1998 book of barbecue recipes: "I tasted these unusual hot dogs at a samba school in Rio. From midnight to 4 A.M., the cavernous concrete hall reverberates with the thunderous rhythm of samba. An army of street vendors stands by to assuage the hunger of the dancers, and I was particularly intrigued by the hot dog stand: The vendor crowned her hot dogs with a luscious relish of corn, tomatoes, peas, black and green olives, and hard-cooked eggs."

Mental Health Food

Edward Nishball, Poughkeepsie, New York

A licensed psychologist in private practice, Nishball has had a lifelong love affair with hot dogs. "I have never mistaken hot dogs for health food," he says. "But for me they are *mental health food*, always associated with family, friends, and good times.

"I love hot dogs—but only some hot dogs. They shouldn't be boiled, steamed, or fried in a pan. Broiled or griddled is good. Best of all is cooked briefly in hot oil, then placed on a hot griddle. Any or all of the following should be spread on top: bacon bits, mustard (spicy brown, not yellow), sweet relish (green), sauerkraut (warm) and fresh chopped onion. People who eat hot dogs with ketchup or chili on top are highly suspect—they probably don't really like hot dogs. I have never eaten a hot dog with ketchup."

Frankfurter, Apple and Cheese Pie
The Great Book of Sausages, 1996

British food writers Antony and Araminta Coxe cover the world of sausages in this impressive book— from Aberdeen sausages (Scotland) to *Zwyczajna* (Poland). In a brief passage on the American frank-furter, they describe a pie that combines eight franks, mustard, three apples, and two tablespoons of Parmesan or Romano cheese. The ingredients are placed in a greased baking dish and baked in a moderate oven for 20 minutes, and then grilled until the cheese is bubbling and browned.

Chapter Seven

POP GOES THE HOT DOG

THE SWEEP OF THE HOT dog encompasses literature, movies, music, advertising, the workplace, and politics. Here are some snapshots of the hot dog in American society and pop culture:

A CONFEDERACY OF DUNCES

Hot dogs are an important part of this award-winning 1980 novel by the late John Kennedy Toole. The book's protagonist, Ignatius J. Reilly, is an oversized New Orleans resi-

dent whose love of hot dogs is so ardent that he takes a job with a local pushcart company called Paradise Vendors, Inc. Ignatius tends to eat most of the inventory, so his sales are modest, but he enjoys his work.

The novel has this memorable passage in which Ignatius introduces himself to the head of Paradise Vending, located in a former garage on the ground floor of a commercial building on Poydras Street:

Stopping before the narrow garage, [Ignatius] sniffed the fumes from

Before Jayne Mansfield got her big break in Hollywood, she won a feature role in 1950 as Miss Hot Dog Ambassador

Paradise with great sensory pleasure. . . . analyzing, cataloging, categorizing, and classifying the distinct odors of hot dogs, mustard, and lubricant. Breathing deeply he wondered whether he also detected the more delicate odor, the fragile scent of hot dog buns. He looked at the

"I would like to buy one of your hot dogs. They smell rather tasty. I was wondering if I could buy just one."

"Sure."

"May I select my own?" Ignatius asked, peering down over the top of the pot. . . . "I shall pretend that I am

> *"I would like to buy one of your hot dogs. They smell rather tasty. I was wondering if I could buy just one."*
>
> – IGNATIUS J. REILLY

white-gloved hands of his Mickey Mouse wristwatch and noticed that he had eaten lunch only an hour before. Still the intriguing aromas were making him salivate actively.

"Pardon me, sir," Ignatius called. "Do you retail here?"

The man's watering eyes turned toward the large visitor.

"What do you want?"

in a smart restaurant and that this is the lobster pond."

BASEBALL

There's plenty of baseball lore concerning the food most closely associated with the national pastime. Babe Ruth was known for enjoying

Babe Ruth was known for enjoying dozen or so hot dogs
between games of a doubleheader

a dozen or so dogs between games of a doubleheader. Baseball players use the term "hot dog" to describe a flashy, exhibitionistic player; when slugger Reggie Jackson joined the New York Yankees, a teammate told a sportswriter, "There's not enough mustard in New York to cover that hot dog."

A classic moment in baseball's hot-dog history involved Gates Brown, an outfielder who played 13 years for the Detroit Tigers. Brown was once called upon to pinch-hit while sitting on the bench and eating a hot dog. To escape the wrath of his manager, Mayo Smith, he stuffed the hot dog inside his shirt, stepped up to the plate, and lined a double into right field. Unfortunately, upon sliding into second base, the squashed hot dog splattered all over his uniform. Smith, while grateful for his timely hit, nevertheless fined Brown for eating on the bench.

Rabbi David Senter, a graduate of the Kol Yakkov Torah Center in Monsey, New York, opened the first for-profit Orthodox Kosher hot-dog concessions in the major leagues in 1998. "Senter's operations at Yankee and Shea Stadiums, where Jewish and non-Jewish fans have lined up 10 deep for hot dogs and knishes, are the latest craze in ballpark food," reported Bloomberg News Service.

In a 1998 *Sports Illustrated* article, writer Steve Rustin described his time on the road, watching sports events at offbeat stadiums across America. "I watched a fat man in a minor league ballpark in Colorado Springs spoon chopped onions and pickle relish onto his jumbo frank

> *"Sports is becoming an extension of the hot-dog business."*
>
> – CHRIS BIGELOW

and then turn to me, a complete stranger, and say, 'Vegetables.' And scarier still, I had shared his pride, for I too had come to view the stadium condiment bar as a veritable vegetable garden."

In baseball, as in other professional sports, the revenues from hot-dog concession sales are a critical income stream in an era of escalating player salaries and expensive new facilities. A hot dog and soft drink at some stadiums can cost more than $8, according to a *The Wall Street Journal* story in February 1999. "Sports is becoming an extension of the hot dog business," said Chris Bigelow, a Kansas City foodservice consultant. "Some architects tell me they've building concession stands that just happen to have a baseball game next door."

Chicago's own: A Vienna Beef frankfurter topped with tomato, green relish, yellow mustard, chopped onions, pickles, and sport peppers, served on a poppyseed bun

TV AND MOVIES

Hot dogs frequently appear in Hollywood depictions of American life, both in the movies and on television. An episode of *The Honeymooners*, "The Hot Dog Stand," concerned Ralph Kramden's efforts to enter the hot-dog business, assisted by his loyal friend, Ed Norton. *The Hollywood Shuffle* (1987), starring Robert Townsend and Keenan Wayans, involved an enterprising actor who worked at a hot-dog stand and aspired to be a big-time star.

Their marriage may have been in turmoil, but Lucille Ball and Desi Arnaz shared a hot dog at Santa Anita Race Track in this 1945 photo

In the classic baseball movie *Field of Dreams*, the characters of Kevin Costner and James Earl Jones have an amusing exchange at a baseball stadium's concession (the joke is based on a misunderstanding of the question, "What do you want on the hot dog?") In another

Chris Patak, Gerry Beyer, and Susannah Ludwig have spent six weeks traveling around America to make their two-hour documentary on "the subculture that surrounds hot dogs." Among their subjects are the Hot Dog Ministry in Columbus, Ohio, a shelter that offers hot dogs

"I had a vision of my own hot dog stand. It was as exciting to me as having my own yacht."

– HOWARD JONAS

part of the movie, a hot dog is a central reason why the Doctor, played by Burt Lancaster, decides to leave the dream field of his youth abruptly.

Three young filmmakers are producing a documentary called *Footlong*, which concerns the influence of the hot dog on American society.

and prayers, and the Hot Dog Hall of Fame in Fairfield, California.

"ON A ROLL"

Howard Jonas is chief executive officer of International Discount Telecommunications, a publicly

traded telecommunications company and Internet service provider. He
began in a much different industry—hot dogs. As Jonas described
in his 1998 autobiography, *On A
Roll*, the lessons he learned selling
hot dogs in New York City would be
invaluable when he graduated from
Harvard and launched his "real" career:

> I had a vision of my own hot dog
> stand. It was as exciting to me as
> having my own yacht. I could see it
> in my mind's eye, all polished,
> gleaming chrome, with the smell of
> boiling hot dogs, sauerkraut, and
> onions wafting out in small puffs
> from beneath the chrome food
> doors. . . . Working hard and run-
> ning my own business was fun. That
> was even more important than the
> money I made. For the first six years
> I was in the telecommunications
> business, I didn't take a dime in
> salary or profits. Many times I didn't
> know whether I'd still be in business
> in two months. But I loved what I

was doing, just like I loved selling
hot dogs.

The teenaged Jonas began selling
hot dogs on a corner in a tough
urban neighborhood, across the
street from a bar called the Tender
Trap:

> At first the bar hostesses would
> come running across the street to
> pick up hot dogs for their patrons.
> Soon they would just yell the order
> across the two-way, six-lane street
> and I would prepare the hot dogs
> and run them over. . . . Eventually
> the bar and I developed a signaling
> system similar to that between a
> major league catcher and pitcher.
> The hostesses would go to the win-
> dow and on the right hand hold up
> fingers to signal the number of hot
> dogs needed. Then, on the left, they
> put up one finger for onions, two for
> sauerkraut, three for mustard only,
> or four for plain. After receiving the
> signal, I'd prepare the dogs and de-
> liver them pronto to the bar.

Smoke rise at Campobello—Eleanor Roosevelt cooks hot dogs at the Roosevelt summer home on Campobello Island in July 1933, shortly after her husband's inauguration as president

HOT DOG POLITICS

In June 1998 the mighty *New York Times* editorial page rose to the defense of hot-dog pushcarts after Mayor Rudolph Giuliani proposed banning sidewalk vendors from 144 blocks in Manhattan.

"Do we really want to outlaw the corner hot dog stand?" thundered the *Times* in an editorial titled, "And Now, the Hot Dog War."

"In [the Mayor's] zeal for order and obedience, he must not destroy the lively street scene that is part of the city's historic flavor," continued

A New York City hot-dog vendor surveys his domain, April 1936

the *Times.* "There must be a better way for the city to hear the voice of the hot dog vendors and their customers, not just those who sell sandwiches or real estate nearby." As *Hot Dog Companion* went to press, the Manhattan hot-dog controversy still was unresolved.

dons a chef's hat and apron, wheels the cart to an indoor courtyard, and cooks free hot dogs for everyone in the company. If customers or suppliers are in the building, they are welcome to have a hot dog, too. "The purpose is to create a more informal atmosphere. It

> *Once a month, Zeid dons a chef's hat and apron, wheels the cart to an indoor courtyard, and cooks free hot dogs for everyone in the company.*

DOGS IN THE WORKPLACE

Philip Zeid is president of Universal Scrap Metals, a recycling business in Chicago. Last year, after his family gave him a hot-dog cart as a birthday present, he brought "Phil's Wiener Wagon" to his company and instituted Wiener Wednesdays. Once a month Zeid

generates a family, friendly feeling—people come in, talk with one another, and get a hot dog," Zeid says.

Asked which brand of hot dog he cooks on Wiener Wednesdays, Zeid freely confesses to a Fluky bias: his son is married into the Drexler family that owns Fluky's, a Chicago hot-dog shrine.

"A HIGHER AUTHORITY"

Hebrew National introduced one of advertising's most memorable campaigns for its kosher franks. The original television commercial in 1976 portrayed a top-hatted Uncle Sam character eating a hot dog, while a voice-over explained that Hebrew National's standards were "higher" than that of the U.S. government. The punch line, "We answer to a higher authority," has become the marketing theme for all of Hebrew National's products. A new line of humorous commercials, featuring the voice of comedian Robert Klein emanating from behind a hot-dog cart, further develops the slogan.

"Consumers today are so concerned about what they are eating," says Steven Silk, president of Hebrew National. "Kosher is the first quality assurance system for meat known to mankind. We've tried to integrate that into the essence of our advertising."

Incidentally, the single biggest customer of Hebrew National kosher franks is Costco, the warehouse retailer. Costco customers can enjoy a Hebrew National hot dog, toppings, and a soft drink for $1.50.

ACKNOWLEDGMENTS

Many people have helped me on this literary expedition through the lore and legends of the hot dog. A special thanks to the following persons, who were especially generous with their time and hot dog expertise:

Richard Riemann, Top Dog, Berkeley, California

Steven Silk, president, Hebrew National, New York

Professor Gerald Cohen, University of Missouri, Rolla

Dennis Tase, president, Wienerschnitzel, Newport Beach, California

Bruce Bunch and the Weenie Wanderers, Fairfield, Connecticut

Jim Mosle, Saags Products, San Leandro, California

Ed Vohasek, Chicago, Illinois

Ed and Patricia Nishball, Poughkeepsie, New York

Steve Rushmore, HVS International, Mineola, New York

Barbara Pisani and Christi Nelson, Lebhar-Friedman, New York, researchers for the *Companion* series

Beth G. Klein, librarian, California Culinary Academy, San Francisco

Craig Jackson and Lucinda Walker, reference specialists, Mechanics' Institute Library, San Francisco

Janet Reilly, National Hot Dog & Sausage Council, American Meat Institute, Arlington, Virginia

Geoff Golson and Paul Frumkin at Lebhar-Friedman Books, New York, who had the original vision and enthusiasm for the *Companion* series.

PHOTO CREDITS

INDEX

Index

ABOUT THE AUTHOR

DAVID GRAULICH writes a nationally syndicated humor column, performs regular commentaries on National Public Radio, and is most recently the author of *Dial 9 to Get Out!,* a humorous look at office life. An avid and enthusiastic fan of hamburgers, french fries, and hot dogs, he resides with his family in San Bruno, California.

15 COLORFUL BLANKETS IN DIFFERENT TECHNIQUES AND STYLES

COSY CROCHET BLANKETS

TO SNUGGLE UNDER

ANA MORAIS SOARES

TUVA

This book is dedicated to the amazing woman who taught me to crochet when I was just a little girl - my beloved grandmother. I thank her for all the times she made me frog my work when a stitch was not right. And for turning me into a crochet addict!

3

Tuva Publishing
www.tuvapublishing.com

Address Merkez Mah. Cavusbasi Cad. No:71
Cekmekoy - Istanbul 34782 / Turkey
Tel: +9 0216 642 62 62

Cosy Crochet Blankets To Snuggle Under

First Print 2020 / February

All Global Copyrights Belong To
Tuva Tekstil ve Yayıncılık Ltd.

Content Crochet

Editor in Chief Ayhan DEMİRPEHLİVAN
Project Editor Kader DEMİRPEHLİVAN
Designer Ana Morais SOARES
Technical Editors Leyla ARAS, Büşra ESER
Crochet Tech Editor Wendi CUSINS
Graphic Designers Ömer ALP
Abdullah BAYRAKÇI, Tarık TOKGÖZ
Photograph Tuva Publishing

ISBN 978-605-9192-69-9

 TuvaYayincilik TuvaPublishing
 TuvaYayincilik TuvaPublishing

Thank you *Scheepjes*
for supporting this book with your yarn.

THANK YOU

I met so many extraordinary people during this book journey and I can never thank all of them for the amazing help and support along the way.

It all started when one day I received an email from TUVA Publishing, inviting me to write a book of crochet blankets. At first I was puzzled – but absolutely thrilled. Wow! Me writing a book? That's a big reponsibility. (For many years, I worked at a Portuguese schoolbook publisher, and I came to treasure and respect books.) I will always be grateful to Kader Demirpehlivan for this marvelous opportunity, and for her trust and support. Also, a giant Thank You to Wendi Cusins for all her extraordinary work as well as her patience and dedication. A true honor and big pleasure to work with this lady.

A huge "thank you" to all the ladies who helped me with the edits and blankets' testing – Caroline, Felicia, Lynette, Mary, Stacey, Tanie, Tawnya, Michele, Jane and The Incredibles – Jo, Margaret, Silvana and Laurene (all from the Facebook group, CAL-Crochet Along). They are all amazing and I am eternally grateful.

Also, a big "thank you" to two beautiful ladies that have tested my patterns for some time now – Julia Veloso and Samantha Janke. They were the first ones to know about this massive project and went through each and every pattern - handling them with discretion and in secrecy.

Thank you to Scheepjes for sponsoring the yarn for the blankets.

Finally, but most importantly, I am immensely grateful to:

My dear friend, Lynnette Wilkie, who welcomed me into her crochet world and always supported, helped and encouraged me;

My mother and sister, who helped make some of the blankets (I would still be making them without their help), and my husband and children, for all their patience in dealing with my lack of time, my nerves and my self-doubts.

CONTENTS

PROJECTS

INTRODUCTION

Crafting has always been part of my life. As a child, daytime was spent at school or playing in the fields with friends. But the evenings were magical! After dinner, my mother and grandmother would sit together chatting – sometimes knitting, sometimes crocheting. My sister and I would join them for these "ladies nights". And this is where I picked up the crochet bug!

Color fascinates me, and instead of using the neutral colors favored by the older women, I picked up every colorful ball of yarn I could lay my hands on. I remember the joy I felt when seeing all the heavenly colors in the yarn shops.

My first attempts at crochet were clothes for my dolls, granny squares, and corner-to-corner (C2C) cushions. In my mother's home there are still some of my early projects. Others are only in my childhood memories.

Most of my late adolescence was spent knitting (a skill my mother taught me). Besides the countless scarves, cowls, sweaters and cardigans I made, I also learnt to knit socks – using five needles!

During my school career, I was enchanted by the craft classes learnt many different skills and techniques. I made a lot of cross-stitch, macramé, punch needle and quilting pieces. In fact, quilting is my second passion after crochet, perhaps because of all the colorful fabrics available.

Designing is a new element in my life. Even though, in the past, I created unique crochet and knitting items, I had never written out the patterns before. Recently some crochet friends challenged me to do it. And here I am, embracing that challenge!

I hope you have as much joy crocheting these blankets as I have had creating them. It was fun experimenting with the various crochet techniques.

Sending love

Ana

Hearts Full of Grace 20

Everlasting Love 28

Purple Mist 34

Flower Patches 40

Crush on You 48

Fluttering in the Breeze 60

Rainbows in Tunisia 66

Little Boxes of Joy 72

Spring Field 78

Where the Wild Roses Grow 84

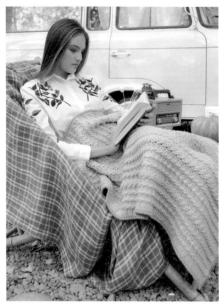

Cables and Puffs 94

All the Oceans Blue 100

Painting the Woods 104

Twinkling Star 112

Daigo-ji Garden 138

CROCHET TERMINOLOGY

This book is written using US crochet terminology.

US Crochet Terms		UK Crochet Terms	
⬭	Chain	⬭	Chain
•	Slip Stitch	•	Slip Stitch
+	Single Crochet	+	Double Crochet
T	Half-Double Crochet	T	Half-Treble Crochet
⊤	Double Crochet	⊤	Treble Crochet
⊤	Treble Crochet	⊤	Double Treble Crochet
⊤	Double Treble	⊤	Triple Treble
⬭	Double Crochet Bobble	⬭	Treble Crochet Bobble
◯	Magic Ring	◯	Magic Ring

Crochet Hook Sizes (Rather use this updated table)

Metric	US	UK/Canada
2.00 mm	—	14
2.25 mm	B-1	13
2.50 mm	—	12
2.75 mm	C-2	—
3.00 mm	—	11
3.125 mm	D	—
3.25 mm	D-3	10
3.50 mm	E-4	9
3.75 mm	F-5	—
4.00 mm	G-6	8
4.25 mm	G	—
4.50 mm	#7	7
5.00 mm	H-8	6
5.25 mm	I	—
5.50 mm	I-9	5
6.00 mm	J-10	4
6.50 mm	K-10 ½	3
7.00 mm		2
8.00 mm	L-11	0
9.00 mm	M/N-13	00
10.00 mm	N/P-15	000

Abbreviations of Basic Stitches

ch	Chain Stitch
sl st	Slip Stitch
sc	Single Crochet Stitch
hdc	Half-Double Crochet Stitch
dc	Double Crochet Stitch
tr	Treble (or Triple) Crochet Stitch

Standard Symbols Used in Patterns

[ ]	Work instructions within brackets as many times as directed
( )	Work instructions within parentheses in same stitch or space indicated
*	Repeat the instructions following the single asterisk as directed
**	1) Repeat instructions between asterisks as many times as directed; or 2) Repeat from a given set of instructions
♥ ♥ ♥	Repeat instructions between hearts as many times as directed

Concise Action Terms

dec	Decrease (reduce by one or more stitches)
inc	Increase (add one or more stitches)
join	Join two stitches together, usually with a slip stitch. (Either to complete the end of a round or when introducing a new ball or color of yarn)
rep	Repeat (the previous marked instructions)
turn	Turn your crochet piece so you can work back for the next row/round
yo	Yarn over the hook. (Either to pull up a loop or to draw through the loops on hook)

YARNS AND MATERIALS

  Fingering Weight

Scheepjes Whirl / Whirlette
(60% Cotton & 40% Acrylic)

Scheepjes Catona
(100% Cotton Mercerized)

Scheepjes Sunkissed
(100% Cotton)

Sport Weight

Stone Washed
(78% Cotton & 22% Acrylic)

River Washed
(78% Cotton & 22% Acrylic)

DK Weight

Scheepjes Merino Soft
(50% Wool Superwash Merino,
25% Microfiber & 25% Acrylic)

Scheepjes Softfun / Softfun Denim
(60% Cotton & 40% Acrylic)

Scheepjes Colour Crafter
(100% Premium Acrylic)

Scheepjes Linen Soft
(27% Linen, 47% Cotton & 26% Acrylic)

Scheepjes Wanderlust
(100% single spun Acrylic yarn)

 Aran Weight

 Bulky Weight

Scheepjes Stone Washed XL / River Washed XL
(70% Cotton & 30% Acrylic)

Scheepjes Cahlista
(100% natural cotton)

Scheepjes Namaste
(50% Virgin Wool & 50% Acrylic)

CROCHET BASICS

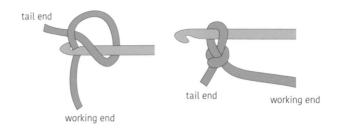

Slip Knot

Almost all crochet projects start with a slip knot on the hook. This is rarely mentioned in the pattern - it is assumed.

To make a slip knot, form a loop with the yarn (the tail end to the back of the loop) and insert hook in the loop pulling the working end (attached to the ball) of the yarn through the loop.

Tugging on the tail end tightens the knot and tugging of the working yarn, closes the loop.

Chain Stitch (ch)

The chain stitch is the foundation of most crochet projects. The foundation chain is a series of chain stitches in which the first row of stitches is worked. To make a chain stitch, start with a slip knot (or loop) on hook. Yarn over and draw the yarn through the loop on the hook.

Hint: When making a foundation chain, do not work too tightly as it will then be difficult to work the first row of stitches.

When counting chain stitches, do not count the slip knot nor the loop on hook. Only count the number of visible "v"s at the front of the chain string, or the ridges at the back.

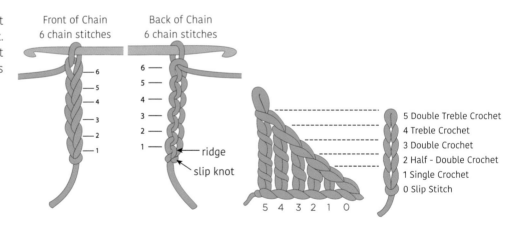

Yarn Over (yo)

This is a common term in crochet, where you wrap the working end of the yarn around the hook (however many times is needed), from back to front around the shaft of the hook.

Slip Stitch (sl st)

Slip stitches do not have any height to them. They are used for closing joined rounds or when attaching a new color or ball of yarn. They can also be used to position the yarn for the next row or round.

With a loop on the hook, insert the hook in the stitch or space specified and pull up the yarn through the stitch or space, drawing the yarn through the loop on hook (slip stitch made).

12

Single Crochet (sc)

The height of the single crochet stitch is one chain high.
When starting the first row of single crochet stitches, working into the foundation chain, skip one chain, and start working in the second chain from hook. This skipped chain does not count as a stitch, but brings the stitches up to the correct height.

Similarly, at the beginning of a row or round, make one chain stitch (to get the height) before working the single crochet stitches, starting in the first stitch.

With a loop on the hook, insert the hook in the stitch or space specified and pull up a loop (two loops on hook). Yarn over hook and draw through both the loops on hook (one loop remains on hook) to make a single crochet stitch.

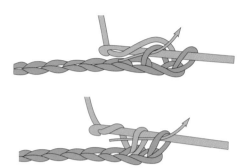

Half-Double Crochet (hdc)

The height of a half-double crochet stitch is two chains high. When working into the foundation chain, skip two chains, and start working in the third chain from hook. These skipped chain stitches do not count as the first stitch, but brings the stitches up to the correct height. Similarly, at the beginning of a row or round, make two chain stitches (to get the height) before working the half-double crochet stitches, starting in the first stitch.

(Note: Some patterns might state that the first two chain stitches do count as the first half-double crochet stitch. In that case, the subsequent rounds or rows are started in the second stitch.)

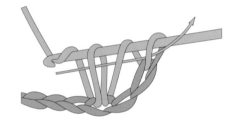

To make a half-double crochet stitch, start with a loop on the hook. Yarn over and insert the hook in the stitch or space specified and pull up a loop (three loops on hook). Yarn over hook and draw through all three loops on hook (one loop remains on hook).

Double Crochet (dc)

The height of a double crochet stitch is three chains high. When working into the foundation chain, skip three chains, and start working in the fourth chain from hook. These three skipped chain stitches (which bring up the height) count as the first double crochet stitch. At the beginning of a row or round, make three chain stitches (which count as the first

double crochet stitch, as well as to get the height). Skip the first stitch of the previous row and work the double crochet stitches, starting in the next stitch.

To make a double crochet stitch, start with a loop on the hook. Yarn over and insert the hook in the stitch or space specified and pull up a loop (three loops on hook).

Yarn over hook and draw through two loops on hook (two loops remain). Yarn over hook and draw through remaining two loops on hook (one loop remains on hook)

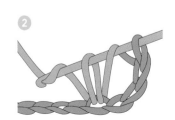

Treble (or Triple) Crochet (tr)

The height of a treble crochet stitch is four chains high.

When working into the foundation chain, skip four chains, and start working in the fifth chain from hook. These four skipped chain stitches (which bring up the height) count as the first treble crochet stitch. At the beginning of a row or round, make four chain stitches (which count as the first treble crochet stitch, as well as to get the height). Skip the first stitch of the previous row and work the treble crochet stitches, starting in the next stitch.

To make a treble crochet stitch, start with a loop on the hook. Wrap the yarn over the hook twice and insert the hook in the stitch or space specified and pull up a loop (four loops on hook). Yarn over hook and draw through two loops on hook (three loops remain). Again, yarn over hook and draw through two loops on hook (two loops remain). And once more, yarn over hook and draw through remaining two loops on hook (one loop remains on hook).

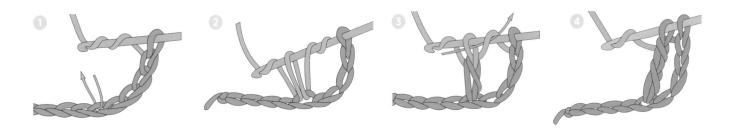

Double Treble (or Double Triple) Crochet (dtr)

The height of a Double Treble is five chains high.

Starting with a loop on hook, wrap the yarn over hook three times before inserting hook in stitch or space specified and pull up a loop (five loops on hook). Yarn over hook and draw through two loops on hook (four loops on hook). Repeat: Yarn over hook and draw through two loops on hook – three times more until only one loop remains on hook.

Triple Treble (or Triple Triple) Crochet (trtr)

The height of a Triple Treble is six chains high.

Starting with a loop on hook, wrap the yarn over hook four times before inserting hook in stitch or space specified and pull up a loop (six loops on hook). Repeat: Yarn over hook and draw through two loops on hook - five times until only one loop remains on hook.

STITCHES & TECHNIQUES

Changing Colors / Attaching New Yarn

Instead of fastening off and then starting the next row or round with a new color (either by joining with a slip stitch or by making a standing stitch), one can change to the new color in the last step of the final stitch before the new color change.

For the basic stitches, the final step of the stitch, is the yarn over and drawing through remaining loops on hook, leaving one loop on hook.

With the current color, work the last stitch before the color change up to the last step of the stitch. Using the new color, yarn over hook and draw new color through remaining loops on hook (one new color loop on hook).

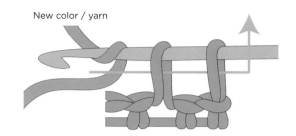

New color / yarn

Front Loop Only (FLO) and Back Loop Only (BLO)

To identify the loops at the top of the stitch:

Back loop - insert the hook from front to back under only the loop furthest from you.

Both loops - insert the hook from front to back under both the front and back loops (the "v") at the top of the stitch.

Front loop - insert the hook from front to back under only the loop nearest to you.

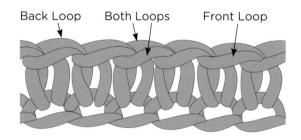

Back Loop   Both Loops   Front Loop

Magic Ring

1 Form a loop with the yarn, keeping the tail end of the yarn behind the working yarn (the yarn attached to the ball).

2 Insert the hook through the loop (from front to back), and pull the working yarn through the loop (from back to front). Do not tighten up the loop.

3 Using the working yarn, make a chain stitch (to secure the ring). This chain stitch does NOT count as first stitch.

4 Work the required stitches into the ring (over the tail strand). When all the stitches are done, gently tug the tail end to close the ring, before joining the round (if specified). Remember, make sure this tail is firmly secured before weaving in the end.

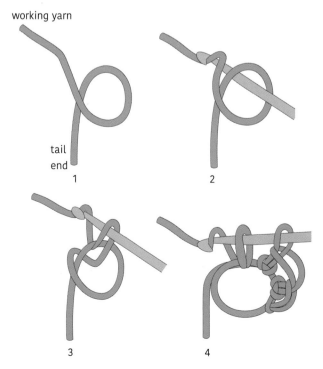

working yarn

tail end

1

2

3

4

Post Stitches

Instead of working in the top loops of previously made stitches, post stitches are worked around the post of the previously made stitch.

To work a Front Post stitch (FP), insert the hook from front to back to front around the post of the specified stitch.

For a Back Post (BP) stitch, insert the hook from back to front to back around the post of the specified stitch.

Any stitch, including complex stitches, can be worked around the posts of previously made stitches.

Unless noted otherwise, always skip the stitch behind a Front Post stitch (or in front of a Back Post stitch).

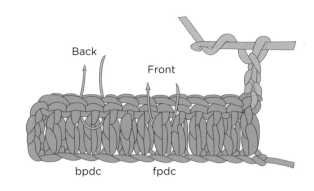

Front Post Single Crochet (FPsc)

Insert hook from front to back to front around post of specified stitch and pull up a loop (2 loops on hook), yarn over and draw through both loops on hook.

Back Post Single Crochet (BPsc)

Insert hook from back to front to back around post of specified stitch and pull up a loop (2 loops on hook), yarn over and draw through both loops on hook.

Front Post Half-Double Crochet (FPhdc)

Yarn over, insert hook from front to back to front around post of specified stitch and pull up a loop (3 loops on hook), yarn over and draw through all 3 loops on hook.

Back Post Half-Double Crochet (BPhdc)

Yarn over, insert hook from back to front to back around post of specified stitch and pull up a loop (3 loops on hook), yarn over and draw through all 3 loops on hook.

Front Post Double Crochet (FPdc)

Yarn over, insert hook from front to back to front around post of specified stitch and pull up a loop (3 loops on hook), [yarn over, draw through 2 loops on hook] twice.

Back Post Double Crochet (BPdc)

Yarn over, insert hook from back to front to back around post of specified stitch and pull up a loop (3 loops on hook), [yarn over, draw through 2 loops on hook] twice.

Front Post Treble (FPtr)

Yarn over twice, insert hook from front to back to front around post of specified stitch and pull up a loop (4 loops on hook), [yarn over, draw through 2 loops on hook] 3 times.

Front Post Double Treble (FPdtr)

Yarn over 3 times, insert hook from front to back to front around post of specified stitch and pull up a loop (5 loops on hook), [yarn over, draw through 2 loops on hook] 4 times.

Front Post Triple Treble (FPtrtr)

Yarn over 4 times, insert hook from front to back to front around post of specified stitch and pull up a loop (6 loops on hook), [yarn over, draw through 2 loops on hook] 5 times.

Picots

Picots form decorative (and sometimes functional) chain loops.

For each picot: Make three chain stitches, then slip stitch through both the front loop and side bar together of the base stitch (picot made).

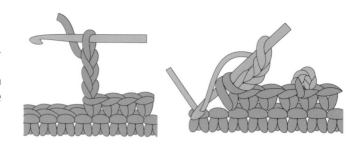

Puff Stitch (puff-st)

The crochet puff stitch is so named, because the finished stitch is a gently puffed up oval shape, adding texture to your project. It is made from a group of unfinished half-double crochets, before joining them all together to finish.

Working in the same stitch or space specified, repeat: Yarn over hook, insert hook and pull up a long loop (to the height of a half-double crochet – 2 chains high) - four times. There are now nine loops on hook. Yarn over and draw through all nine loops on hook. Make one chain – to secure the puff-stitch.

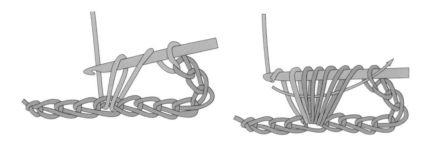

Standing Stitches

Instead of joining a new color yarn with a slip stitch and then working chain stitches to the height needed, one can make the stitch from the top down - a standing stitch.

All standing stitches start by placing a slip knot on the hook. The required stitch is then made following the normal instructions. Any stitch, including complex stitches, can be made into a standing stitch – even popcorns, bobbles, and also post stitches.

Standing Single Crochet

With a slip knot on the hook, insert the hook in the stitch or space specified and pull up a loop (two loops on hook). Yarn over hook and draw through both loops on hook (single crochet stitch made).

Standing Double Crochet

With a slip knot on the hook, yarn over and insert the hook in the stitch or space specified and pull up a loop (three loops on hook). Yarn over hook and draw through two loops on hook (two loops remain). Yarn over hook and draw through remaining two loops on hook (double crochet stitch made).

Standing Treble Bobble (with 3 tr)

With slip knot on hook, yarn over twice, and insert hook in stitch or space specified and pull up a loop (four loops on hook). [Yarn over and draw through two loops on hook] twice (two loops remain on hook). Repeat: Yarn over twice and insert hook in

same stich or space and pull up a loop. [Yarn over and draw through two loops on hook] twice - twice more (four loops on hook). Yarn over and draw through remaining four loops on hook (treble bobble made).

Hint: Hold the slip knot in place with your thumb before wrapping the yarn over the hook.

PROJECTS

HEARTS FULL OF GRACE

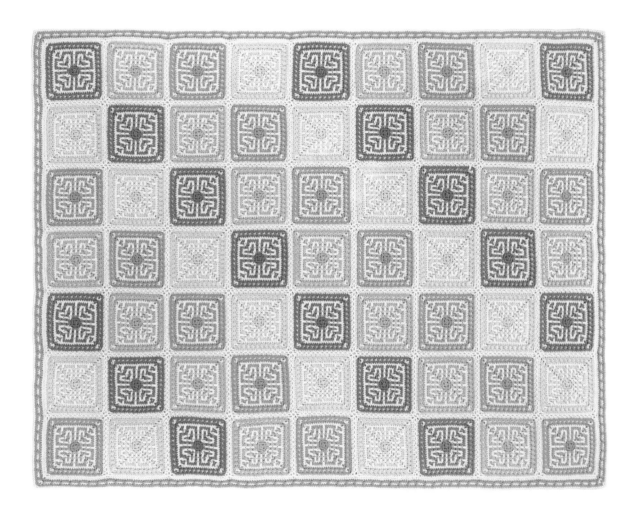

Materials

Scheepjes Softfun
Main Color (MC): Cream (2622) - 11 balls

Contrasting Colors (CC):
Color A: Lilac (2618) - 3 balls
Color B: Wine (2624) - 3 balls
Color C: Gold (2621) - 3 balls
Color D: Blue Grey (2625) - 3 balls

#7 (4.50 mm) Crochet Hook – for Motifs and Border
I-9 (5.50 mm) Crochet Hook – for joining Motifs together

Size

About 43" wide by 57" long (109 cm by 145 cm)

Gauge

Each Motif: About 6" (15 cm) square.

Pattern Notes

1 Motifs and Border of this blanket are worked using the Mosaic Crochet technique.

2 Each Motif is worked in rounds using Main Color and one of the other four colors.

3 From Round 3, all single crochet stitches are worked in the back loops only (BLO) of stitches. (The corners are still worked into the chain-spaces.) The double crochet stitches are worked in the front loop only (FLO) of the corresponding stitch two rounds below.

4 All rounds are worked with right side facing. Do NOT fasten off at the end of each round (after making the ch-3 string).

MOTIF

(MAKE 63 – 16 MOTIFS EACH USING COLOR A, B & C, AND 15 MOTIFS USING COLOR D)

Round 1: (Right Side) Using CC and smaller hook, make a magic ring; ch 1, [sc in ring, ch 2] 4 times; join with sl st in first sc. (4 sc & 4 corner ch-2 sps)

Round 2: Ch 1, [(sc, ch 2, sc) in next ch-2 sp, sc in next st] 4 times; join with sl st in first sc. Ch 3 and remove hook. (12 sc, 4 corner ch-2 sps & 1 ch-3 string)

Round 3: (see Pattern Note 3) Join MC with standing sc in the corner ch-2 sp opposite the ch-3 string, ch 2, sc in same sp, *working in BLO, sc in each of next 3 sts, (sc, ch 2, sc) in next corner ch-2 sp*, sc in each of next 2 sts, working over the ch-3 string from previous round, sc in next st, sc in next corner ch-2 sp (string is in position for next round), ch 2, (not working over string) sc in same ch-2 sp; rep from * to * once, sc in each of next 3 sts; join with sl st in first sc. Ch 3 and remove hook. (20 sc, 4 corner ch-2 sps & 1 ch-3 string)

Round 4: (see Pattern Note 3) Insert hook in CC loop (from Rnd 2), (sc, ch 2, sc) in corner ch-2 sp, *sc in next st, dc in first sc after ch-2 corner (Rnd 2), skip next st, sc in next st, dc in last sc before ch-2 corner (Rnd 2), skip next st, sc in next st**, (sc, ch 2, sc) in next corner ch-2 sp; repeat from * around (remember to work over ch-3 string with last sc before third corner and the first sc in corner), ending at ** on final repeat; join with sl st in first sc. Ch 3 and remove hook. (20 sc, 8 dc, 4 corner ch-2 sps & 1 ch-3 string)

Round 5: (see Pattern Note 3) Insert hook in MC loop (from Rnd 3), (sc, ch 2, sc) in corner ch-2 sp, *sc in next st, dc in first sc after ch-2 corner (Rnd 3), skip next st, sc in next st, dc in corresponding st (Rnd 3),

skip next st, sc in next st, dc in last st before corner (Rnd 3), skip next st, sc in next st**, (sc, ch 2, sc) in next corner ch-2 sp; repeat from * around (remember to work over ch-3 string with last sc before third corner and the first sc in corner), ending at ** on final repeat; join with sl st in first sc. Ch 3 and remove hook. (24 sc, 12 dc, 4 corner ch-2 sps & 1 ch-3 string)

Round 6: (see Pattern Note 3) Insert hook in CC loop (from Rnd 4), (sc, ch 2, sc) in corner ch-2 sp, *sc in next st, dc in first sc after ch-2 corner (Rnd 4), [skip next st, sc in next st, dc in corresponding st (Rnd 4)] twice, skip next st, sc in next st, dc in last st before corner (Rnd 4), skip next st, sc in next st**, (sc, ch 2, sc) in next corner ch-2 sp; repeat from * around (remember to work over ch-3 string with last sc before third corner and the first sc in corner), ending at ** on final repeat; join with sl st in first sc. Ch 3 and remove hook. (28 sc, 16 dc, 4 corner ch-2 sps & 1 ch-3 string)

Round 7: (see Pattern Note 3) Insert hook in MC loop (from Rnd 5), (sc, ch 2, sc) in corner ch-2 sp, *sc in next st, dc in first sc after ch-2 corner (Rnd 5), [skip next st, sc in next st, dc in corresponding st (Rnd 5)] 3 times, skip next st, sc in next st, dc in last st before corner (Rnd 5), skip next st, sc in next st**, (sc, ch 2, sc) in next corner ch-2 sp; repeat from * around (remember to work over ch-3 string with last sc before third corner and the first sc in corner), ending at ** on final repeat; join with sl st in first sc. Ch 3 and remove hook. (32 sc, 20 dc, 4 corner ch-2 sps & 1 ch-3 string)

Round 3

Round 3

Round 4

Round 4

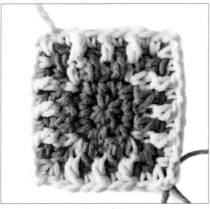

Round 5

Round 8: (see Pattern Note 3) Insert hook in CC loop (from Rnd 6), (sc, ch 2, sc) in corner ch-2 sp, *sc in next st, dc in first sc after ch-2 corner (Rnd 6), skip next st, sc in each of next 3 sts, dc in corresponding st (Rnd 6), skip next st, sc in next st, dc in corresponding st (Rnd 6), skip next st, sc in each of next 3 sts, dc in last st before corner (Rnd 6), skip next st, sc in next st**, (sc, ch 2, sc) in next corner ch-2 sp; repeat from * around (remember to work over ch-3 string with last sc before third corner and the first sc in corner), ending at ** on final repeat; join with sl st in first sc. Ch 3 and remove hook. (44 sc, 16 dc, 4 corner ch-2 sps & 1 ch-3 string)

Round 9: (see Pattern Note 3) Insert hook in MC loop (from Rnd 7), (sc, ch 2, sc) in corner ch-2 sp, *sc in next st, dc in first sc after ch-2 corner (Rnd 7), skip next st, sc in each of next 5 sts, dc in corresponding st (Rnd 7), skip next st, sc in each of next 5 sts, dc in last st before corner (Rnd 7), skip next st, sc in next st**, (sc, ch 2, sc) in next corner ch-2 sp; repeat from * around (remember to work over ch-3 string with last sc before third corner and the first sc in corner), ending at ** on final repeat; join with sl st in first sc. Ch 3 and remove hook. (56 sc, 12 dc, 4 corner ch-2 sps & 1 ch-3 string)

Round 10: (see Pattern Note 3) Insert hook in CC loop (from Rnd 8), (sc, ch 2, sc) in corner ch-2 sp, *sc in each of next 17 sts**, (sc, ch 2, sc) in next corner ch-2 sp; repeat from * around (remember to work over ch-3 string with last sc before third corner and the first sc in corner), ending at ** on final repeat; join with sl st in first sc. Ch 3 and remove hook. (76 sc, 4 corner ch-2 sps & 1 ch-3 string)

Round 11: (see Pattern Note 3) Insert hook in MC loop (from Rnd 9), (sc, ch 2, sc) in corner ch-2 sp, *sc in each of next 19 sts**, (sc, ch 2, sc) in next corner ch-2 sp; repeat from * around (remember to work over ch-3 string with last sc before third corner and the first sc in corner), ending at ** on final repeat; join with sl st in first sc. Ch 3 and remove hook. (84 sc, 4 corner ch-2 sps & 1 ch-3 string)

Round 12: (see Pattern Note 3) Insert hook in CC loop (from Rnd 10), (sc, ch 2, sc) in corner ch-2 sp, *sc in next st, dc in first sc after ch-2 corner (Rnd 10), [skip next st, sc in next st, dc in corresponding st (Rnd 10)] 8 times, skip next st, sc in next st, dc in last st before corner (Rnd 10), skip next st, sc in next st**, (sc, ch 2, sc) in next corner ch-2 sp; repeat from * around (remember to work over ch-3 string with last sc before third corner and the first sc in corner), ending at ** on final repeat; join with sl st in first sc. (52 sc, 40 dc, 4 corner ch-2 sps & 1 ch-3 string) Fasten off CC and weave in all ends.

Round 13: (see Pattern Note 3) Insert hook in MC loop (from Rnd 11), (sc, ch 2, sc) in corner ch-2 sp, *sc in each of next 23 sts**, (sc, ch 2, sc) in next corner ch-2 sp; repeat from * around, ending at ** on final repeat; join with sl st in first sc. (100 sc, 4 corner ch-2 sps & 1 ch-3 string) Fasten off MC and weave in all ends.

Round 8

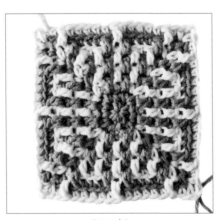

Round 9

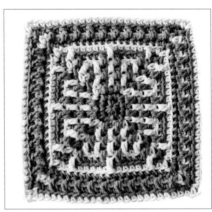

Round 13

JOINING MOTIFS

Lay the motifs out (right side facing) to form a rectangle – 7 motifs wide by 9 motifs long - with the same colors running diagonally.

The motifs are crocheted together through both loops of the stitches, using the larger hook. Following the chart, first join motifs together horizontally, and then join them vertically.

C	A	B	D	C	A	B
A	B	D	C	A	B	D
B	D	C	A	B	D	C
D	C	A	B	D	C	A
C	A	B	D	C	A	B
A	B	D	C	A	B	D
B	D	C	A	B	D	C
D	C	A	B	D	C	A
C	A	B	D	C	A	B

FIRST JOINING ROW

Holding first two motifs with right sides together (wrong side facing), working through both thicknesses, using larger hook, join MC with standing sc in any corner ch-2 sp, *[ch 1, skip next st, sc in next st] 12 times, ch 1, skip next st, sc in next corner ch-2 sp**, ch 1 (connection between motifs), holding next two motifs with right sides together, sc in corner ch-2 sp; repeat from * 6 times more, ending at ** on final repeat. Fasten off and weave in all ends.

NEXT JOINING ROW

Open the joined motifs, with right sides facing (check that the ch-1 connections are not twisted), following the diagram, place next new motif on top of joined motif (right sides together), working through both thicknesses, join MC with standing sc in any corner ch-2 sp, *[ch 1, skip next st, sc in next st] 12 times, ch 1, skip next st, sc in next corner ch-2 sp**, ch 1 (connection between motifs), holding next new motif on next joined motif, with right sides together, sc in corner ch-2 sp; repeat from * 6 times more, ending at ** on final repeat. Fasten off and weave in all ends.

Repeat Next Joining Row until all motifs are joined horizontally. Then repeat the procedure for all the vertical joins, where the ch-1 connection goes over the horizontal ch-1 connection.

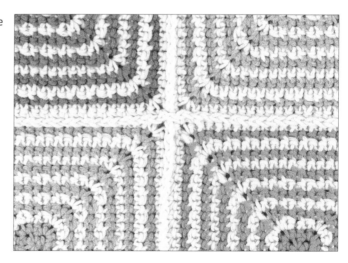

BORDER

Note: All rounds are worked in BLO.

Round 1: With right side of joined blanket facing, using smaller hook, join MC with standing sc in any corner ch-2 sp, ch 2, sc in same sp (**corner made**), ♥ working in BLO, sc in each of next 25 sts (**do not skip hidden st**), *sc in next ch-2 sp, hdc in BLO of joining st (**see image below**), sc in next corner ch-2 sp, sc in each of next 25 sts (**do not skip hidden st**); repeat from * across to next corner, (sc, ch 2, sc) in corner ch-2 sp; repeat from ♥ around, omitting final corner on last repeat; join with sl st in first sc. (189 sc & 6 hdc across short sides & 243 sc & 8 hdc across long sides & 4 corner ch-2 sps) Fasten off and weave in all ends.

Round 2: With right side facing, join Color C with standing sc in any corner ch-2 sp, ch 2, sc in same sp (**corner made**), working in BLO, *[sc in next st] across to next corner, (sc, ch 2, sc) in next corner ch-2 sp; repeat from * around, omitting last corner on final repeat; join with sl st in first sc. (197 sc across short sides & 253 sc across long sides & 4 corner ch-2 sps) Fasten off and weave in all ends.

Round 3: Using MC, repeat Round 2. (199 sc across short sides & 255 sc across long sides & 4 corner ch-2 sps)

Round 4: (**see Pattern Note 3**) With right side facing, join Color C with standing sc in any corner ch-2 sp, ch 2, sc in same sp (**corner made**), *sc in next st, dc in first sc after ch-2 corner (**Rnd 2**), skip next st, [sc in each of next 3 sts, dc in corresponding st (**Rnd 2**)] across to next corner (**last dc is in the sc before corner of Rnd 2**), skip next st, sc in next st, (sc, ch 2, sc) in next corner ch-2 sp; repeat from * around, omitting last corner on final repeat; join with sl st in first sc. (151 sc & 50 dc across short sides & 193 sc & 64 dc across long sides & 4 corner ch-2 sps) Fasten off and weave in all ends.

Round 5: Using MC, repeat Round 2. (203 sc across short sides & 259 sc across long sides & 4 corner ch-2 sps)

Round 1
Marked stitch shows the hdc worked in the back loop of joining stitch.

Round 5

CHART NOTES

1. Motifs for the Blanket are worked in rounds, from a center point.

2. The gold-colored blocks represent the contrasting color, and the light grey blocks the main color.

3. Each round is worked in one color only. From Round 3, colors are alternated every round.

4. Each block on the chart represents one stitch – either a single crochet (empty block) or a double crochet (block with x), which is worked in the same color two rounds below - except for the corner blocks (with ∞) which represent two chain stitches.

∞∞ ch2 corner sp	X dc - double crochet	V hdc - half double crochet	✕ sc in joining
sc - single crochet	MR MR - magic ring		ch1 in joining

EVERLASTING LOVE

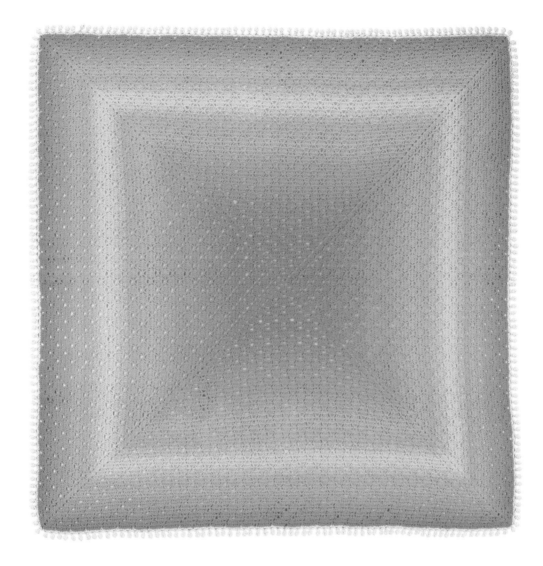

Materials

Scheepjes Whirl – Ombré Collection
Color A: Coral Catastrophe (557) – 2 cakes
Scheepjes Whirlette
Color B: Grapefruit (862) – 1 cake

B-1 (2.25 mm) Crochet Hook

Tapestry Needle

Size
About 47" (120 cm) square (including pompom border)

Gauge
Rounds 1 through 8: About 6¼" (16 cm) square

Pattern Notes

1 This blanket is made with turned joined rounds.

2 Instead of the usual three chains for the turning chain, only two chains are used. These two chains count as the first double crochet stitch throughout the pattern.

3 For Color A (Whirl), start first cake from center pull and second cake from outside end.

4 Color B (Whirlette) is used only for Border.

Double Crochet Decrease (over 5 stitches) (dc2tog): Yarn over, insert hook in stitch or space specified and pull up a loop, (3 loops on hook), yarn over, draw through 2 loops on hook (2 loops remain on hook); skip next 3 sts, yarn over, insert hook in next stitch and pull up a loop (4 loops on hook), yarn over, draw through 2 loops on hook, yarn over, draw through remaining 3 loops on hook (decrease made).

V-Stitch (v-st): (Dc, ch 3, dc) in stitch or space specified.

Pompom Stitch (pom-st): [Ch 3, dc-bob in 3rd ch from hook] twice (images 1-3); fold second bobble forward over first bobble, sl st in same ch in which first bobble was worked (images 4-5).

Double Crochet Bobble (with 4 dc) (dc-bob): Yarn over, insert hook in stitch or space specified and pull up a loop (3 loops on hook), yarn over, draw through 2 loops on hook (2 loops remain on hook); [yarn over, insert hook in same stich and pull up a loop, yarn over, draw through 2 loops on hook] 3 times more (5 loops on hook); yarn over, draw through remaining 5 loops.

Image 1

Image 2

Image 3

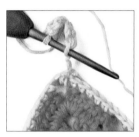

Image 4

Image 5

BLANKET

Round 1: (Right Side) Using Color A, make a magic ring, ch 5 (counts as first dc & ch-3, now and throughout), dc in ring, [ch 3, dc in ring] twice; ch 1, join with dc in first dc (2nd ch of beg ch-5). (4 dc & 4 corner ch-3 sps)

Note: The dc-join counts as the last ch-3 sp and positions the yarn for the next round.

Round 2: Ch 2 (counts as first dc, now and throughout), DO NOT TURN, dc in sp under hook, dc in next st, [(2 dc, ch 3, 2 dc) in next ch-3 sp, dc in next st] 3 times, 2 dc in first ch-sp, ch 1; join with dc in first dc (2nd ch of beg ch-2) (20 dc & 4 corner ch-3 sps)

Round 3: Ch 2, turn, 2 dc in sp under hook, ch 2, dc2tog (using first and last dc of 5-dc group), ch 2, [(3 dc, ch 3, 3 dc) in corner ch-3 sp, ch 2, dc2tog, ch 2] 3 times, 3 dc in first corner sp, ch 1; join with dc in first dc. (24 dc, 4 dc2tog, 8 ch-2 sps & 4 corner ch-3 sps)

Round 4: Ch 2, turn, 2 dc in sp under hook, *dc in each of next 2 sts, skip next st & ch-2 sp, v-st in sp under dc2tog, skip next ch-2 sp & next st, dc in each of next 2 sts**, (3 dc, ch 3, 3 dc) in next corner ch-3 sp; repeat from * around, ending at ** on final repeat, 3 dc in first corner sp, ch 1; join with dc in first dc. (40 dc, 4 v-sts & 4 corner ch-3 sps)

Round 5: Ch 2, turn, 2 dc in sp under hook, *ch 2, dc2tog (using first and last dc of 5-dc group), ch 2, dc in next st, 3 dc in next ch-3 sp, dc in next st, ch 2, dc2tog, ch 2**, (3 dc, ch 3, 3 dc) in corner ch-3 sp; repeat from * around, ending at ** on final repeat, 3 dc in first corner sp, ch 1; join with dc in first dc. (44 dc, 8 dc2tog, 16 ch-2 sps & 4 corner ch-3 sps)

Round 6: Ch 2, turn, 2 dc in sp under hook, *dc in each of next 2 sts, skip next st & sp, v-st in sp under dc2tog, skip next sp & st, dc in each of next 5 sts, skip next st & sp, v-st in sp under dc2tog, skip next sp & st, dc in each of next 2 sts**, (3 dc, ch 3, 3 dc) in next corner ch-3 sp; repeat from * around, ending at ** on final repeat, 3 dc in first corner sp, ch 1; join with dc in first dc. (60 dc, 8 v-sts & 4 corner ch-3 sps)

Round 7: Ch 2, turn, 2 dc in sp under hook, *[ch 2, dc2tog, ch 2, dc in next st, 3 dc in next ch-3 sp, dc in next st] across to corner, ending with ch 2, dc2tog, ch 2**, (3 dc, ch 3, 3 dc) in corner ch-3 sp; repeat from * around, ending at ** on final repeat, 3 dc in first corner sp, ch 1; join with dc in first dc. (64 dc, 12 dc2tog, 24 ch-2 sps & 4 corner ch-3 sps)

Round 8: Ch 2, turn, 2 dc in sp under hook, *dc in each of next 2 sts, skip next st & ch-2 sp, v-st in sp under dc2tog, [skip next ch-2 sp, dc in each of next 5 sts, skip next ch-2 sp, v-st in sp under dc2tog] across to corner, ending with skip next ch-2 sp & next st, dc in each of next 2 sts**, (3 dc, ch 3, 3 dc) in next corner ch-3 sp; repeat from * around, ending at ** on final repeat, 3 dc in first corner sp, ch 1; join with dc in first dc. (80 dc, 12 v-sts & 4 corner ch-3 sps)

Rounds 9-64: Repeat Rounds 7 & 8.
At the end of Round 64, there are 222 dc & 31 ch-3 sps across each side & 4 corner ch-3 sps. Fasten off and weave in all ends.

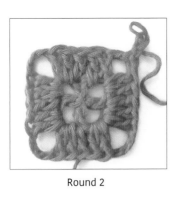

Round 2

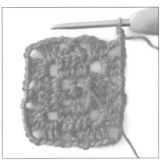

Round 3

Round 3

Round 4

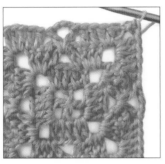

Round 4

Round 5

Round 6

Round 8

BORDER

Round 1: With right side facing, join Color B with standing sc in any corner ch-3 sp, ch 2, sc in same sp (corner made), *sc in each of next 6 sts, 2 sc in next ch-3 sp, [sc in each of next 7 sts, 2 sc in next ch-3 sp] 30 times, sc in each of next 6 sts, (sc, ch 2, sc) in next corner ch-3 sp; repeat from * around, omitting last corner on final repeat; join with sl st in first sc. (286 sc across each side & 4 ch-2 corners)

Round 2: *Ch 3, pom-st, ch 4, skip next corner ch-2 sp, sl st in next st (sc after ch-2 corner), [ch 3, pom-st, ch 4, skip next 3 sts, sl st in next st] 70 times, ch 3, pom-st ch 4, skip next 4 sts, sl st in next st (last sc before corner ch-2 sp); repeat from * around. (71 pompom on each side & 1 pompom across each corner.) Fasten off and weave in all ends.

Round 1

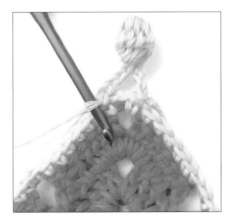

Round 2

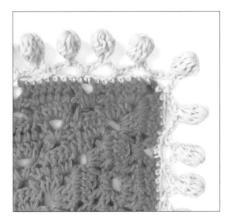

Round 2

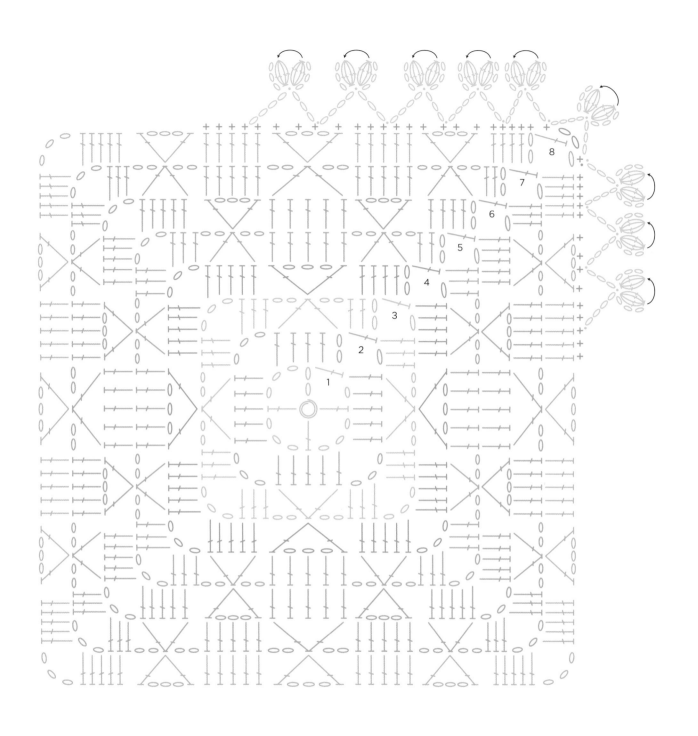

1
2
3
4
5
6
7
8

- **sl st -** slip stitch
- **ch -** chain
- **sc -** single crochet
- **dc -** double crochet

v-st

dc2tog - double crochet two together

4-dc bobble

pom-st - pompom stitch

PURPLE MIST

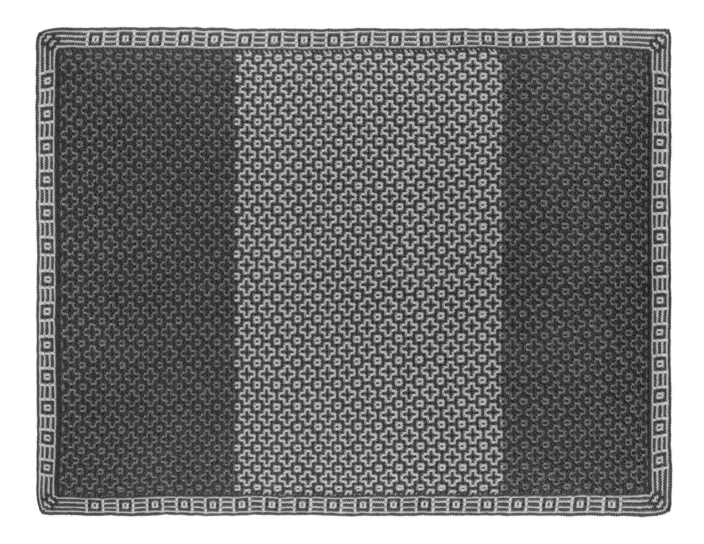

Materials

Scheepjes Colour Crafter
Main Color (MC): Zutphen (1828) - 4 balls
Color A: Wolvega (1099) - 2 balls (for Blanket)
Color B: Verviers (2017) - 2 balls (for Blanket and Border)

#7 (4.50 mm) Crochet Hook

Tapestry Needle

Size
About 38" wide by 55" long (96 cm by 140 cm)

Gauge
Using the Mosaic Crochet pattern stitch -
19 sts & 18 rows = 4" (10 cm)

Pattern Notes

❶ The Blanket and Border are worked using the Mosaic Crochet technique.

❷ Blanket Rows and Border Rounds are all worked with right side facing. At the end of each row or round, the yarn is fastened off and the ends woven in.

❸ Colors are alternated with the Main Color throughout. All odd-numbered rows and rounds are in Main Color. Even-numbered rows and rounds are in either Color A or Color B (as specified).

BLANKET

Row 1: (Right Side) Using MC, ch 168; sc in 2nd ch from hook and in each ch across. (167 sc) Fasten off and weave in all ends.

Row 2: (See Pattern Notes) With right side facing, join Color A with standing sc in both loops of first sc, working in BLO, [sc in next st] across to last st, sc in both loops of last st. (167 sc) Fasten off and weave in all ends.

For Each of the Following Rows:

>>> Start with right side facing (do not turn the work).

>>> The first (standing) stitch and last single crochet stitch of the row are worked through both loops.

>>> Across the row, work single crochets in the back loops (BLO) of stitches and work the double crochets in the front loops (FLO) of corresponding stitch two rows below. (The stitch behind the double crochet stitch is skipped.)

>>> At the end of the row, fasten off and weave in all ends.

Row 3: Join MC with standing stitch in first st, dc in next st (2nd front loop on Row 1), [sc in each of next 3 sts, (skip next 3 front loops on Row 1) dc in next st] 41 times, sc in last st. (125 sc & 42 dc)

Row 4: Join Color A with standing stitch in first st, sc in each of next 5 sts, [dc in next st, sc in next st, dc in next st, sc in each of next 5 sts] 20 times, sc in last st. (127 sc & 40 dc)

Row 5: Join MC with standing stitch in first st, sc in each of next 2 sts, [dc in next st, sc in each of next 3 sts] across. (126 sc & 41 dc)

Row 6: Join Color A with standing stitch in first st, [sc in next st, dc in next st] twice, *sc in each of next 5 sts, dc in next st, sc in next st, dc in next st] 20 times, sc in each of last 2 sts. (125 sc & 42 dc)

Row 7: Join MC with standing stitch in first st, sc in each of next 2 sc, [dc in next st, sc in each of next 3 sts] across. (126 sc & 41 dc)

Row 8: Join Color A with standing stitch in first st, sc in each of next 5 sts, [dc in next st, sc in next st, dc in next st, sc in each of next 5 sts] 20 times, sc in last st. (127 sc & 40 dc)

Row 9: Join MC with standing stitch in first st, [dc in next st, sc in each of next 3 sts] 41 times, dc in next st, sc in last st. (125 sc & 42 dc)

Row 10: Join Color A with standing stitch in first st, [sc in next st, dc in next st] twice, *sc in each of next 5 sts, dc in next st, sc in next st, dc in next st] 20 times, sc in each of last 2 sts. (125 sc & 42 dc)

Rows 11-66: Repeat Rows 3 to 10 seven times.

Rows 67-73: Repeat Rows 3 to 9 once more. After Row 73, Color B replaces Color A.

Row 74: Using Color B, repeat Row 10.

Rows 75-170: Using MC and Color B in alternating rows, repeat Rows 3 to 10 twelve times.

Row 171-177: Using same colors, repeat Rows 3 to 9 once. After Row 177, Color A replaces Color B.

Row 178: Using Color A, repeat Row 10.

Rows 179-226: Using MC and Color A in alternating rows, repeat Rows 3 to 10 six times.

Rows 227-233: Using same colors, repeat Rows 3 to 9 once. At the end of Row 233, fasten off and weave in all ends.

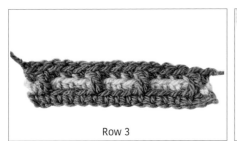

Row 3

Row 4

Row 5

Row 6

Row 7

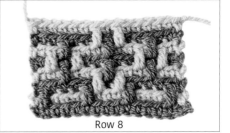

Row 8

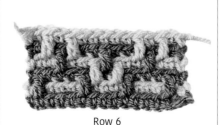

Row 10

BORDER

Round 1: With right side facing, working in both loops, join MC with standing sc in first st, ch 2, sc in same st (corner made), [sc in next st] across to last st, (sc, ch 2, sc) in last st; *working in sides of rows, skip first row, sc in each row across to last row, skip last row*; working in unused loops on other side of starting chain, (sc, ch 2, sc) in first ch, [sc in next ch] across to last ch, (sc, ch 2, sc) in last ch; repeat from * to * once; join with sl st in first sc. (167 sc across short sides, 233 sc across long sides & 4 corner ch-2 sps) Fasten off and weave in all ends.

For each of the following rounds:

>>> Start with right side facing.

>>> Between corners, work single crochets in the back loops (BLO) of stitches and work the double crochets in the front loops (FLO) of the corresponding stitch two rows below. (The stitch behind the double crochet stitch is skipped.)

>>> At the end of the round, fasten off and weave in all ends.

Round 2: Join Color B with standing sc in any corner ch-2 sp, ch 2, sc in same sp (corner made), working in BLO, *[sc in next st] across to next corner**, (sc, ch 2, sc) in next corner ch-2 sp; repeat from * around, ending at ** on final repeat; join with sl st in first sc. (169 sc across short sides & 235 sc across long sides & 4 corner ch-2 sps) Fasten off and weave in all ends.

Round 3: With MC, repeat Round 2. (171 sc across short sides & 237 sc across long sides & 4 corner ch-2 sps Fasten off and weave in all ends.

Round 4: Join Color B with standing sc in corner ch-2 sp at beginning of any short side, ch 2, sc in same sp; *Short Side: sc in each of next 10 sts, dc in next st, [sc in each of next 5 sts, dc in next st] 25 times, sc in each of next 10 sts, (sc, ch 2, sc) in corner ch-2 sp; Long Side: sc in each of next 13 sts, dc in next st, [sc in each of next 5 sts, dc in next st] 35 times, sc in each of last 13 sts*, (sc, ch 2, sc) in next corner; repeat from * to * once; join with sl st in first sc. (147 sc & 26 dc across short sides & 203 sc & 36 dc across long sides & 4 corner ch-2 sps) Fasten off and weave in all ends.

Round 5: Join MC with standing sc in corner ch-2 sp at beginning of any short side, ch 2, sc in same sp; *Short Side: sc in each of next 2 sts, dc in next st, sc in each of next 9 sts, dc in next st, sc in each of next 3 sts, dc in next st, [sc in each of next 7 sts, dc in next st, sc in each of next 3 sts, dc in next st] 12 times, sc in each of next 9 sts, dc in next st, sc in each of next 2 sts, (sc, ch 2, sc) in corner ch-2 sp; Long Side: sc in each of next 2 sts, dc in next st, sc in each of next 12 sts, dc in next st, sc in each of next 3 sts, dc in next st, [sc in each of next 7 sts, dc in next st, sc in each of next 3 sts, dc in next st] 17 times, sc in each of next 12 sts, dc in next st, sc in each of next 2 sts*, (sc, ch 2, sc) in corner ch-2 sp; repeat from * to * once; join with sl st in first sc. (147 sc & 28 dc across short sides & 203 sc & 38 dc across long sides & 4 corner ch-2 sps) Fasten off and weave in all ends.

Round 1

Round 1

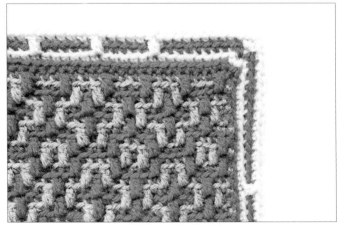

Round 4

Round 4

Round 6: Join Color B with standing sc in corner ch-2 sp at beginning of any short side, ch 2, sc in same sp; ***Short Side:** sc in each of next 12 sts, dc in next st, [sc in next st, dc in next st] 3 times, *sc in each of next 5 sts, dc in next st, [sc in next st, dc in next st] 3 times; repeat from * 11 times more, sc in each of next 12 sts, (sc, ch 2, sc) in corner ch-2 sp; **Long Side:** sc in each of next 15 sts, dc in next st, [sc in next st, dc in next st] 3 times, **sc in each of next 5 sts, dc in next st, [sc in next st, dc in next st] 3 times; repeat from ** 16 times more, sc in each of next 15 sts***, (sc, ch 2, sc) in corner ch-2 sp; repeat from *** to *** once; join with sl st in first sc. (125 sc & 52 dc across short sides & 171 sc & 72 dc across long sides & 4 corner ch-2 sps) Fasten off and weave in all ends.

Round 7: Join MC with standing sc in corner ch-2 sp at beginning of any short side, ch 2, sc in same sp; *Short Side:** sc in each of next 2 sts, dc in next st, sc in each of next 11 sts, dc in next st, sc in each of next 3 sts, dc in next st, [sc in each of next 7 sts, dc in next st, sc in each of next 3 sts, dc in next st] 12 times, sc in each of next 11 sts, dc in next st, sc in each of next 2 sts, (sc, ch 2, sc) in corner ch-2 sp;

Long Side: sc in each of next 2 sts, dc in next st, sc in each of next 14 sts, dc in next st, sc in each of next 3 sts, dc in next st, [sc in each of next 7 sts, dc in next st, sc in each of next 3 sts, dc in next st] 17 times, sc in each of next 14 sts, dc in next st, sc in each of next 2 sts*, (sc, ch 2, sc) in corner ch-2 sp; repeat from * to * once; join with sl st in first sc. (151 sc & 28 dc across short sides & 207 sc & 38 dc across long sides & 4 corner ch-2 sps) Fasten off and weave in all ends.

Round 8: Join Color B with standing sc in corner ch-2 sp at beginning of any short side, ch 2, sc in same sp; *Short Side:** sc in each of next 14 sts, dc in next st, [sc in each of next 5 sts, dc in next st] 25 times, sc in each of next 14 sts, (sc, ch 2, sc) in corner ch-2 sp;

Long Side: sc in each of next 17 sts, dc in next st, [sc in each of next 5 sts, dc in next st] 35 times, sc in each of next 17 sts*, (sc, ch 2, sc) in corner ch-2 sp; repeat from * to * once; join with sl st in first sc. (155 sc & 26 dc across short sides & 211 sc & 36 dc across long sides & 4 corner ch-2 sps) Fasten off and weave in all ends.

Round 9: Join MC with standing sc in any corner ch-2 sp, ch 2, sc in same sp **(corner made)**, working in BLO, *[sc in next st] across to next corner**, (sc, ch 2, sc) in next corner ch-2 sp; repeat from * around, ending at ** on final repeat; join with sl st in first sc. (183 sc across short sides & 249 sc across long sides & 4 corner ch-2 sps) Fasten off and weave in all ends.

Round 6

Round 6

Round 7

Round 8

Round 9

Round 9

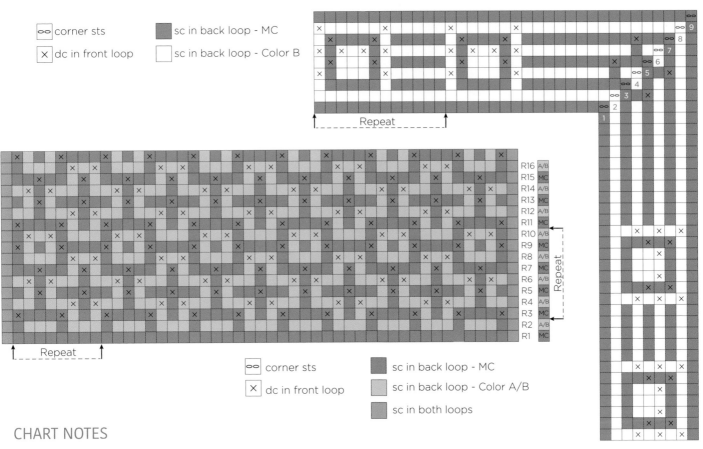

Legend (top):
- ∞ corner sts
- ✕ dc in front loop
- ■ sc in back loop - MC
- □ sc in back loop - Color B

Legend (middle):
- ∞ corner sts
- ✕ dc in front loop
- ■ sc in back loop - MC
- ■ sc in back loop - Color A/B
- ■ sc in both loops

Rows (right to left): R16 A/B, R15 MC, R14 A/B, R13 MC, R12 A/B, R11 MC, R10 A/B, R9 MC, R8 MC, R7 MC, R6 MC, R5 A/B, R4 A/B, R3 MC, R2 A/B, R1 MC

CHART NOTES

① The Blanket is worked in right-side facing rows – following the chart from right to left and from bottom to top.

② The purple-colored blocks represent the Main Color, and the light grey blocks the contrasting color (either Color A or Color B). The white blocks (border) represent Color B.

③ Each row is worked in one color only.

④ Each block on the chart represents one stitch - either a single crochet (empty block) or a double crochet (block with x), which is worked in the same color two rows/rounds below - except for the corner blocks (with ∞) which represent two chain stitches.

FLOWER PATCHES

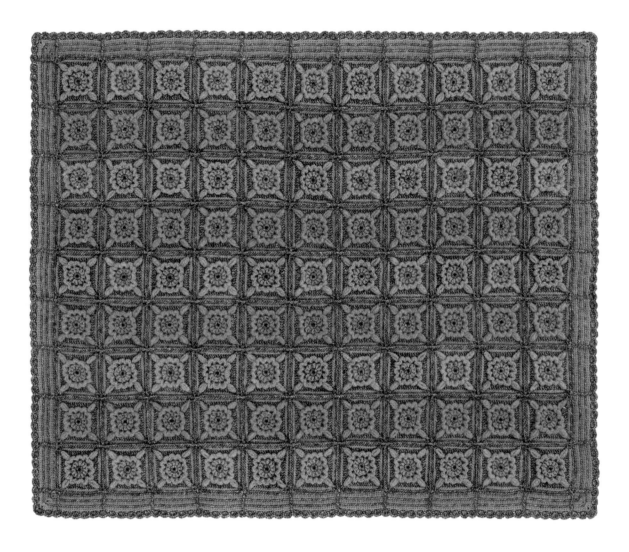

Materials

Scheepjes Stone Washed
Main Color (MC): Black Onyx (803) – 13 balls

Scheepjes River Washed
Color A: Rhine (952) – 3 balls
Color B: Nile (944) – 3 balls
Color C: Narmada (962) – 3 balls
Color D: Mekong (943) – 3 balls

E-4 (3.50 mm) Crochet Hook – for Blanket & Border
G-6 (4.00 mm) Crochet Hook - for Joining Motifs
Tapestry Needle

Size
About 35½" wide by 45¼" long (90 cm by 115 cm)

Gauge
Each Motif: About 4" (10 cm) square.

Pattern Notes

1 Motifs and Border are worked in right-side facing joined rounds.

2 Two colors are used in each Motif – the Main Color and one of the other four colors.

3 Motifs are joined together using the Zipper Join technique.

Front Post Double Treble Bobble (FPdtr-bob):
*Yarn over 3 times (image 1), insert hook from front to back to front around post of specified stitch (image 2) and pull up a loop, [yarn over, draw through 2 loops on hook] 3 times (image 3); *yarn over 3 times, insert hook from front to back to front in same stitch and pull up a loop, [yarn over, draw through 2 loops on hook] 3 times; repeat from * once more (image 4); yarn over, draw through all 4 loops on hook (bobble made) (image 5). Unless noted otherwise, always skip the stitch behind the post stitch.

| Image 1 | Image 2 | Image 3 | Image 4 | Image 5 |

Zipper Join
With both motifs lying side-by-side, with right sides facing, keeping yarn to the back, *insert hook in back loop from front to back in the next stitch on the first piece and then insert in the back loop of the corresponding stitch (also from front to back) on the second piece, pull yarn up through both stitches and draw through the loop on hook (slip stitch made). Repeat from * across.

Hint: Use the same order for each pair of stitches. (If one first starts on the right motif and then the left one, continue this way for every stitch.)

BLANKET

MOTIFS (MAKE 99 – 22 EACH OF COLOR A & COLOR B, 28 OF COLOR C & 27 OF COLOR D)

Round 1: Using MC, ch 6; join with sl st in first ch to form ring; ch 1, 12 sc in ring; join with sl st in first sc. (12 sc) Fasten off and weave in all ends.

Round 2: With right side facing, join Color with standing hdc in any st, [ch 1, hdc in next st] around, ch 1, join with sl st in first hdc. (12 hdc & 12 ch-1 sps) Fasten off and weave in all ends.

Round 3: With right side facing, join MC with standing hdc in any ch-1 sp, [ch 2, hdc in next ch-1 sp] around, ch 2, join with sl st in first hdc. (12 hdc & 12 ch-2 sps) Fasten off and weave in all ends.

Round 4: With right side facing, join Color with standing dc in any ch-2 sp, 3 dc in same sp, [FPsc around next st, 4 dc in next ch-2 sp] around, FPsc around last st; join with sl st in first dc. (48 dc & 12 FPsc) Fasten off and weave in all ends.

Round 5: With right side facing, working in Round 3 (in front of Round 4), join MC with standing dc in ch-2 sp before any FPsc (after 4-dc group), ch 2, dc in next ch-2 sp (after next FPsc and before 4-dc group - corner made),

*ch 2, skip next 4 dc, hdc in same sp (before next FPsc), ch 2, skip next ch-2 sp (with 6 sts - FPsc, 4-dc, FPsc), hdc in next ch-2 sp (after FPsc), ch 2, skip next 4 dc**, dc in same ch-2 sp (before next FPsc), ch 2, dc in next ch-2 sp (after FPsc – corner made); repeat from * around, ending at ** on final repeat; join with sl st in first dc. (8 dc, 8 hdc & 16 ch-2 sps) DO NOT FASTEN OFF.

Round 6: Sl st in next ch-2 sp, ch 3 (counts as first dc, now and throughout), (dc, ch 2, 2 dc) in same sp, *dc in next st, [2 dc in next ch-2 sp, dc in next st] 3 times**, (2 dc, ch 2, 2 dc) in next ch-2 sp; repeat from * around, ending at ** on final repeat; join with sl st in first dc. (56 dc & 4 corner ch-2 sps) Fasten off and weave in all ends.

Round 7: With right side facing, join Color with standing sc in any corner ch-2 sp, (FPdtr-bob, sc) in same sp, *sc in each of next 14 st, (sc, FPdtr-bob, sc) in next corner ch-2 sp; repeat from * around, omitting last sc on final repeat; join with sl st in first sc. (64 sc & 4 corner FPdtr-bobbles)

Round 8: With right side facing, working in BLO, join MC with standing sc in any st before FPdtr-bob, *(FPdc, ch 2, FPdc) around the FPdtr-bob, sc in each of next 16 sts; repeat from * around, omitting last sc on final repeat; join with sl st in first sc. (64 sc, 8 FPdc & 4 corner ch-2 sps) Fasten off and weave in all ends.

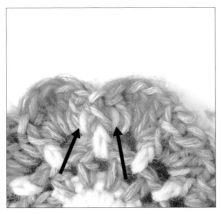
Round 5

Round 7

Round 8

JOINING MOTIFS

Following the color chart, lay out the motifs (with right side facing) on a flat surface, in a 9 by 11 grid.

Image 1

Image 2

Image 3

Image 4

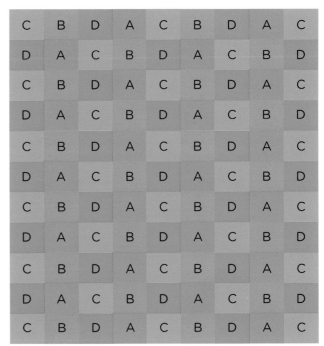

C	B	D	A	C	B	D	A	C
D	A	C	B	D	A	C	B	D
C	B	D	A	C	B	D	A	C
D	A	C	B	D	A	C	B	D
C	B	D	A	C	B	D	A	C
D	A	C	B	D	A	C	B	D
C	B	D	A	C	B	D	A	C
D	A	C	B	D	A	C	B	D
C	B	D	A	C	B	D	A	C
D	A	C	B	D	A	C	B	D
C	B	D	A	C	B	D	A	C

HORIZONTAL JOIN

Using MC and larger hook, working from right to left across chart, taking care not to twist Motifs, place a slip knot on hook, insert hook from front to back in corner ch-2 sp of first Motif (image 1), insert hook from front to back in corresponding ch-2 sp of second Motif (image 2), keeping yarn at back, pull yarn through spaces and draw through loop on hook (sl st made) (image 3); *Zipper Join in each st across to next corner, sl st in next corner ch-2 sp (image 4)**, picking up next 2 Motifs, sl st in corner ch-2 sp; repeat from * across, ending at ** on final repeat. Fasten off and weave in all ends.

VERTICAL JOIN

Repeat Horizontal Join until all Motifs are connected. Using MC and larger hook, working from top to bottom across chart, place a slip knot on hook, insert hook from front to back in corner ch-2 sp of first Motif, insert hook from front to back in corresponding ch-2 sp of second Motif, keeping yarn at back, pull yarn through both spaces (2 loops on hook) and draw through both loops on hook (sl st made); *Zipper Join in each st across to next corner (image 4), sl st in next corner ch-2 sp**, ch 1, sl st in corner ch-2 sp of next Motif pair; repeat from * across, ending at ** on final repeat. Fasten off and weave in all ends. Repeat Vertical Join until all Motifs are connected.

BORDER

Round 1: With right side facing, using smaller hook, working in BLO, join MC with standing sc in any corner ch-2 sp, ch 2, sc in same sp (corner made), ♥*sc in each of next 18 sts**, sc in next ch-2 sp, hdc in join, sc in next ch-2 sp; repeat from * across to next corner, ending at ** on final repeat, (sc, ch 2, sc) in next corner ch-2 sp; repeat from ♥ around, omitting last corner on final repeat; join with sl st in first sc. (180 sc & 8 hdc across short sides, 220 sc & 10 hdc across long sides & 4 corner ch-2 sps) Fasten off and weave in all ends.

Round 2: With right side facing, working in BLO, join Color A with standing hdc in any corner ch-2 sp, (hdc, ch 2, 2 hdc) in same sp, [hdc in next hdc] around, working (2 hdc, ch 2, 2 hdc) in each corner ch-2 sp; join with sl st in first hdc. (192 hdc across short sides, 234 hdc across long sides & 4 corner ch-2 sps) Fasten off and weave in all ends.

Round 3: With right side facing, working in BLO, join MC with standing sc in any corner ch-2 sp, ch 2, sc in same sp, *skip next st, [sc in next st] across to corner, (sc, ch 2, sc) in next corner ch-2 sp; repeat from * around, omitting last corner on final repeat; join with sl st in first sc. (193 sc across short sides, 235 sc across long sides & 4 corner ch-2 sps) Fasten off and weave in all ends.

Round 4: With right side facing, working in BLO, join Color B with standing hdc in any corner ch-2 sp, (hdc, ch 2, 2 hdc) in same sp, [hdc in next hdc] around, working (2 hdc, ch 2, 2 hdc) in each corner ch-2 sp; join with sl st in first hdc. (197 hdc across short sides, 239 hdc across long sides & 4 corner ch-2 sps) Fasten off and weave in all ends.

Round 5: With right side facing, working in BLO, join MC with standing sc in any corner ch-2 sp, ch 2, sc in same sp, *skip next st, sc in each of next 4 sts, FPdtr around corresponding corner sc on Round 1, sc in each of next 19 sts, FPdtr around corresponding hdc (in join) on Round 1, [sc in each of next 20 sts, FPdtr around next hdc (from Rnd 1)] 7 times (for short sides) or 9 times (for long sides), sc in each of next 19 sts, FPdtr around corresponding corner sc on Round 1, sc in each of next 4 sts, (sc, ch 2, sc) in corner ch-2 sp; repeat from * around, omitting last corner on final repeat; join with sl st in first sc. (188 sc & 10 FPdtr across short sides, 228 sc & 12 FPdtr across long sides & 4 corner ch-2 sps) Fasten off and weave in all ends.

Round 6: With right side facing, working in BLO, join Color C with standing hdc in any corner ch-2 sp, (hdc, ch 2, 2 hdc) in same sp, [hdc in next st] around, working (2 hdc, ch 2, 2 hdc) in each corner ch-2 sp; join with sl st in first hdc. (202 hdc across short sides, 244 hdc across long sides & 4 corner ch-2 sps) Fasten off and weave in all ends.

Round 7: With right side facing, working in BLO, starting at beginning of any short side, join MC with standing sc in corner ch-2 sp, ch 2, sc in same sp, *skip next st, sc in each of next 7 sts, FPtr around corresponding FPdtr on Round 5, sc in each of next 19 sts, FPtr around corresponding FPdtr on Round 5, [sc in each of next 20 sts, FPtr around next FPdtr (from Rnd 5)] 7 times (for short sides) or 9 times (for long sides), sc in each of next 19 sts, FPtr around corresponding FPdtr on Round 5, sc in each of next 6 sts, (sc, ch 2, sc) in corner ch-2 sp; repeat from * around, omitting last corner on final repeat; join with sl st in first sc. (191 sc & 10 FPtr across short sides, 231 sc & 12 FPtr across long sides & 4 corner ch-2 sps) DO NOT FASTEN OFF.

Round 1

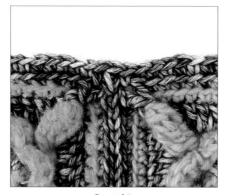

Round 1

Round 5

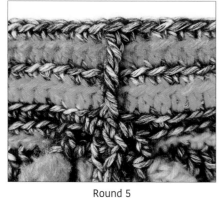

Round 5

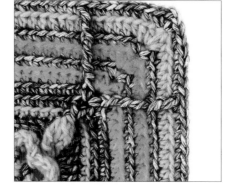

Round 7

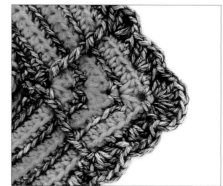

Round 8

Round 8: Sl st in next corner ch-2 sp, ch 3 (counts as first dc), 7 dc in same sp (corner made);
**Short Side: skip next st, FPhdc around next st, [skip next st, 4 dc in next st, skip next st, FPhdc in next st] across to last st, skip last st, 8 dc in corner ch-2 sp;

Long Side: FPhdc around first st, [skip next st, 4 dc in next st, skip next st, FPhdc in next st] across**, 8 dc in corner ch-2 sp; repeat from ** to ** once; join with sl st in first dc (3rd ch of beg ch-3). (51 FPhdc & 50 dc-4 groups across short sides, 62 FPhdc & 61 dc-4 groups across long sides & 4 corner dc-8 groups)

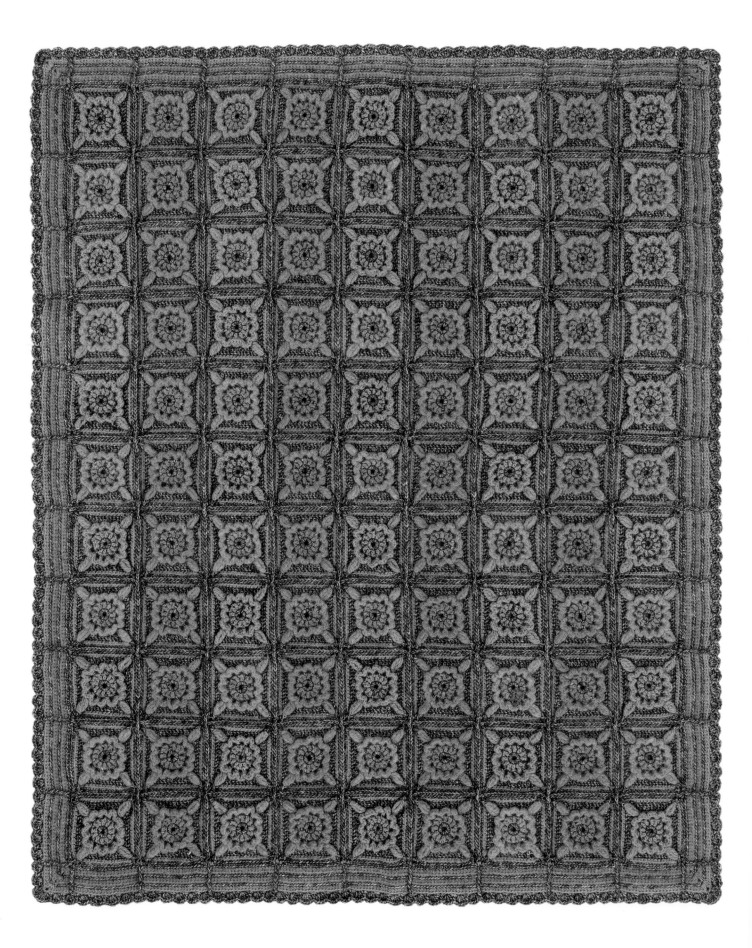

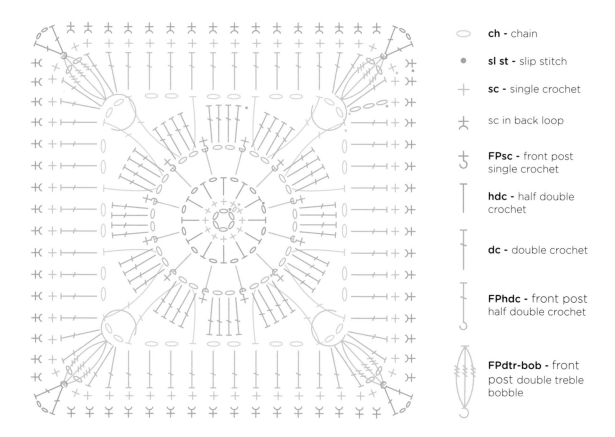

- ◯ **ch -** chain
- ● **sl st -** slip stitch
- + **sc -** single crochet
- ⊥ sc in back loop
- **FPsc -** front post single crochet
- | **hdc -** half double crochet
- | **dc -** double crochet
- **FPhdc -** front post half double crochet
- **FPdtr-bob -** front post double treble bobble

Short Side

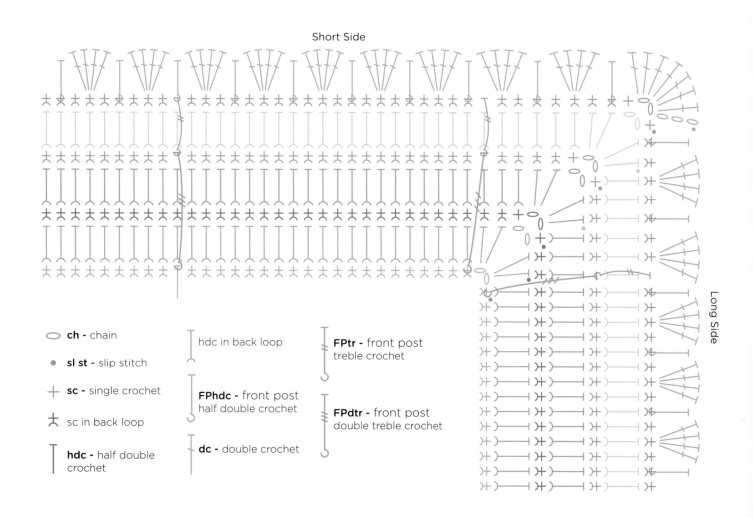

Long Side

- ◯ **ch -** chain
- ● **sl st -** slip stitch
- + **sc -** single crochet
- ⊥ sc in back loop
- | **hdc -** half double crochet
- hdc in back loop
- **FPhdc -** front post half double crochet
- | **dc -** double crochet
- **FPtr -** front post treble crochet
- **FPdtr -** front post double treble crochet

47

CRUSH ON YOU

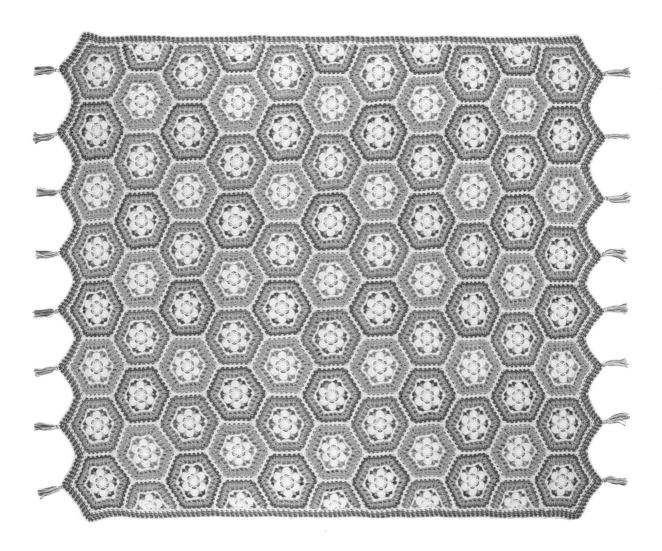

Materials

Scheepjes Catona
Color A: Old Lace (130) - 10 balls
Color B: Silver Green (402) - 10 balls
Color C: Saffron (249) - 3 balls
Color D: Moon Rock (254) - 3 balls
Color E: Rosewood (258) - 3 balls

E-4 (3.50 mm) Crochet Hook

Tapestry Needle

Size
About 39" wide by 47" long (99 cm by 119 cm)

Gauge
Each Hexagon Motif measures 5" (13 cm) from point to
point (without Edging).

Pattern Notes

① The hexagons are worked in right-side facing joined
rounds.

② The half-hexagons are worked in rows – some rows
worked on right side, others on wrong side.

③ All the motifs are joined together using the join-as-
you-go (JAYGO) technique.

④ For an extra special touch, add small fringes to the
points of the hexagons across the top and bottom of the
blanket.

Single Crochet Cluster (over 3 stitches) (sc3tog)
Insert hook in stitch or space specified and pull up a loop; [insert hook in next specifed stitch or space and pull up a loop] twice (4 loops on hook), yarn over and draw through all 4 loops on hook (cluster made).

Join As You Go (JAYGO)
Ch 1, remove hook, working on previous Motif, insert hook (from right side to wrong side) in stitch specified, place loop back on hook (image A) and pull loop through stitch or space (image B), ch 1 (image C) and continue working on current Motif (image D).

Image A

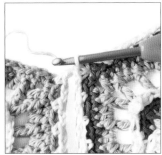
Image B

Image C

Image D

BLANKET

HEXAGON MOTIF (MAKE 83 – 27 WITH COLOR C, 28 EACH WITH COLOR D & COLOR E)

Round 1: (Right Side) Using Color A, make a magic ring, ch 3 (counts as first dc), 11 dc in ring; join with sl st in first dc (3rd ch of beg ch-3). (12 dc) DO NOT FASTEN OFF.

Round 2: Ch 1, sc in same st as joining, [ch 4, skip next st, sc in next st] around, ch 4; join with sl st in first sc. (6 sc & 6 ch-4 loops) DO NOT FASTEN OFF.

Round 3: Ch 1, [(sc, hdc, 4 dc, hdc, sc) in next ch-4 lp] around; join with sl st in first sc. (6 petals – each with 2 sc, 2 hdc & 4 dc) Fasten off and weave in all ends.

Round 4: With right side facing, working behind the petals in the skipped sts on Rnd 1, join Color B with standing sc in any skipped st, [ch 4, sc in next skipped st] around, ch 4; join with sl st in first sc. (6 sc & 6 ch-4 loops) DO NOT FASTEN OFF.

Round 5: Working in the ch-4 lps on Rnd 4, ch 1, [(sc, hdc, 2 dc) in next ch-4 lp, tr between corresponding 2 sc on Rnd 3, (2 dc, hdc, sc) in same lp] around; join with sl st in first sc. (6 petals – each with 2 sc, 2 hdc, 4 dc & 1 tr) Fasten off and weave in all ends.

Round 3

Round 4

Round 4

Round 5

Round 5

Round 5

Round 5

Round 6: With right side facing, join Color C (or D or E) with standing sc in first sc of any petal on Rnd 5, sc in each of next 3 sts, [(sc, FPhdc, sc)] in next tr, sc in each of next 8 sts] around, omitting last 4 sc on final repeat; join with sl st in first sc. (60 sc & 6 FPhdc) Fasten off and weave in all ends.

Round 7: With right side facing, working in BLO, join Color A with standing sc in 4th st before any FPhdc, sc in each of next 3 sts, *(sc, picot, sc) in next FPhdc, sc in each of next 4 sts, hdc between corresponding center 2-dc on Rnd 3, skip next 2 sts**, sc in each of next 4 sts; repeat from * around, ending at ** on final repeat; join with sl st in first sc. (60 sc, 6 hdc & 6 picots) Fasten off and weave in all ends.

Round 8: With right side facing, working in Rnd 6 behind Rnd 7, join Color B with standing dc in any FPhdc (between the 2-sc already there), *ch 2, dc in same st (corner made), ch 2, skip next 2 sts, dc in next st, ch 2, skip next 2 sts, BPdc around next hdc on Rnd 7, ch 2, dc in next corresponding st on Rnd 6, ch 2, skip next 2 sts**, (dc, ch 2, dc) in next FPhdc (between the 2-sc already there); repeat from * around, ending at ** on final repeat; join with sl st in first dc. (24 dc, 6 BPdc, 24 ch-2 sps & 6 corner ch-2 sps) DO NOT FASTEN OFF.

Round 9: Sl st in next corner ch-2 sp, ch 4 (counts as first hdc & ch-2), hdc in same sp, *FPhdc around next st, [2 hdc in next ch-2 sp, FPhdc around next st] 4 times**, (hdc, ch 2, hdc) in next corner ch-2 sp; repeat from * around, ending at ** on final repeat; join with sl st in first hdc (2nd ch of beginning ch-4). (60 hdc, 30 FPhdc & 6 corner ch-2 sps) Fasten off and weave in all ends.

Round 10: With right side facing, join Color C (or D or E) with standing sc in any corner ch-2 sp, ch 2, sc in same sp, *sc in each of next 15 sts**, (sc, ch 2, sc) in next corner sp; repeat from * around, ending at ** on final repeat; join with sl st in first sc. (102 sc & 6 corner ch-2 sps) Fasten off and weave in all ends.

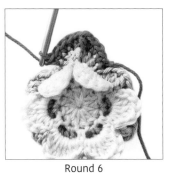
Round 6

Round 6

Round 7

Round 7

Round 7

Round 7

Round 8

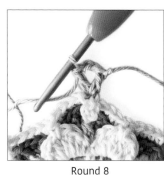
Round 8

Round 8

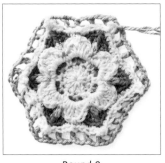
Round 8

Round 9

Round 10

HALF HEXAGON (MAKE 10 – 5 EACH WITH COLOR D & COLOR E)

Row 1: (Right Side) Using Color A, make a magic ring, ch 3 (counts as first dc), 8 dc in ring; DO NOT JOIN. (9 dc)

Row 2: Ch 2, turn, skip first st, sc in next st, [ch 4, skip next st, sc in next st] 3 times, ch 2, sl st in last dc (3rd ch of ch-3). (4 sc, 3 ch-4 loops & 2 ch-2 sps)

The markers indicate the ch-2 sps.

Row 3: Ch 1, turn, sc in first ch-2 sp, [(sc, hdc, 4 dc, hdc, sc) in next ch-4 lp] across, sc in last ch-2 sp. (2 sc & 3 petals – each with 2 sc, 2 hdc & 4 dc) Fasten off and weave in all ends.

Row 4: Turn (wrong side facing), working in Row 1, join Color B with standing sc in first dc, ch 2, sc in next skipped st, [ch 4, sc in next skipped st] twice, ch 2, sc in last dc (3rd ch of ch-3 – with sl st). (5 sc, 2 ch-4 loops & 2 ch-2 sps) DO NOT FASTEN OFF.

Row 5: Ch 2, turn, tr between corresponding 2 sc on Rnd 3, (2 dc, hdc, sc) in next ch-2 sp, [(sc, hdc, 2 dc) in next ch-4 lp, tr between corresponding 2 sc on Rnd 3, (sc, hdc, 2 dc) in same lp] twice, (sc, hdc, 2 dc) in next ch-2 sp, tr between corresponding 2 sc on Rnd 3. (2 petals – each with 2 sc, 2 hdc, 4 dc & 1 tr; & 2 half-petals - each with sc, hdc, 2 dc & 1 tr)

Row 6: With right side facing, join Color D (or E) with standir   FPhdc around first tr, sc in same tr, sc in each of next 8 sts, [(sc, FPhdc, sc)] in next tr, sc in each of next 8 sts] twice, (sc, FPhdc) in last tr. (24 sc & 4 FPhdc) Fasten off and weave in all ends.

Row 7: With right side facing, working in BLO, join Color A with standing sc in first FPhdc, (picot, sc) in same st, sc in each of next 4 sts, hdc between corresponding center 2-dc on Row 3, *skip next 2 sts, sc in each of next 4 sts, (sc, picot, sc) in next FPhdc, sc in each of next 4 sts, hdc between center 2-dc on Row 3; repeat from * once more, skip next 2 sts, sc in each of next 4 sts, (sc, picot, sc) in last FPhdc. (32 sc, 3 hdc & 4 picots) Fasten off and weave in all ends.

Row 8: Turn (wrong side facing), working in Row 6 (in front of Row 7), join Color B with standing dc in first FPhdc (between the 2-sc already there), ch 2, dc in same st (corner made), *ch 2, skip next 2 sts, dc in next st, ch 2, skip next 2 sts, FPdc around next hdc on Row 7, ch 2, dc in next corresponding st on Row 6, ch 2, skip next 2 sts, (dc, ch 2, dc) in next FPhdc (between the 2-sc already there); repeat from * twice more. (14 dc, 3 BPdc, 12 ch-2 sps & 4 corner ch-2 sps) DO NOT FASTEN OFF.

Row 9: Turn, sl st in ch-2 sp, ch 4 (counts as first hdc & ch-2), hdc in same sp, *FPhdc around next st, [2 hdc in next ch-2 sp, FPhdc around next st] 4 times, (hdc, ch 2, hdc) in next corner ch-2 sp; repeat from * across. (32 hdc, 15 FPhdc & 4 corner ch-2 sps) Fasten off and weave in all ends.

Row 10: With right side facing, join Color D (or E) with standing sc in first corner ch-2 sp, ch 2, sc in same sp, [sc in each of next 15 sts, (sc, ch 2, sc) in next corner sp] 3 times. (53 sc & 4 corner ch-2 sps) Fasten off and weave in all ends.

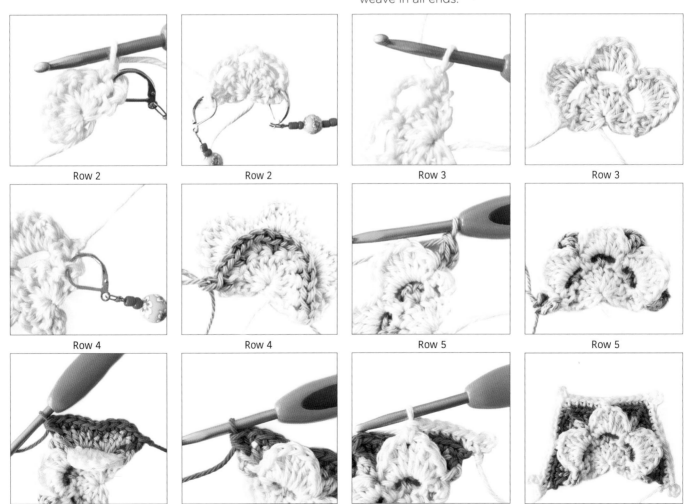

Row 2	Row 2	Row 3	Row 3
Row 4	Row 4	Row 5	Row 5
Row 6	Row 6	Row 7	Row 7

Row 8

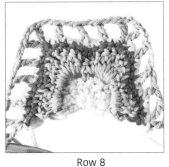

Row 8

Row 9

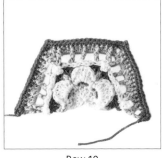

Row 10

JOINING MOTIFS

Following the color distribution chart, join the Hexagons and Half-Hexagons together using the join-as-you-go (JAYGO) method on the Edging Round.

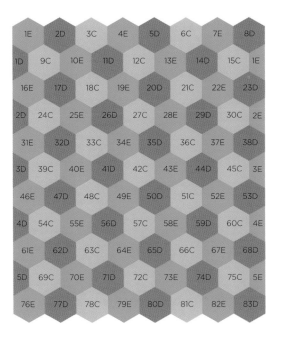

1E	2D	3C	4E	5D	6C	7E	8D
1D	9C	10E	11D	12C	13E	14D	15C	1E
16E	17D	18C	19E	20D	21C	22E	23D
2D	24C	25E	26D	27C	28E	29D	30C	2E
31E	32D	33C	34E	35D	36C	37E	38D
3D	39C	40E	41D	42C	43E	44D	45C	3E
46E	47D	48C	49E	50D	51C	52E	53D
4D	54C	55E	56D	57C	58E	59D	60C	4E
61E	62D	63C	64E	65D	66C	67E	68D
5D	69C	70E	71D	72C	73E	74D	75C	5E
76E	77D	78C	79E	80D	81C	82E	83D

FOR FIRST MOTIF ONLY

Edging Round: With right side facing, join Color A with standing sc in any corner ch-2 sp, ch 2, sc in same sp, *ch 2, skip next 2 sts, [sc in next st, ch 2, skip next 2 sts] 5 times**, (sc, ch 2, sc) in corner ch-2 sp; repeat from * around, ending at ** on final repeat; join with sl st in first sc. (42 sc, 36 ch-2 sps & 6 corner ch-2 sps) Fasten off and weave in all ends.

ONE-SIDED JOIN (2 MOTIFS)

Repeat the Edging Round until you reach the corner before the side to be joined, (sc, JAYGO in corresponding corner ch-2 sp, sc) in next corner ch-2 sp, [JAYGO in next corresponding ch-sp, skip next 2 sts, sc in next st] across to corner, (sc, JAYGO in next corner, sc) in corner ch-2 sp; continue with Edging Round. (42 sc, 30 ch-2 sps, 4 corner ch-2 sps & 8 JAYGO joins)

TWO-SIDED JOIN (3 MOTIFS – 2 MOTIFS ALREADY JOINED)

Repeat the Edging Round until you reach the corner before the first side to be joined, (sc, JAYGO in corresponding corner ch-2 sp on previously joined motif, sc) in next corner ch-2 sp, [JAYGO in next corresponding ch-sp, skip next 2 sts] across to next corner, (sc, JAYGO in st connecting joined motifs, sc) in corner ch-2 sp, [JAYGO in next corresponding ch-sp, skip next 2 sts, sc in next st] across to next corner, (sc, JAYGO in next corresponding corner, sc) in corner ch-2 sp; continue with Edging Round. (42 sc, 24 ch-2 sps, 3 corner ch-2 sps & 15 JAYGO joins)

THREE-SIDED JOIN (HALF-HEXAGON & 3 JOINED MOTIFS)

Half-Hexagon Edging Round: With right side facing, join Color A with standing sc in first corner ch-2 sp, JAYGO in corresponding corner ch-2 sp, sc in same sp, *[JAYGO in next corresponding ch-sp on first motif, skip next 2 sts, sc in next st] across to next corner, (sc, JAYGO in st connecting joined motifs, sc) in corner ch-2 sp; repeat from * once more, [JAYGO in next corresponding ch-sp, skip next 2 sts, sc in next st] across to next corner, (sc, JAYGO in corresponding ch-sp, sc) in corner ch-2 sp; working across sides of rows, ch 2, sc in Row 8 (over dc-st), ch 2, sc in Row 6 (over FPhdc), ch 2, sc in Row 5 (over tr-st), ch 2, sc in Row 2 (ch-2sp), ch 2, sc in Row 1 (over dc-st)ch 2, sc in Row 1 (over dc-st), ch 2, sc in Row 2 (ch-2sp), ch 2, sc in Row 5 (over tr-st), ch 2, sc in Row 6 (over FPhdc), ch 2, sc in Row 8 (over dc-st), ch 2; join with sl st in first sc. (12 sc, 11 ch-2 sps & 21 JAYGO joins) Fasten off and weave in all ends.

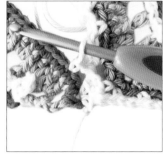

BORDER

Round 1: With right side of blanket facing, join Color A with standing sc in any corner ch-2 sp before short side, ch 2, sc in same sp, ♥*ch 2, [sc in next ch-2 sp, ch 2] 6 times, (sc, ch 2, sc) in next peak ch-2 sp, ch 2, [sc in next ch-2 sp, ch 2] 6 times**, sc in joining sp; repeat from * across short side, ending at ** on final repeat, (sc, ch 2, sc) in corner ch-2 sp; working across long side, ch 2, [sc in next ch-2 sp, ch 2] across to next corner, (sc, ch 2, sc) in corner ch-2 sp; repeat from ♥ around, omitting last corner on final repeat; join with sl st in first sc. (121 sc & 120 ch-2 sps across short sides, 103 sc & 102 ch-2 sps across long sides & 4 corner ch-2 sps) Fasten off and weave in all ends.

Round 2: With right side facing, join Color D with standing sc in any corner ch-2 sp before short side, ch 2, sc in same sp, ♥ch 2, [sc in next ch-2 sp, ch 2] 7 times, (sc, ch 2, sc) in next peak ch-2 sp, *ch 2, [sc in next ch-2 sp, ch 2] 14 times, (sc, ch 2, sc) in peak ch-2 sp; repeat from * 6 times more, ch 2, [sc in next ch-2 sp, ch 2] 7 times, (sc, ch 2, sc) in next corner ch-2 sp; working across long side, ch 2, [sc in next ch-2 sp, ch 2] across to next corner, (sc, ch 2, sc) in corner ch-2 sp; repeat from ♥ around, omitting last corner on final repeat; join with sl st in first sc. (130 sc & 129 ch-2 sps across short sides, 104 sc & 103 ch-2 sps across long sides & 4 corner ch-2 sps) Fasten off and weave in all ends.

Round 3: With right side facing, join Color C with standing sc in any corner ch-2 sp before short side, ch 2, sc in same sp, ♥ch 2, [sc in next ch-2 sp, ch 2] 8 times, (sc, ch 2, sc) in next peak ch-2 sp, *ch 2, [sc in next ch-2 sp, ch 2] 15 times, (sc, ch 2, sc) in peak ch-2 sp; repeat from * 6 times more, ch 2, [sc in next ch-2 sp, ch 2] 8 times, (sc, ch 2, sc) in next corner ch-2 sp; working across long side, ch 2, [sc in next ch-2 sp, ch 2]

across to next corner, (sc, ch 2, sc) in corner ch-2 sp; repeat from ♥ around, omitting last corner on final repeat; join with sl st in first sc. (139 sc & 138 ch-2 sps across short sides, 105 sc & 104 ch-2 sps across long sides & 4 corner ch-2 sps) Fasten off and weave in all ends.

Round 4: With right side facing, join Color E with standing sc in any corner ch-2 sp before short side, ch 2, sc in same sp, ♥ch 2, [sc in next ch-2 sp, ch 2] 9 times, (sc, ch 2, sc) in next peak ch-2 sp, *ch 2, [sc in next ch-2 sp, ch 2] 16 times, (sc, ch 2, sc) in peak ch-2 sp; repeat from * 6 times more, ch 2, [sc in next ch-2 sp, ch 2] 9 times, (sc, ch 2, sc) in next corner ch-2 sp; working across long side, ch 2, [sc in next ch-2 sp, ch 2] across to next corner, (sc, ch 2, sc) in corner ch-2 sp; repeat from ♥ around, omitting last corner on final repeat; join with sl st in first sc. (148 sc & 147 ch-2 sps across short sides, 106 sc & 105 ch-2 sps across long sides & 4 corner ch-2 sps) Fasten off and weave in all ends.

Round 5: With right side facing, join Color A with standing sc in any corner ch-2 sp before short side, ♥ [ch 2, sc in next ch-2 sp] 10 times, (no ch-2) (sc, ch 2, sc) in next peak ch-2 sp, *(no ch-2) sc in next ch-2 sp, [ch 2, sc in next ch-2 sp] 6 times, ch 1, sc3tog (**using next 3 ch-2 sps**), ch 1, sc in next ch-2 sp, [ch 2, sc in next ch-2 sp] 6 times, (no ch-2) (sc, ch 2, sc) in peak ch-2 sp; repeat from * 6 times more, (no ch-2) [sc in next ch-2 sp, ch 2] 10 times, sc in corner ch-2 sp; working across long side, ch 2, [sc in next ch-2 sp, ch 2] across to next corner, sc in corner ch-2 sp; repeat from ♥ around, omitting last corner on final repeat; join with sl st in first sc. (134 sc, 112 ch-2 sps, 14 ch-1 sps & 7 sc3tog across short sides, 105 sc & 106 ch-2 sps across long sides & 4 corner sc-sts) Fasten off and weave in all ends.

| Round 1 | Round 4 | Round 4 | Round 5 | Round 5 |

FINAL TOUCH

FRINGE

A fringe is attached to each ch-2 sp across the short sides.

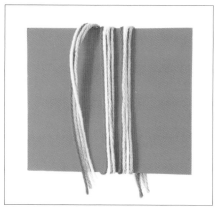

Step 1

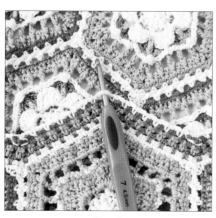

Step 2

Step 2

Step 1: Cut a 3" (8 cm) square piece of cardboard. For each color (except Color D), cut a 20" (50 cm) length of yarn. Holding the 4 strands together, wind around the card about 3 times.

Step 2: Remove the yarn from the card. With right side of blanket facing, insert hook from back to front in ch-2 space and pull the folded ends of yarn half-way through. (The folded strands form a loop at the back, with the tails and other folds in front.)

Step 3

Step 3

Step 3: Thread the tail end of the strands through the folded loop. Pull tight to secure. Trim the ends.

57

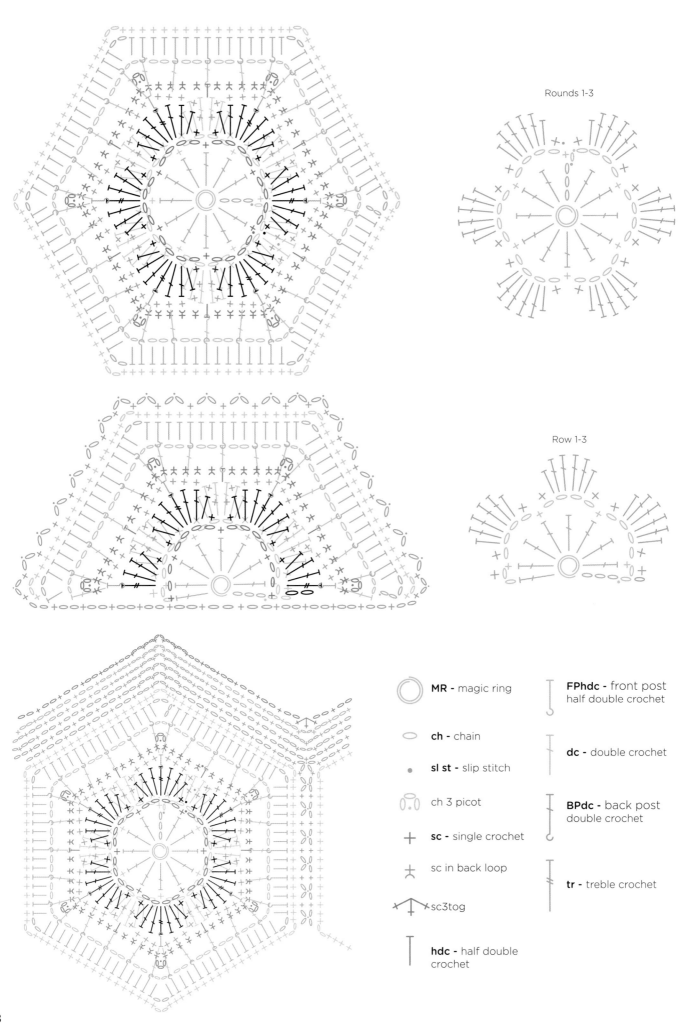

Rounds 1-3

Row 1-3

MR - magic ring

ch - chain

sl st - slip stitch

ch 3 picot

sc - single crochet

sc in back loop

sc3tog

hdc - half double crochet

FPhdc - front post half double crochet

dc - double crochet

BPdc - back post double crochet

tr - treble crochet

FLUTTERING IN THE BREEZE

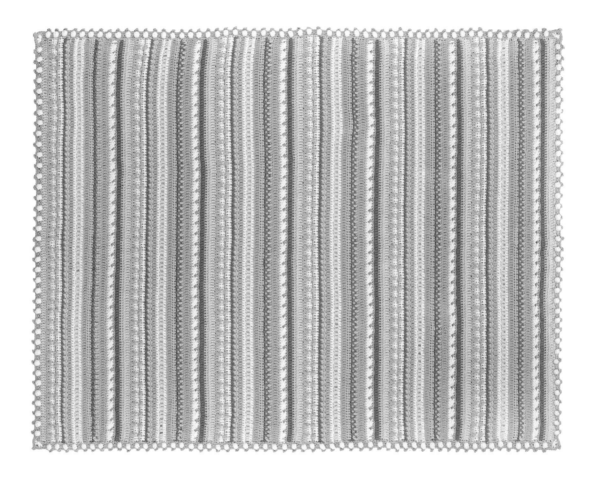

Materials

Scheepjes Cahlista
Color A: Lime Juice (392) - 3 balls
Color B: Old Rose (408) - 5 balls
Color C: Cherry (413) - 4 balls
Color D: Saffron (249) - 4 balls
Color E: Old Lace (130) - 6 balls
Color F: Lime (512) - 5 balls

H-8 (5.00 mm) Crochet Hook

Tapestry Needle

Size
About 41" wide by 54" long (104 cm by 137 cm)

Gauge
15 sts & 12 pattern rows ([dc next row,
hdc next row]) rows = 4" (10 cm)

Pattern Notes

1. The Blanket is worked in turned rows, each row using a different color.

2. The odd-numbered rows are worked with right side facing, and even-numbered rows are worked wrong side facing.

3. The Border is worked in right-side facing joined rounds.

Popcorn Stitch with three Half-Double Crochets

(pop-3hdc): Work 3 hdc in specified stitch or space. Remove hook from loop and insert hook in first hdc (of 3-hdc group). Place loop on hook and draw loop through first stitch. Ch 1 to secure.

Popcorn Stitch with four Half-Double Crochets (pop-4hdc): Work 4 hdc in specified stitch or space. Remove hook from loop and insert hook in first hdc (of 4-hdc group). Place loop on hook and draw loop through first stitch. Ch 1 to secure.

Double Crochet Double Cross Stitch (dc-XX): Worked over 4 stitches. Skip next 2 sts, dc in each of next 2 sts, dc in each of skipped 2 sts (working in front of stitches just made).

Long Single Crochet (long-sc): Insert hook in the corresponding stitch on the specified row or round below, pulling up the loop to the height of current row's stitches, draw through both loops on hook.

(Long (or spike) stitches are worked in one or more rows/rounds below the current row/round to create vertical "spikes".)

BLANKET

Note: Fasten off and weave in all ends at the end of each and every row.

Row 1: (Right Side) Using Color A, ch 158, dc in 4th ch from hook (skipped ch count as first dc), [dc in next ch] across. (156 dc)

Row 2: Turn (wrong side facing), working in FLO across, join Color B with standing hdc in first st, [hdc in next st] across. (156 hdc)

Row 3: Turn, join Color C with standing dc in first st, [dc in next st] across. (156 dc)

Row 4: Turn, join Color D with standing sc in first st, [sc in next st] across. (156 sc)

Row 5: Turn, join Color E with standing dc in first st, dc in next st, [dc-XX (using next 4 sts)] across to last 2 sts, dc in each of last 2 sts. (4 dc & 38 dc-XX)

Row 6: Turn, join Color D with standing sc in first st, [sc in next st] across. (156 sc)

Row 7: Turn, join Color F with standing dc in first st, [dc in next st] across. (156 dc)

Row 8: Turn, working in FLO across, join Color B with standing dc in first st, [dc in next st] across. (156 dc)

Row 9: Turn, join Color C with standing hdc in first st, hdc in next st, [FPhdc in next st, BPhdc in next st] across to last 2 sts, dc in each of last 2 sts. (4 hdc, 76 FPhdc & 76 BPhdc)

Row 10: Turn, join Color B with standing hdc in first st, [hdc in next st] across. (156 hdc)

Row 11: Turn, join Color F with standing dc in first st, [dc in next st] across. (156 dc)

Row 12: Turn, working in FLO across, join Color E with standing sc in first st, [sc in next st] across. (156 sc)

Row 13: Turn, join Color A with standing dc in first st, dc in each of next 3 sts, [ch 1, skip next st, dc in each of next 2 sts] across to last 5 sts, ch 1, skip next st, dc in each of last 4 sts. (106 dc & 50 ch-1 sps)

Row 14: Turn, join Color E with standing sc in first st, sc in each of next 3 sts, [sc in next ch-1 sp, sc in each of next 2 sts] across, ending with sc in last ch-1 sp, sc in each of last 4 sts. (156 sc)

Row 15: Turn, join Color D with standing dc in first st, [dc in next st] across. (156 dc)

Row 16: Turn, join Color B with standing sc in first st, dc in next st, [sc in next st, dc in next st] across. (78 sc & 78 dc)

Row 17: Turn, join Color C with standing sc in first st, dc in next st, [sc in next st, dc in next st] across. (78 sc & 78 dc)

Row 18: Turn, join Color E with standing hdc in first st, [hdc in next st] across. (156 hdc)

Row 19: Turn, join Color D with standing sc in first st, sc in each of next 3 sts, [pop-3hdc in next st, sc in each of next 3 st] across. (118 sc & 38 popcorns)

Row 20: Turn, join Color E with standing hdc in first st, hdc in each of next 2 sts, [BPhdc in next st (popcorn), hdc in each of next 3 sts] across to last st, hdc in last st. (118 hdc & 38 BPhdc)

Row 1 to Row 6

Row 4 to Row 10

Row 7 to Row 11

Row 11 to Row 16

Row 14 to Row 18

Row 17 to Row 23

Row 21: Turn, join Color B with standing hdc in first st, [hdc in next st] across. (156 hdc)

Row 22: Turn, join Color F with standing sc in first st, sc in each of next 2 sts, [BPdc around next st 2 rows below (BPhdc), sc in last st. (118 sc & 38 BPdc)

Row 23: Turn, join Color A with standing dc in first st, [dc in next st] across. (156 dc)

Rows 24-133: Repeat Rows 2-23 five times more. At the end of Row 133, fasten off and weave in all ends.

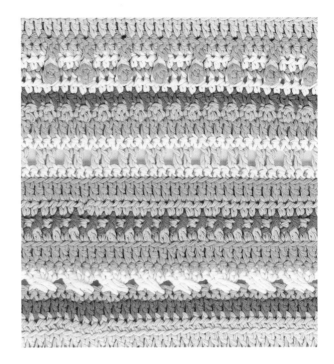

BORDER

Round 1: With right side facing (do not turn), working in last row, join Color F with standing sc in first st, ch 2, sc in same st (corner made), [sc in next st] across to last st, (sc, ch 2, sc) in last st; *working across long side to next corner, work 1 sc in each sc-row, 2 sc in each hdc- or dc- row, and randomly add 2 additional sc-sts*; working in unused loops on other side of starting ch, (sc, ch 2, sc) in first ch, [sc in next ch] across to last ch, (sc, ch 2, sc) in last ch; repeat from * to *; join with sl st in first sc. (156 sc across short sides, 228 sc across long sides & 4 corner ch-2 sps) Fasten off and weave in all ends.

Round 2: With right side facing, join Color E with standing hdc in any corner ch-2 sp, (hdc, ch 2, 2 hdc) in same sp, *ch 3, skip next 3 sts, [pop-4hdc in next st, ch 3 (do NOT count the popcorn ch), skip next 3 sts] across to next corner**, (2 hdc, ch 2, 2 hdc) in corner ch-2 sp;

repeat from * around, ending at ** on final repeat; join with sl st in first hdc. (38 popcorns, 39 ch-3 sps & 4 hdc across short sides, 56 popcorns, 57 ch-3 sps & 4 hdc across long sides & 4 corner ch-2 sps) Fasten off and weave in all ends.

Round 3: With right side facing, join Color F with standing sc in any corner ch-2 sp, (sc, picot, sc) in same sp, **sc in each of next 2 sts, *sc in next ch-3 sp, working in Round 1, long-sc in center st of skipped 3-sc (over the ch-3 loop), working in current round, sc in same ch-3 sp, FPsc around next st (popcorn), picot; rep from * across to last 2 sts, sc in each of last 2 sts**, (2 sc, picot, sc) in corner ch-2 sp; repeat from ** around, ending at ** on final repeat; join with sl st in first sc. (123 sc, 38 FPsc & 38 picots across short sides, 177 sc, 56 FPsc & 56 picots across long sides & 4 corner sc with picot)

Round 1

Round 2

Round 3

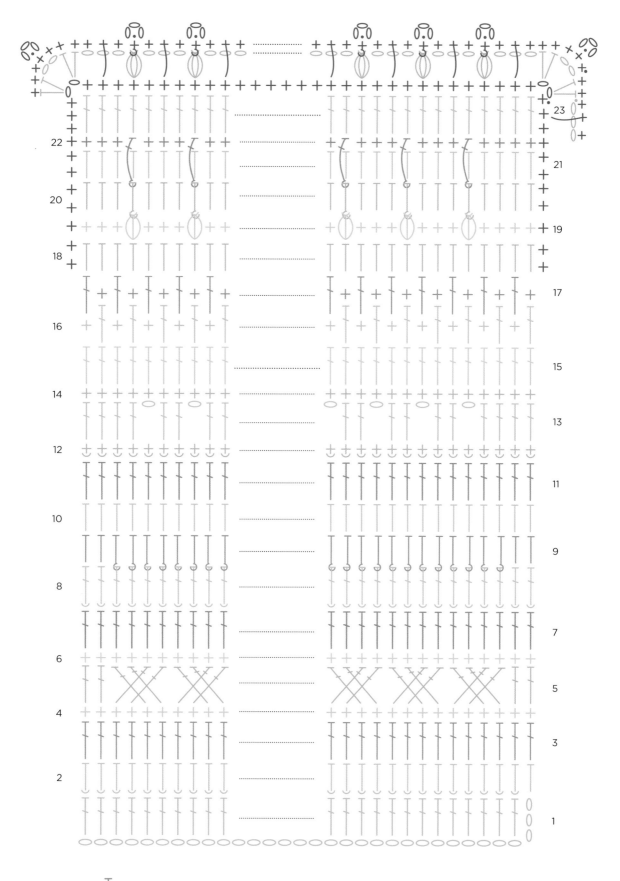

ch - chain

sl st - slip stitch

ch 3 picot

sc - single crochet

sc in front loop

hdc - half double crochet

hdc - hdc front loop

FPhdc - front post half double crochet

BPhdc - back post half double crochet

dc - double crochet

dc in front loop

BPdc - back post double crochet

pop-3hdc - popcorn stitch with three half-double crochets

pop-4hdc - popcorn stitch with four half-double crochets

FPsc - front post single crochet

64

RAINBOWS IN TUNISIA

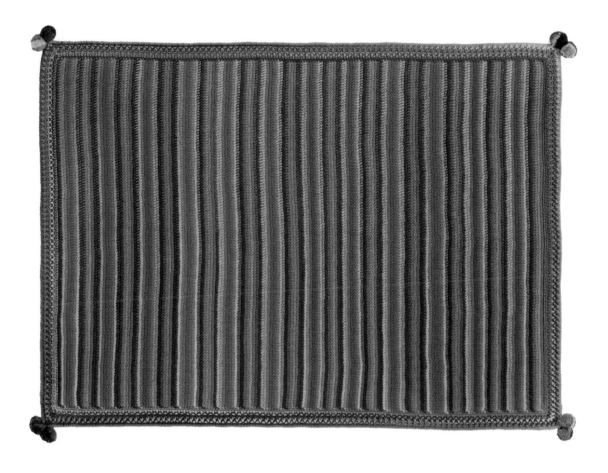

Materials

Scheepjes Wanderlust
Main Color (MC): Hawaii (457) - 11 balls

I-9 (5.50 mm) Tunisian Crochet Hook (with extensions)
#7 (4.50 mm) Crochet Hook – for Border

Tapestry Needle

Size
About 37½" wide by 51" long (95 cm by 130 cm)

Gauge
Using Tunisian Simple Stitch – 17 sts & 14 rows = 4"
(10 cm)

Pattern Notes

1 This blanket is made using the Tunisian Simple Stitch, also known as Basic Afghan Stitch, Royal Princess Stitch, or Tricot Stitch.

2 Each row of Tunisian Crochet consists of two passes – a forward pass (pulling up loops) and a return pass (working off the loops).

3 Tunisian Crochet is a one-sided fabric and is worked with right side facing on all rows – both forward and return passes.

4 Projects made in Tunisian Crochet tend to curl at the base and top. To minimize this, try using a larger hook and/or blocking the finished project. Another tip is to work the foundation row into the back ridges (or back bumps) of the chain stitches.

Hint: Before starting the project, make test swatches using different sizes of Tunisian hooks to determine which size reduces the curling the most.

5 The Blanket Border is worked in right-side facing, joined rounds.

Tunisian Simple Stitch (TSS)

Forward Pass: (Right Side) Insert hook from right to left under 2nd vertical bar and pull up a loop (image 1), keeping all loops on hook, [insert hook under vertical bar of next stitch and pull up a loop (image 2)] across to last st (image 3), insert hook through both side loops of last ch and pull up loop.

Image 1

Image 2

Image 3

Return Pass: (Right Side) Ch 1 loosely, [yo and draw through 2 loops on hook] across, until only 1 loop remains on hook.

BLANKET

Foundation Row (Row 1): Using Tunisian hook, ch 131.

Forward Pass: (Right Side) (see Pattern Notes) Insert hook in 2nd ch from hook, and pull up loop (2 loops on hook); keeping loops on hook (image 1), [insert hook in next ch and pull up loop] across (image 2). (131 loops on hook)

Image 1 - Stitch marker indicates back ridge of chain stitch.

Image 2

Return Pass: (Right Side) Ch 1 loosely (using first loop on hook) (image 1), [yo (image 2), draw through 2 loops on hook (image 3)] across, until only 1 loop remains on hook (image 4).

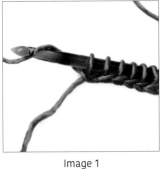

Image 1

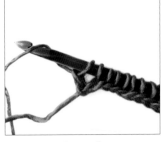

Image 2

Image 3

Image 4

Tips:

1 For a neater edge, pull up the last loop of forward pass through both side loops of first chain of previous return pass.

2 The right hand edge tends to be loose. Take care and tighten yarn before picking up stitches.

3 Do not work the beginning ch of the return pass too tightly.

Row 2: TSS in each st across (forward & return pass).
(131 loops on hook after Forward Pass)

Rows 3-174: Repeat Row 2.

Row 175: (Bind Off - Forward Pass Only) Insert hook from right to left under 2nd vertical bar and pull up loop, drawing through loop on hook (first sl st made), [sl st in next st] across to last st, sl st through both side loops of last ch. (1 loop on hook) Fasten off and weave in all ends.

BORDER

Note: The stitches across the long sides are worked in the lateral side stitch of every row.

Round 1: With right side facing, using smaller crochet hook, join with standing sc in first corner st of last row, 2 sc in same st, [sc in next st] across to corner, 3 sc in next corner st; *working in sides of rows, sc in each row across to corner*; 3 sc in next corner st, working across other side of foundation chain, [sc in next ch] across to corner, 3 sc in next corner st; repeat from * to * once; join with sl st in first sc. (130 sc across short sides, 174 sc across long sides & 4 corner sc-sts)

Round 2: Sl st in next st (center st of corner 3-sc group), ch 4 (counts as first hdc & ch-2, now and throughout), hdc in same st, *[hdc in next st] across to corner st, (hdc, ch 2, hdc) in corner st; repeat from * around, omitting last corner on final repeat; join with sl st in first hdc. (132 hdc across short sides, 176 hdc across long sides & 4 corner ch-2 sps)

Round 3: Sl st to next corner ch-2 sp, ch 4, hdc in same sp, *[FPhdc around next st, BPhdc around next st] across to next corner (hdc, ch 2, hdc) in next corner ch-2 sp; repeat from * around, omitting last corner on final repeat; join with sl st in first hdc. (2 hdc, 66 FPhdc & 66 BPhdc across short sides, 2 hdc, 88 FPhdc & 88 BPhdc across long sides & 4 corner ch-2 sps)

Round 4: Sl st to next corner ch-2 sp, ch 2 (counts as first hdc, now and throughout), (hdc, ch 2, 2 hdc) in same sp, *[BPhdc around next st, FPhdc around next st] across to next corner (2 hdc, ch 2, 2 hdc) in next corner ch-2 sp; repeat from * around, omitting last corner on final repeat; join with sl st in first hdc. (4 hdc, 67 FPhdc & 67 BPhdc across short sides, 4 hdc, 89 FPhdc & 89 BPhdc across long sides & 4 corner ch-2 sps)

Round 5: Sl st to next corner ch-2 sp, ch 4, hdc in same sp, *[BPhdc around next st, FPhdc around next st] across to next corner (hdc, ch 2, hdc) in next corner ch-2 sp; repeat from * around, omitting last corner on final repeat; join with sl st in first hdc. (2 hdc, 69 FPhdc & 69 BPhdc across short sides, 2 hdc, 91 FPhdc & 91 BPhdc across long sides & 4 corner ch-2 sps)

Round 6: Sl st to next corner ch-2 sp, ch 2, (hdc, ch 2, 2 hdc) in same sp, *[FPhdc around next st, BPhdc around next st] across to next corner (2 hdc, ch 2, 2 hdc) in next corner ch-2 sp; repeat from * around, omitting last corner on final repeat; join with sl st in first hdc. (4 hdc, 70 FPhdc & 70 BPhdc across short sides, 4 hdc, 92 FPhdc & 92 BPhdc across long sides & 4 corner ch-2 sps)

Round 7: Sl st to next corner ch-2 sp, ch1, 2 sc in same sp, *[sc in next st] across to corner, 2 sc in next corner ch-2 sp; repeat from * around, omitting last 2 sc on final repeat; join with sl st in first sc. (144 sc across short sides, 188 sc across long sides & 4 corner 2-sc) Fasten off and weave in all ends.

Round 1

Round 1

Round 2

Round 7

FINAL TOUCH

POMPOMS (MAKE 8)

Attach 2 Pompoms to each corner and sew in ends.

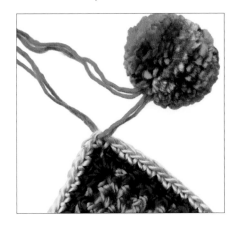

HOW TO MAKE POMPOMS

Designer's Note: I follow my grandmother's method for making pompoms.

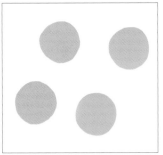
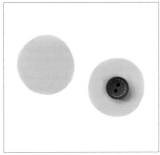

Step 1: Using cardstock or cardboard, cut out 2 circles 1¼" (3 cm) diameter. Cut a hole in the center of each circle about ½" (1 cm) diameter (I draw around a button for the center hole.)

Step 2: Hold the 2 circles together, and start wrapping the yarn around them until there is no more space in the center circle. Use a needle to help with the final wraps. (Instead of working with a very long strand, I cut a few strands of yarn about 2 yds (2 m) long and use each one doubled up.)

Step 3: Insert scissors between the paper circles and cut the yarn around the circumference.

Step 4: Cut a 20" (50 cm) length of yarn, and using it doubled, tie 2 knots very tightly around the cut strands between the circles. Do not trim these tails as they are used to attach the pompoms.

Step 5: Gently remove the card circles. Using scissors, trim to shape the pompom.

Repeat Steps 1-5 for each Pompom.

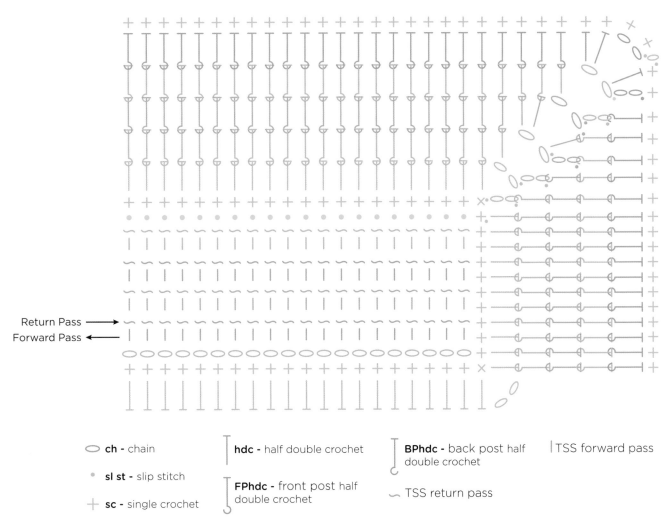

Return Pass ⟶

Forward Pass ⟵

◯	**ch -** chain	│ **hdc -** half double crochet	│ **BPhdc -** back post half double crochet	│ TSS forward pass
•	**sl st -** slip stitch	│ **FPhdc -** front post half double crochet	⌒ TSS return pass	
+	**sc -** single crochet			

LITTLE BOXES OF JOY

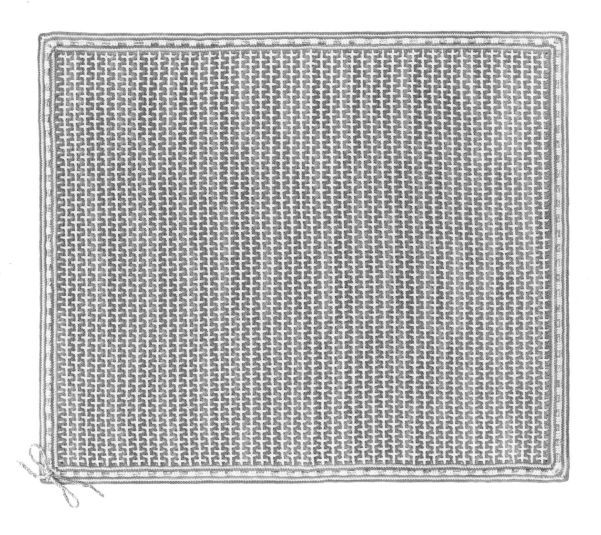

Materials

Scheepjes Softfun
Color A: Cream (2622) - 8 balls

Scheepjes Softfun Denim
Color B: Red (514) - 8 balls

#7 (4.50 mm) Crochet Hook
G-6 (4.00 mm) Crochet Hook – for Border

Tapestry Needle

Stitch Markers

Size
About 40" wide by 49" long (101 cm by 124 cm)

Gauge
Using the pattern stitch – 21 sts & 16 rows = 4" (10 cm)

Pattern Notes

1 The Blanket is worked using Interlocking Crochet™ technique (also known as Double Filet Crochet, Intermeshing or Interweaving). It consists of two layers of filet-style mesh worked simultaneously and woven together to create a reversible fabric.

2 For this pattern, the height of the double crochet stitch is only two chains (not the usual three chains). The turning chain (three chains) counts as the first double crochet and a chain space.

3 To keep edges neater, the last stitch of the row is worked in the second chain of the beginning chain three.

>>> Each row consists of two parts – one for Color A and one for Color B - both worked in the same direction. First work the Color A part, followed by the Color B part of the row. Only when both parts of the row are finished, is the work turned to start on the following row.

>>> Row numbers are labelled with either an A or a B, indicating the color needed. For example: Row 1A (worked using only Color A) or Row 14B (using only Color B).

>>> The stitch pattern for each row of the mesh is: Ch 3, [skip next sp, dc in next dc, ch 1] across, ending with dc in last dc. This creates "windows". (What makes the difference is whether the double crochet is worked in front or at the back of the fabric.)

>>> The dc stitches are always worked in the dc stitches on the previous row of the same color. When using Color A, only work in stitches made with Color A. Similarly, only use Color B to work in Color B stitches.

>>> Never work over another stitch, or wrap another stitch.

>>> At the end of each row part, remove hook and place a stitch marker in the loop of the color not in use.

Note: At the beginning of each row, before starting Color A, it is important to position Color B as per pattern – either to the front or to the back of the work.

INTERLOCKING CROCHET™ STITCHES

Double Crochet in Front (dc-f): When the specified stitch is already in front, work a double crochet as usual. If the stitch needed is at the back, then work the dc by inserting hook through "window" and pulling the stitch through the window to the front to complete.

Double Crochet in Back (dc-b): When the specified stitch is already at the back, work a double crochet as usual. If the stitch needed is in front, then work the dc by inserting hook from back to front through the "window" and pulling the stitch through the window to the back to complete.

BLANKET

FOUNDATION ROW

Color A: Ch 169, dc in 5th ch from hook (skipped ch count as ch-1, first dc & ch-1), [ch 1, skip next ch, dc in next ch] across. (83 ch-1 sps "windows") Remove hook and place marker in loop.

Color B: Ch 167, taking care not to twist chain, weave the chain back and forth through the Color A windows, starting from the first window (image 1) (both chain tails are on the same side), dc-f in 5th ch from hook (image 2 & 3), [ch 1, skip next ch, dc-f in next ch] across. (82 ch-1 sps) Remove hook and place marker in loop. Both loops are on the same side (image 4).

| Image 1 | Image 2 | Image 3 | Image 4 |

FIRST ROW

Turn, drop Color B to front.

Row 1A: Ch 3, [dc-b, ch 1, dc-f, ch 1] across, dc in last dc.

Row 1B: Ch 3, [dc-f, ch 1] across, dc-f in last dc.

Turn, drop Color B to front.

Row 2A: Ch 3, [dc-b, ch 1, dc-f, ch 1] across, dc in last dc.

Row 2B: Ch 3, [dc-f, ch 1] across, dc-f in last dc.

Turn, drop Color B to front.

Row 3A: Ch 3, [dc-f, ch 1, dc-b, ch 1] across, dc in last dc.

Row 3B: Ch 3, [dc-f, ch 1] across, dc-f in last dc.

Turn, drop Color B to front.

Row 4A: Ch 3, [dc-f, ch 1, dc-b, ch 1] across, dc in last dc.

Row 4B: Ch 3, [dc-f, ch 1] across, dc-f in last dc.

Rows 5-96: Repeat Rows 1 through Row 4, 23 times more. At the end of Row 96, there are 97 windows in height for both colors.

Row 1A

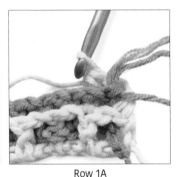
Row 1A

Row 1A

Row 1A

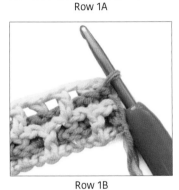
Row 1B

Row 1B

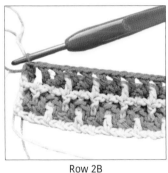
Row 2B

BORDER

Round 1: (Right Side) Do not turn, using Color B and smaller hook, starting across long side, working over both Color A and Color B into ch-1 sps, ch 1, 3 sc in corner window (image 1), [2 sc in next window (placing 1 sc on either side of Color B post) (image 2)] around, working 5 sc in each corner window (image 3), ending with 2 sc in same first window; join with sl st in first sc (image 4). (162 sc across short sides, 191 sc across long sides & 4 corner 5-sc groups) Fasten off and weave in all ends.

Round 2: With right side facing, **working in BLO,** join Color A with standing sc in 3rd (center) sc of any corner 5-sc group, ch 2, sc in same st, [sc in next st] around, working (sc, ch 2, sc) in each center sc of corner ch-5 groups; join with sl st in first sc. (168 sc across short sides, 197 sc across long sides & 4 corner ch-2 sps) Fasten off and weave in all ends.

Round 3: With right side facing, **working in BLO,** join Color B with standing sc in any corner ch-2 sp, ch 2, sc in same sp, [sc in next st] around, working (sc, ch 2, sc) in each corner ch-2 sp; join with sl st in first sc. (170 sc across short sides, 199 sc across long sides & 4 corner ch-2 sps) Fasten off and weave in all ends.

Image 1

Image 2

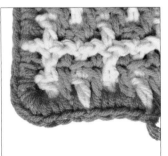
Image 3

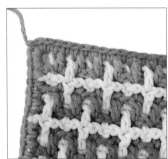
Image 4

Round 4: With right side facing, **working in BLO,** join Color A with standing dc in any corner ch-2 sp, 4 dc in same sp, [dc in next st] around, working 5 dc in each corner ch-2 sp; join with sl st in first dc. (170 dc across short sides, 199 dc across long sides & 4 corner 5-dc groups) Fasten off and weave in all ends.

Round 5: With right side facing, **working in BLO,** join Color B with standing sc in 3rd (center) dc of any corner 5-dc group, ch 2, sc in same sp, [sc in next st] around, working (sc, ch 2, sc) in center dc of each corner 5-dc group; join with sl st in first sc. (176 sc across short sides, 205 sc across long sides & 4 corner ch-2 sps) Fasten off and weave in all ends.

Round 6: With right side facing, **working in BLO,** join Color A with standing sc in any corner ch-2 sp, ch 2, sc in same sp, [sc in next st] around, working (sc, ch 2, sc) in each corner ch-2 sp; join with sl st in first sc. (178 sc across short sides, 207 sc across long sides & 4 corner ch-2 sps) Fasten off and weave in all ends.

Round 7: With right side facing, **working in BLO,** join Color B with standing sc in any corner ch-2 sp, (hdc, sc) in same sp, [sc in next st] around, working (sc, hdc, sc) in each corner ch-2 sp; join with sl st in first sc. (180 sc across short sides, 209 sc across long sides & 4 corner hdc) Fasten off and weave in all ends.

Round 2 to Round 7

FINAL TOUCH

Holding 2 strands of yarn together (one of each color), using smaller hook, work a chain string about 5½ yards (5 meters) long.

Starting at bottom right hand corner, weave the chain string all around through the dc-sts of Border Round 4. Tie ends in a bow.

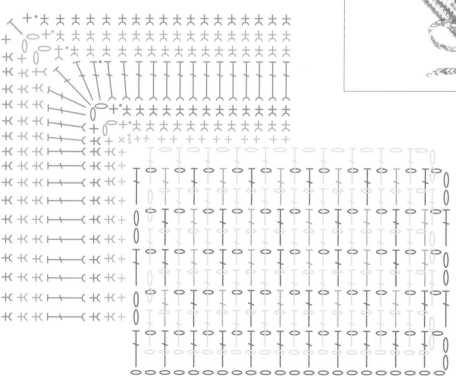

◯ **ch** - chain

• **sl st** - slip stitch

+ **sc** - single crochet

⅄ sc in back loop

hdc - half double crochet

dc - double crochet

dc in back loop

SPRING FIELD

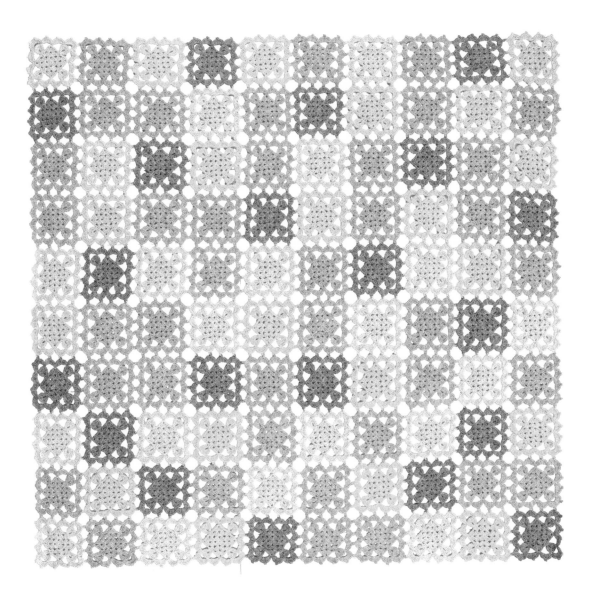

Materials

Scheepjes Sunkissed
Color A: Morning Sunrise (22) - 3 balls
Color B: Candy Floss (19) - 3 balls
Color C: Peach Ice (11) - 3 balls
Color D: Beach Hut Pink (20) - 3 balls
Color E: Moonday Sun (15) - 3 balls

D-3 (3.25 mm) Crochet Hook

Tapestry Needle

Size
About 42" (107 cm) square.

Gauge
Each Motif: About 4½" (11 cm) square.

Pattern Notes

1 The center of each Motif is a 3-round granny square, worked in turned joined rounds.

2 Motifs are joined by connecting the picots on the last round using the join-as-you-go (JAYGO) technique. Each joined side has four connected picots.

Loop Shell (lp-shell)

Ch 7, sl st in first ch to form loop (image 1), (sc, hdc, 7 dc, hdc sc) in ch-7 loop (images 2 & 3), sl st in last dc worked before the loop (image 4).

Image 1

Image 2

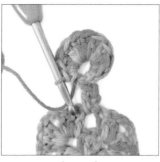

Image 3

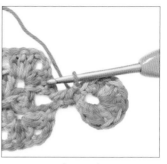

Image 4

Join As You Go (JAYGO)

(Picot joining) Ch 1, remove hook, working on previous Motif, insert hook (from right side to wrong side) in corresponding picot (image A), place loop back on hook and pull loop through picot, ch 2 (image B), sl st in both front loop and side bar together of base stitch to complete picot (image C).

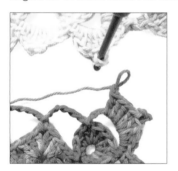

Image A

Image B

Image C

BLANKET

MOTIFS (MAKE 100 - 20 IN EACH COLOR)

Hint: To follow the original blanket color scheme, the first Motif is worked in Color A.

Round 1: (Right Side) Make a magic ring; ch 3 (counts as first dc, now and throughout), 2 dc in ring, [ch 2, 3 dc in ring] 3 times, ch 2; join with sl st in first dc (3rd ch of beg ch-3). (12 dc & 4 corner ch-2 sps)

Round 2: Ch 3, turn, (2 dc, ch 2, 3 dc) in first corner ch-2 sp, [ch 1, skip next 3 dc, (3 dc, ch 2, 3 dc) in next corner ch-2 sp] 3 times, ch 1, skip next 3 dc; join with sl st in first dc. (24 dc, 4 ch-1 sps & 4 corner ch-2 sps)

Round 3: Ch 3, turn, (dc, lp-shell, dc) in first ch-1 sp, *ch 1, skip next 3 dc, (3 dc, ch 2, 3 dc) in corner ch-2 sp, ch 1**, skip next 3 dc, (2 dc, lp-shell, dc) in next ch-1 sp; repeat from * around, ending at ** on final repeat; join with sl st in first dc. (36 dc, 8 ch -1 sps, 4 loop-shells & 4 corner ch-2 sps)

Round 4: Turn, sl st in each of next 6 sts (ch, 3 dc & 2 ch-sts); ch 1, turn, sc in corner ch-2 sp (under hook), *ch 6, working in lp-shell, sl st in 2nd dc made, ch 8, skip next 3 dc, sl st in next dc, ch 6, sc in next corner ch-2 sp; repeat from * around, omitting last sc on final repeat; join with sl st in first sc. (4 sc, 8 ch-6 lps, 4 ch-8 lps & 8 sl sts) DO NOT FASTEN OFF.

Round 3

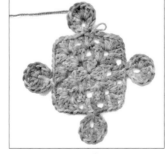

Round 3

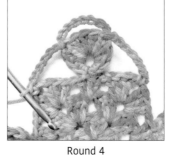

Round 4

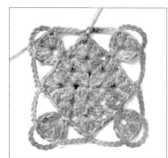

Round 4

JOINING MOTIFS

Following the color chart, lay out the Motifs to form a 10 by 10 square. Make sure the motifs are all right side facing. Starting from the top row, after the first motif (Color A), make and join the motifs together sequentially, following the required joining method.

1 Col. A	2 Col. C	3 Col. E	4 Col. D	5 Col. E	6 Col. B	7 Col. A	8 Col. C	9 Col. D	10 Col. E
11 Col. D	12 Col. B	13 Col. C	14 Col. A	15 Col. C	16 Col. D	17 Col. E	18 Col. B	19 Col. A	20 Col. C
21 Col. C	22 Col. A	23 Col. D	24 Col. E	25 Col. B	26 Col. A	27 Col. C	28 Col. D	29 Col. B	30 Col. E
31 Col. B	32 Col. E	33 Col. B	34 Col. C	35 Col. D	36 Col. E	37 Col. B	38 Col. E	39 Col. C	40 Col. D
41 Col. A	42 Col. D	43 Col. A	44 Col. B	45 Col. A	46 Col. C	47 Col. D	48 Col. A	49 Col. E	50 Col. B
51 Col. E	52 Col. B	53 Col. C	54 Col. A	55 Col. E	56 Col. B	57 Col. A	58 Col. C	59 Col. D	60 Col. A
61 Col. D	62 Col. C	63 Col. B	64 Col. D	65 Col. C	66 Col. D	67 Col. E	68 Col. B	69 Col. A	70 Col. C
71 Col. A	72 Col. D	73 Col. A	74 Col. E	75 Col. B	76 Col. A	77 Col. C	78 Col. A	79 Col. D	80 Col. E
81 Col. C	82 Col. E	83 Col. D	84 Col. C	85 Col. A	86 Col. B	87 Col. E	88 Col. D	89 Col. C	90 Col. B
91 Col. A	92 Col. C	93 Col. A	94 Col. E	95 Col. D	96 Col. C	97 Col. B	98 Col. A	99 Col. E	100 Col. D

FOR FIRST MOTIF ONLY

Round 5: Ch 1 (do not turn), *(sc, hdc, 3 dc, picot, 3 dc, hdc, sc) in next ch-6 lp, (sc, hdc, 2 dc, picot, 4 dc, picot, 2 dc, hdc, sc) in next ch-8 lp, (sc, hdc, 3 dc, picot, 3 dc, hdc, sc) in next ch-6 lp; repeat from * around; join with sl st in first sc. (24 sc, 24 hdc, 80 dc & 16 picots)

ONE-SIDE VERTICAL JOINING (MOTIFS #2 – #10)

Note: This join is made across the third side of the Motif.

Round 5: Ch 1 (do not turn);
First Half-Side: (sc, hdc, 3 dc, picot, 3 dc, hdc, sc) in next ch-6 lp, (sc, hdc, 2 dc, picot, 2 dc) in next ch-8 lp;
Second Side: (2 dc, picot, 2 dc, hdc, sc) in same ch-8 lp, [(sc, hdc, 3 dc, picot, 3 dc, hdc, sc) in next ch-6 lp] twice; (sc, hdc, 2 dc, picot, 2 dc) in next ch-8 lp;

Third Side: (2 dc, JAYGO, 2 dc, hdc, sc) in same ch-8 lp, [(sc, hdc, 3 dc, JAYGO, 3 dc, hdc, sc) in next ch-6 lp] twice, (sc, hdc, 2 dc, JAYGO, 2 dc) in next ch-8 lp;
Fourth Side: Repeat Second Side;
Finish First Side: (2 dc, picot, 2 dc, hdc, sc) in same ch-8 lp, (sc, hdc, 3 dc, picot, 3 dc, hdc, sc) in next ch-6 lp; join with sl st in first sc. (24 sc, 24 hdc, 80 dc, 12 picots & 4 joined picots)

ONE-SIDE HORIZONTAL JOINING (MOTIFS #11, #21, #31, #41, ETC.)

Note: This join is made across the second side of the Motif.

Round 5: Ch 1 (do not turn);
First Half-Side: (sc, hdc, 3 dc, picot, 3 dc, hdc, sc) in next ch-6 lp, (sc, hdc, 2 dc, picot, 2 dc) in next ch-8 lp;
Second Side: (2 dc, JAYGO, 2 dc, hdc, sc) in same ch-8 lp, [(sc, hdc, 3 dc, JAYGO, 3 dc, hdc, sc) in next ch-6 lp] twice, (sc, hdc, 2 dc, JAYGO, 2 dc) in next ch-8 lp;

Third Side: (2 dc, picot, 2 dc, hdc, sc) in same ch-8 lp, [(sc, hdc, 3 dc, picot, 3 dc, hdc, sc) in next ch-6 lp] twice; (sc, hdc, 2 dc, picot, 2 dc) in next ch-8 lp;
Fourth Side: Repeat Third Side;
Finish First Side: (2 dc, picot, 2 dc, hdc, sc) in same ch-8 lp, (sc, hdc, 3 dc, picot, 3 dc, hdc, sc) in next ch-6 lp; join with sl st in first sc. (24 sc, 24 hdc, 80 dc, 12 picots & 4 joined picots)

TWO-SIDED JOINING-REMAINING MOTIFS

Note: These joins are made across the second and third sides of the Motif.

Round 5: Ch 1 (do not turn);
First Half-Side: (sc, hdc, 3 dc, picot, 3 dc, hdc, sc) in next ch-6 lp, (sc, hdc, 2 dc, picot, 2 dc) in next ch-8 lp;
Second Side: (2 dc, JAYGO, 2 dc, hdc, sc) in same ch-8 lp, [(sc, hdc, 3 dc, JAYGO, 3 dc, hdc, sc) in next ch-6 lp] twice, (sc, hdc, 2 dc, JAYGO, 2 dc) in next ch-8 lp;

Third Side: Repeat Second Side;
Fourth Side: (2 dc, picot, 2 dc, hdc, sc) in same ch-8 lp, [(sc, hdc, 3 dc, picot, 3 dc, hdc, sc) in next ch-6 lp] twice; (sc, hdc, 2 dc, picot, 2 dc) in next ch-8 lp;
Finish First Side: (2 dc, picot, 2 dc, hdc, sc) in same ch-8 lp, (sc, hdc, 3 dc, picot, 3 dc, hdc, sc) in next ch-6 lp; join with sl st in first sc. (24 sc, 24 hdc, 80 dc, 8 picots & 8 joined picots)

MR - magic ring • **sl st** - slip stitch + **sc** - single crochet   **dc** - double crochet

ch - chain   ch 3 picot   **hdc** - half double crochet

WHERE THE WILD ROSES GROW

Materials

Scheepjes Linen Soft
Main Color (MC): Off-White (616) - 11 balls
Color A: Dark Pink (626) - 4 balls
Color B: Sea Green (623) - 4 balls
Color C: Light Pink (628) - 4 balls

G-6 (4.00 mm) Crochet Hook

Tapestry Needle

Stitch Markers

Size
About 41" wide by 50" long (105 cm by 128 cm)

Gauge
Using Seed Stitch - 18 sts ([dc in next sc, sc in next dc]
9 times) & 14 rows = 4" (10 cm)

Pattern Notes

1 The main body of the Blanket is worked in Seed Stitch.

2 The wide border is worked in right-side facing joined rounds.

3 On the Border, when the stitches differ between the Short and Long sides, the long side numbers will be after the slash. For example: dc in each of next 3/5 sts, means that on the short side, three stitches are worked; and on the long side, five stitches are worked. Similarly, [dc in next st] 6/8 times, means that the instructions within the brackets are repeated 6 times across short sides and 8 times across long sides.

4 The Popcorn Embellishments are worked onto the finished blanket – and are optional.

Working in Third Loops

Besides the Back and Front Loops of any basic stitch, there is also a "third loop". This loop looks like a horizontal bar. When the front of the stitches are facing you, it is found behind and below the back loop.

Stitch marker indicating the third loop behind the back loop.

Double Crochet Bobble (with 2 dc) (dc2-bob)

Yarn over, insert hook in stitch or space specified and pull up a loop (3 loops on hook), yarn over, draw through 2 loops on hook (2 loops remain on hook); yarn over, insert hook in same stitch and pull up a loop (4 loops on hook), yarn over, draw through 2 loops on hook, yarn over, draw through remaining 3 loops on hook.

Double Crochet Bobble (with 3 dc) (dc3-bob)

Yarn over, insert hook in stitch or space specified and pull up a loop (3 loops on hook), yarn over, draw through 2 loops on hook (2 loops remain on hook); [yarn over, insert hook in same stitch and pull up a loop, yarn over, draw through 2 loops on hook] twice more (4 loops on hook); yarn over, draw through remaining 4 loops.

Double Crochet Cluster (over 3 stitches) (dc-cl)

Yarn over, insert hook in stitch or space specified and pull up a loop (3 loops on hook), yarn over, draw through 2 loops on hook (2 loops remain on hook); [yarn over, insert hook in next specified stich or space and pull up a loop, yarn over, draw through 2 loops on hook] twice (4 loops on hook); yarn over, draw through remaining 4 loops.

Front Post Double Crochet Bobble (with 5 dc) (FPdc5-bob)

Yarn over, insert hook from front to back to front around post of specified stitch and pull up a loop (3 loops on hook), yarn over, draw through 2 loops on hook (2 loops remain on hook); [yarn over, insert hook around same stich and pull up a loop, yarn over, draw through 2 loops on hook] 4 times more (6 loops on hook); yarn over, draw through remaining 6 loops. Unless noted otherwise, always skip the stitch behind the post stitch.

Front Post Double Treble Decrease (FPdtr2tog)

Yarn over 3 times, insert hook from front to back to front around post of specified stitch and pull up a loop (5 loops on hook), [yarn over, draw through 2 loops on hook] 3 times (2 loops remain on hook), yarn over 3 times, insert hook around post of next indicated stitch and pull up a loop, [yarn over, draw through 2 loops on hook] 3 times more (3 loops on hook); yarn over, draw through remaining 3 loops. Unless noted otherwise, always skip the stitch behind the post stitch.

Front Post Double Treble/Single Crochet Decrease (FP(dtr-sc)tog)

Yarn over 3 times, insert hook from front to back to front around post of specified stitch and pull up a loop (5 loops on hook), [yarn over, draw through 2 loops on hook] 3 times (2 loops remain on hook), insert hook around post of next indicated stitch and pull up a loop, yarn over, draw through remaining 3 loops.
Unless noted otherwise, always skip the stitch behind the post stitch.

Front Post Single Crochet/ Double Treble Decrease (FP(sc-dtr)tog)

Insert hook from front to back to front around post of specified stitch and pull up a loop (2 loops on hook), yarn over 3 times, insert hook from front to back to front around post of next specified stitch and pull up a loop (6 loops on hook), [yarn over, draw through 2 loops on hook] 3 times (3 loops on hook), yarn over, draw through remaining 3 loops. Unless noted otherwise, always skip the stitch behind the post stitch.

Popcorn Stitch (with 4 dc) (pop)

Work 4 dc in specified stitch or space. Remove hook from loop and insert hook in first dc (of 4-dc group). Place loop on hook and draw loop through first stitch. Ch 1 to secure.

BLANKET

Row 1: (Right Side) Using MC, ch 101, sc in 2nd ch from hook, dc in next ch, [sc in next ch, dc in next ch] across. (50 sc & 50 dc)

Rows 2-126: Ch 1, turn, sc in first dc, dc in next sc, [sc in next dc, dc in next sc] across. (50 sc & 50 dc) At the end of Row 126, DO NOT FASTEN OFF.

BORDER

Round 1: Ch 1, turn (right side facing), 3 sc in first dc (corner made – mark 2nd (center) sc), [sc in next st] across to last st, 3 sc in last st (corner); *working in sides of rows, sc in each row across*; working in unused loops on other side of starting chain, 3 sc in first ch (corner), [sc in next ch] across to last ch, 3 sc in last ch (corner); repeat from * to * once; join with sl st in first sc. (100 sc across short sides, 126 sc across long sides & 4 corner 1-sc) Fasten off and weave in all ends.

Note: All following Rounds start with Right Side Facing.

Round 2: Working in BLO, Join Color A with standing sc in marked st, ch 2, sc in same st (corner made), [sc in next st] around, working (sc, ch 2, sc) in each corner st (center sc of 3-sc group); join with sl st in first sc. (102 sc across short sides, 128 sc across long sides & 4 corner ch-2 sps) Fasten off and weave in all ends.

Round 3: With right side facing, join Color B with standing hdc in any corner ch-2 sp, ch 2, hdc in same sp, working in BLO, [hdc in next st] around, working (hdc, ch 2, hdc) in each corner ch-2 sp; join with sl st in first hdc. (104 hdc across short sides, 130 hdc across long sides & 4 corner ch-2 sps) Fasten off, weave in all ends.

Round 4: With right side facing, join Color C with standing hdc in any corner ch-2 sp, ch 2, hdc in same sp, working in third loops only, [hdc in next st] around, working (hdc, ch 2, hdc) in each corner ch-2 sp; join with sl st in first hdc. (106 hdc across short sides, 132 hdc across long sides & 4 corner ch-2 sps) Fasten off and weave in all ends.

Round 5: With right side facing, join Color A with standing dc2-bob in any corner ch-2 sp, (ch 2, dc2-bob, ch 2, dc2-bob) in same sp, *ch 2, skip next 2 sts, [dc3-bob in next st, ch 2, skip next st] across to corner**, (dc2-bob, [ch 2, dc2-bob] twice) in corner ch-2 sp; repeat from * around, ending at ** on final repeat; join with sl st in first bob. (52 dc3-bobbles

across short sides, 65 dc3-bobbles across long sides & 4 corner 3-dc2-bobbles groups) Fasten off and weave in all ends.

Round 6: With right side facing, join Color C with standing FPhdc around first bobble of any corner 3-bobble group, 2 hdc in next ch-2 sp, (FPhdc, ch 2, FPhdc) around next st (center bobble), 2 hdc in next ch-2 sp, FPhdc around next st, *working in front of ch-2 sp, tr in 2nd skipped st on Round 4, [FPhdc around next st (bobble), working in front of ch-2 sp, tr in next skipped st on Round 4] across to corner**, FPhdc around next st (first bobble of corner group), 2 hdc in next ch-2 sp, (FPhdc, ch 2, FPhdc) around next st (center bobble), 2 hdc in next ch-2 sp, FPhdc around next st; repeat from * around, ending at ** on final repeat; join with sl st in first FPhdc. (56 FPhdc, 53 tr & 4 hdc across short sides, 69 FPhdc, 66 tr & 4 hdc across long sides & 4 corner ch-2 sps) Fasten off and weave in all ends.

Round 7: With right side facing, join MC with standing dc in any corner ch-2 sp, (dc, ch 2, 2 dc) in same sp, *FPdc around next st, dc in each of next 2 sts, FPdc around next st, [dc in next st, FPdc around next st (tr)] across to next corner**, (2 dc, ch 2, 2 dc) in next corner ch-2 sp; repeat from * around, ending at ** on final repeat; join with sl st in first dc. (57 FPdc, & 60 dc across short sides, 70 FPdc 73 dc across long sides & 4 corner ch-2 sps) Fasten off and weave in all ends.

Round 8: With right side facing, join Color B with standing dc in any corner ch-2 sp, (dc, ch 2, 2 dc) in same sp, *[dc in each of next 2 sts, FPdc around next st] twice, [dc in next st, FPdc around next st] across to last 5 sts before next corner, dc in each of next 2 sts, FPdc around next st, dc in each of next 2 sts**, (2 dc, ch 2, 2 dc) in next corner ch-2 sp; repeat from * around, ending at ** on final repeat; join with sl st in first dc. (56 FPdc, & 65 dc across short sides, 69 FPdc & 78 dc across long sides & 4 corner ch-2 sps) Fasten off and weave in all ends.

Round 4

Round 5

Round 6

Round 9: Join MC with standing dc in any corner ch-2 sp, (dc, ch 2, 2 dc) in same sp, *FPdc around next st, dc in each of next 3 sts, FPdc around next st, dc in each of next 2 sts, FPdc around each of next 2 sts, [dc in next st, FPdc around next st] across to last 10 sts before next corner, dc in next st, FPdc around each of next 2 sts, dc in each of next 2 sts, FPdc around next st, dc in each of next 3 sts, FPdc around next st **, (2 dc, ch 2, 2 dc) in next corner ch-2 sp; repeat from * around, ending at ** on final repeat; join with sl st in first dc. (59 FPdc, & 66 dc across short sides, 72 FPdc & 79 dc across long sides & 4 corner ch-2 sps) Fasten off and weave in all ends.

Round 10: With right side facing, join Color A with standing hdc in any corner ch-2 sp, (hdc, ch 2, 2 hdc) in same sp, *hdc in each of next 2 sts, FPhdc around next st, hdc in each of next 3 sts, FPhdc around next st, hdc in each of next 2 sts, FPhdc around each of next 2 sts, [hdc in next st, puff-st in next st] across to last 12 sts before next corner, hdc in next st, FPhdc around each of next 2 sts, hdc in each of next 2 sts, FPhdc around next st, hdc in each of next 3 sts, FPhdc around next st, hdc in each of next 2 sts**, (2 hdc, ch 2, 2 hdc) in next corner ch-2 sts; repeat from * around, ending at ** on final repeat; join with sl st in first hdc. (70 hdc, 51 puff-st & 8 FPhdc across short sides, 83 hdc, 64 puff-st & 8 FPhdc across long sides & 4 corner ch-2 sps) Fasten off and weave in all ends.

Round 11: With right side facing, join Color B with standing hdc in any corner ch-2 sp, (hdc, ch 2, 2 hdc) in same sp, *[FPhdc around next st, hdc in each of next 3 sts] twice, FPhdc around next st, hdc in each of next 2 sts, FPhdc around each of next 2 sts, [hdc in next st, FPhdc around next st (puff-st)] across to last puff-st before next corner, hdc in next st, FPhdc around each of next 2 sts, hdc in each of next 2 sts, [FPhdc around next st, hdc in each of next 3 sts] twice, FPhdc around next st **, (2 hdc, ch 2, 2 hdc) in next corner ch-2 sp; repeat from * around, ending at ** on final repeat; join with sl st in first hdc. (72 hdc & 61 FPhdc across short sides, 85 hdc & 74 FPhdc across long sides & 4 corner ch-2 sps) Fasten off and weave in all ends.

Round 12: With right side facing, join Color C with standing hdc in any corner ch-2 sp, (hdc, ch 2, 2 hdc) in same sp, *hdc in each of next 2 sts, [FPhdc around next st, hdc in each of next 3 sts] twice, FPhdc around next st, hdc in each of next 2 sts, FPhdc around next st, hdc in next st, [puff-st in next st, hdc in next st] across to last 14 sts, FPhdc around next st (2nd FPhdc of 2-FPhdc group), hdc in each of next 2 sts, [FPhdc around next st, hdc in each of next 3 sts] twice, FPhdc around next st, hdc in each of next 2 sts**, (2 hdc, ch 2, 2 hdc) in next corner ch-2 sp; repeat from * around, ending at ** on final repeat; join with sl st in first hdc. (77 hdc, 52 puff-st & 8 FPhdc across short sides, 90 hdc, 65 puff-st & 8 FPhdc across long sides & 4 corner ch-2 sps) Fasten off and weave in all ends.

Round 13: With right side facing, join Color B with standing hdc in any corner ch-2 sp, (hdc, ch 2, 2 hdc) in same sp, *skip next st, [hdc in each of next 3 sts, FPhdc around next st] 3 times, hdc in each of next 2 sts, [FPhdc around next st, hdc in next st] across to last 16 sts before next corner, FPhdc around next st, hdc in each of next 2 sts, [FPhdc around next st, hdc in each of next 3 sts] 3 times, hdc in next st **, (2 hdc, ch 2, 2 hdc) in next corner ch-2 sp; repeat from * around, ending at ** on final repeat; join with sl st in first hdc. (80 hdc & 60 FPhdc across short sides, 93 hdc & 73 FPhdc across long sides & 4 corner ch-2 sps) Fasten off and weave in all ends.

Round 14: With right side facing, join Color MC with standing hdc in any corner ch-2 sp, (hdc, ch 2, 2 hdc) in same sp, *skip next st, hdc in each of next 4 sts, [FPdc5-bob around next st (FPhdc), hdc in each of next 3 sts] twice, FPdc5-bob around next st, hdc in each of next 2 sts, FPhdc around next st, hdc in each of next 2 sts, [puff-st in next st, hdc in next st] across to last 19 sts before next corner, hdc in next st, FPhdc around next st, hdc in each of next 2 sts, [FPdc5-bob around next st, hdc in each of next 3 sts] twice, FPdc5-bob in next st, skip next st, hdc in each of next 5 sts**, (2 hdc, ch 2, 2 hdc) in next corner ch-2 sp; repeat from * around, ending at ** on final repeat; join with sl st in first hdc. (83 hdc, 51 puff-sts, 2 FPhdc & 6 FPdc5-bob across short sides, 96 hdc, 64 puff-sts, 2 FPhdc & 6 FPdc5-bob across long sides & 4 corner ch-2 sps) Fasten off and weave in all ends.

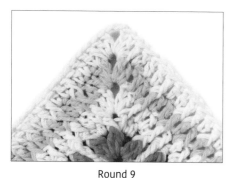

Round 9

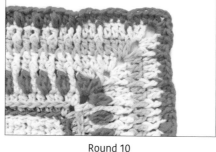

Round 10

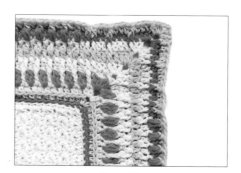

Round 11

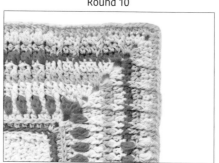

Round 12

Round 13

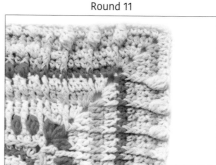

Round 14

Round 15: With right side facing, join Color B with standing hdc in any corner ch-2 sp, (hdc, ch 2, 2 hdc) in same sp, *skip next st, hdc in each of next 5 sts, [FPhdc around next st, hdc in next st, 2 hdc in next st skip next st] twice, [FPhdc around next st, 2 hdc in next st] twice, [FPhdc around next puff, hdc in next st] across to last 20 sts before next corner, hdc in next st, FPhdc around next st, 2 hdc in next st, skip next st, [FPhdc around next st, skip next st, hdc in next st, 2 hdc in next st] twice, FPhdc around next st, hdc in each of next 6 sts, skip next st**, (2 hdc, ch 2, 2 hdc) in next corner ch-2 sp; repeat from * around, ending at ** on final repeat; join with sl st in first hdc. (85 hdc & 59 FPhdc across short sides, 98 hdc & 72 FPhdc across long sides & 4 corner ch-2 sps) Fasten off and weave in all ends.

Round 16: With right side facing, join Color A with standing sc in any corner ch-2 sp, ch 2, sc in same sp, sc in each of next 3 sts, *dtr in ch-2 corner on Rnd 13 (between 2nd & 3rd hdc), skip next st, sc in each of next 4 sts, FPtr around corresponding bobble on Rnd 14, [sc in each of next 3 sts, FPtr around corresponding bobble on Rnd 14] twice, [sc in next st] across to last 16 sts, [FPtr around corresponding bobble on Rnd 14, sc in each of next 3 sts] twice, FPtr around corresponding bobble on Rnd 14, sc in each of next 4 sts, dtr in ch-2 corner on Rnd 13 (between 2nd & 3rd hdc), skip next st, sc in each of next 2 sts**, (sc, ch 2, sc) in corner ch-2 sp; repeat from * around, ending at ** on final repeat; join with sl st in first sc. (138 sc, 6 FPtr & 2 dtr across short sides, 164 sc, 6 FPtr & 2 dtr across long sides & 4 corner ch-2 sps) Fasten off and weave in all ends.

Round 17: With right side facing, join Color C with standing hdc in any corner ch-2 sp, (hdc, ch 2, 2 hdc) in same sp, working in BLO, [hdc in next st] around, working (2 hdc, ch 2, 2 hdc) in each corner ch-2 sp; join with sl st in first hdc. (150 hdc across short sides, 176 hdc across long sides & 4 corner ch-2 sps) Fasten off and weave in all ends.

Round 18: (see Pattern Notes) With right side facing, join Color MC with standing dc2-bob in any corner ch-2 sp, (ch 2, dc2-bob, ch 2, dc2-bob) in same sp, *working in BLO, skip next st, dc in each of next 8 sts, FPdtr around dtr on Rnd 16 (mark this stitch), dc in each of next 3 sts, FPdtr2tog around 1st & 2nd FPtr on Rnd 16, dc in each of next 3 sts, FPdtr2tog around 2nd & 3rd FPtr on Rnd 16, dc in each of next 4 sts, FPdtr around 4th FPhdc on Rnd 15, dc in each of next 4/5 sts, ch 2, skip next st, dc-cl (using next 3 sts), [ch 3, skip next st, dc-cl] 23/29 times, ch 2, skip next st, dc in each of next 4/5 sts, FPdtr around next FPhdc on Rnd 15 (mark this stitch), dc in each of next 4 sts, FPdtr2tog around 1st & 2nd FPtr on Rnd 16, dc in each of next 3 sts, FPdtr2tog around 2nd & 3rd FPtr on Rnd 16, dc in each of next 4 sts, FPdtr around dtr on Rnd 16, dc in each of next 7 sts**, (dc2-bob, [ch 2, dc2-bob] twice in next corner ch-2 sp; repeat from * around, ending at ** on final repeat; join with sl st in first bobble. (44 dc, 4 FPdtr, 4 decreases, 2 ch-2 sps, 24 clusters, 23 ch-3 sp across short sides, 46 dc, 4 FPdtr, 4 decreases, 2 ch-2 sps, 30 clusters, 29 ch-3 sp across long sides & 4 corner 3-dc2-bobbles & 2 ch-2 sps) Fasten off and weave in all ends.

Note: The 8 marked stitches on this round are for the optional Popcorn Embellishments.

Round 19: With right side facing, join Color C with standing FPhdc around first bobble of any corner, *2 hdc in next ch-2 sp, (FPhdc, ch 2, FPhdc) around next (center) bobble, 2 hdc in next ch-2 sp, FPhdc around next bobble, hdc in each of next 12 sts, FPhdc around next FPdtr2tog, hdc in each of next 3 sts, FPhdc around next FPdtr2tog, hdc in each of next 9/10 sts, tr in the corresponding skipped st on Rnd 17 (working in front of ch-2 sp), hdc in ch-2 sp, [FPhdc around next cluster, hdc in next ch-3 sp, tr in next skipped st on Rnd 17 (working in front of ch-sp), hdc in same ch-3 sp] 23/29 times, FPhdc around last cluster, hdc in ch-2 sp, tr in next skipped st on Rnd 17 (working in front of same ch-sp), hdc in each of next 9/10 sts, FPhdc around next FPdtr2tog, hdc in each of next 3 sts, FPhdc around next FPdtr2tog, hdc in each of next 12 sts**, FPhdc around first bobble of next corner; repeat from * around, ending at ** on final repeat; join with sl st in first FPhdc. (100 hdc, 32 FPhdc & 25 tr across short sides, 102 hdc, 38 FPhdc & 31 tr across long sides & 4 corner ch-2 sps) Fasten off and weave in all ends.

Round 17

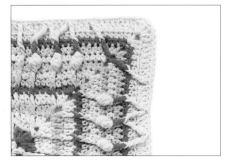

Round 18

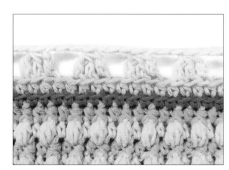

Round 18

Round 19

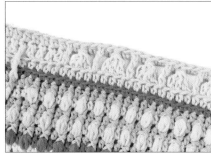

Round 19

Note: Bobbles are worked in both loops.

Round 20: With right side facing, join Color B with standing hdc in any corner ch-2 sp, (hdc, ch 2, 2 hdc) in same sp, *working in BLO, skip next st, hdc in each of next 2 sts, FPhdc around next FPhdc, hdc in each of next 10 sts, skip next 2 sts, (dc3-bob, ch 3, dc3-bob) in next st (which is FPhdc worked around FPdtr2tog on Rnd 18), skip next 3 sts, (dc3-bob, ch 3, dc3-bob) in next st (above FPdtr2tog), skip next 2 sts, hdc in each of next ⅞ sts, FPhdc around next st (tr), [hdc in each of next 3 sts, FPhdc around next st] 24/30 times, hdc in each of next 7/8 sts, skip next 2 sts, (dc3-bob, ch 3, dc3-bob) in next st (above FPdtr2tog), skip next 3 sts, (dc3-bob, ch 3, dc3-bob) in next st (above FPdtr2tog), skip next 2 sts, hdc in each of next 10 sts, FPhdc around next FPhdc, hdc in each of next 3 sts**, (2 hdc, ch 2, 2 hdc) in next corner ch-2 sp; repeat from * around, ending at ** on final repeat; join with sl st in first hdc. (115 hdc, 27 FPhdc & 8 3-bobble groups across short sides, 135 hdc, 33 FPhdc & 8 3-bobble groups across long sides & 4 corner ch-2 sps) Fasten off and weave in all ends.

Round 21: With right side facing, join Color A with standing sc in any corner ch-2 sp, ch 2, sc in same sp, *sc in each of next 15 sts, FP(dtr-sc)tog (working FPdtr around FPdtr on Rnd 18 & FPsc around next bobble), ch 1, pop in same st as bobbles on Rnd 20 (in front of ch-3), ch 1, FPsc around next bob, sc in sp between bobbles, FPsc around next bob, ch 1, pop in same st as bobbles on Rnd 20 (in front of ch-3), ch 1, FPsc around next bobble, skip next st, sc in each st across to next bobble, FPsc around bobble, ch 1, pop in same st as bobbles on Rnd 20 (in front of ch-3), ch 1, FPsc around next bob, sc in sp between bobbles, FPsc around next bob, ch 1,

pop in same st as bobbles on Rnd 20 (in front of ch-3), ch 1, FP(sc-dtr)tog (working FPsc around next dc3-bob & FPdtr around next FPdtr), skip next st, sc in each of next 15 sts**, (sc, ch 2, sc) in next corner ch-2 sp; repeat from * around, ending at ** on final repeat; join with sl st in first sc. (144 sc, 6 FPsc, 4 popcorns 2 decreases & 8 ch-1 sps across short sides, 170 sc, 6 FPsc, 4 popcorns 2 decreases & 8 ch-1 sps across long sides & 4 corner ch-2 sps) Fasten off and weave in all ends.

Round 22: With right side facing, join MC with standing hdc in any corner ch-2 sp, (hdc, ch 2, 2 hdc) in same sp, *skip next st, hdc in each st or sp across to next corner**, (2 hdc, ch 2, 2 hdc) in next corner ch-2 sp; repeat from * around, ending at ** on final repeat; join with sl st in first hdc. (167 hdc across short sides, 193 hdc across long sides & 4 corner ch-2 sps) Fasten off and weave in all ends.

Round 23: With right side facing, join Color C with standing hdc in any corner ch-2 sp, (hdc, ch 2, hdc) in same sp, *working in BLO, hdc in each st across to next corner**, (2 hdc, ch 2, 2 hdc) in next corner ch-2 sp; repeat from * around, ending at ** on final repeat; join with sl st in first hdc. (171 hdc across short sides, 197 hdc across long sides & 4 corner ch-2 sps) Fasten off and weave in all ends.

Round 24: With right side facing, join Color B with standing sc in any corner ch-2 sp, ch 2, sc in same sp, *working in BLO, sc in each st across to next corner**, (sc, ch 2, sc) in next corner ch-2 sp; repeat from * around, ending at ** on final repeat; join with sl st in first sc. (173 sc across short sides, 199 sc across long sides & 4 corner ch-2 sps) DO NOT FASTEN OFF.

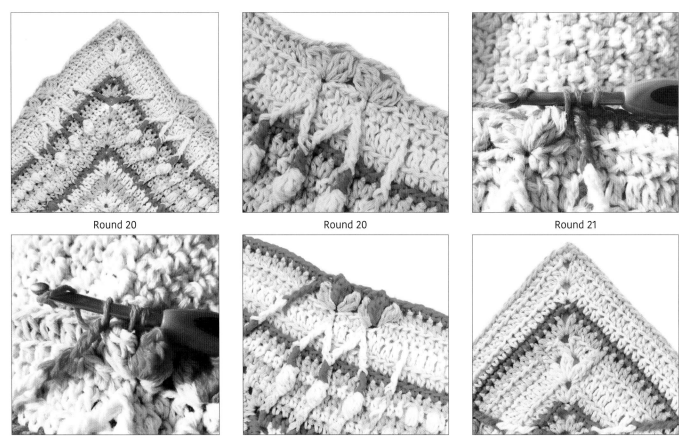

| Round 20 | Round 20 | Round 21 |
| Round 21 | Round 21 | Round 24 |

Round 25: Sl st in corner ch-2 sp, ch 6 (counts as first dc & ch-3), dc in same sp, *skip next 2 sts, (dc3-bob, ch 3, dc3-bob) in next st, [skip next 3 sts, (dc3-bob, ch 3, dc3-bob) in next st] across to last 2/1 st(s), skip last 2/1 sts**, (dc, ch 3, dc) in corner ch-2 sp; repeat from * around, ending at ** on final repeat; join with sl st in first dc (3rd ch of beg ch-6). (86 bobbles, 43 ch-3 sps & 2 dc, 100 bobbles, 50 ch-3 sps & 2 dc & 4 corner ch-3 sps) Fasten off and weave in all ends.

Round 26: With right side facing, join Color A with standing sc in any corner ch-3 sp, *[pop in ch-2 sp on Rnd 24 (in front of ch-3), sc in same corner ch-3 sp] twice, FPsc around next dc, [FPsc around next st, ch 1, pop in same st as bobbles on Rnd 24, ch 1, FPsc around next st] across to last st before corner, FPsc around next dc**, sc in next corner ch-3 sp; repeat from * around, ending at ** on final repeat; join with sl st in first sc. (45 popcorns, 88 FPsc, 86 ch-1 sps & 2 sc across short sides, 52 popcorns, 102 FPsc, 100 ch-1 sps & 2 sc across long sides & 4 corner sc-sts) Fasten off and weave in all ends.

Round 27: With right side facing, join MC with standing sc in any corner sc, *skip next popcorn, sc in each of next 2 sts, [sc in next st, sc in next ch-1 sp, skip next popcorn, sc in next ch-1 sp, sc in next st] across to last FPsc before next corner, sc in last FPsc, sc in next st, skip next popcorn**, sc in next (corner) st; repeat from * around, ending at ** on final repeat; join with sl st in first sc. (176 sc across short sides, 204 sc across long sides & 4 corner sc-sts) Fasten off and weave in all ends.

Round 26

FINAL TOUCH

POPCORN EMBELLISHMENTS (OPTIONAL)

Using Color A, make a standing dc in any of the marked sts on Rnd 18 (to the right of the hdc worked in same st) (image 1). Work 2 more dc in the same place (image 2). Work another 2 dc in the same stitch on the left side of same hdc (image 3). Five dc-sts are in the same stitch (image 4). Remove hook from loop and insert hook in top of standing dc. Place loop on hook and draw loop through stitch. Ch 1 to secure (popcorn made). Cut yarn (image 5). Thread the tails to the back of the blanket - one tail on each side of the hdc on Rnd 20. Tie tails in a knot to secure (image 6) and weave in ends. Repeat until 8 popcorns are made.

Image 1

Image 2

Image 3

Image 4

Image 5

Image 6

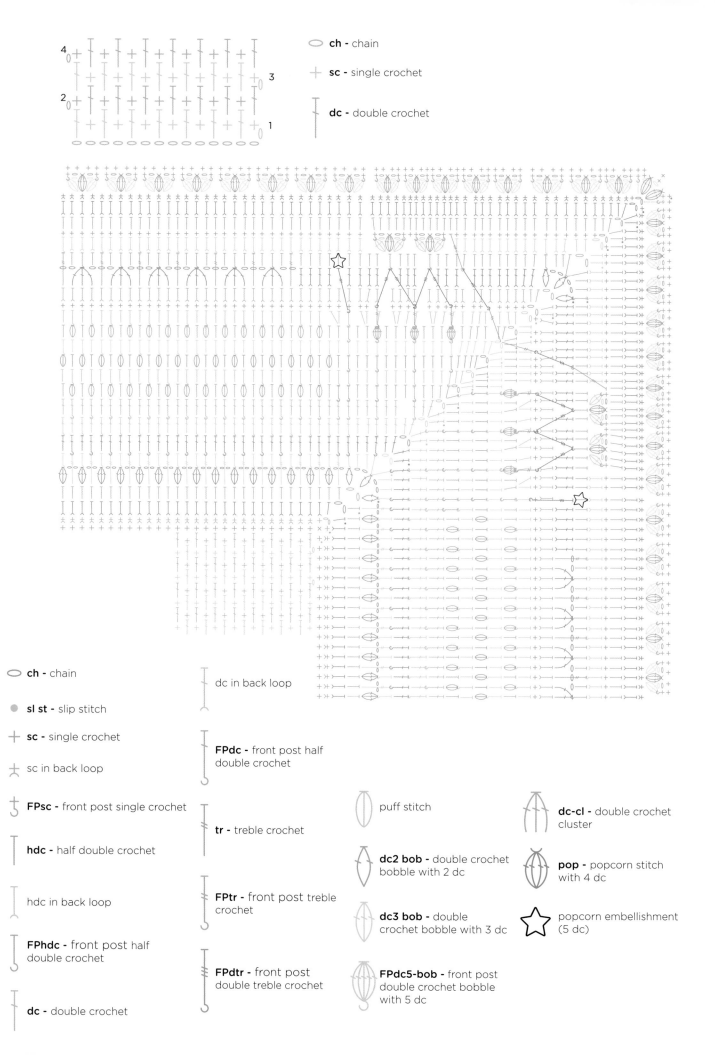

ch - chain

sc - single crochet

dc - double crochet

ch - chain

sl st - slip stitch

sc - single crochet

sc in back loop

FPsc - front post single crochet

hdc - half double crochet

hdc in back loop

FPhdc - front post half double crochet

dc - double crochet

dc in back loop

FPdc - front post half double crochet

tr - treble crochet

FPtr - front post treble crochet

FPdtr - front post double treble crochet

puff stitch

dc2 bob - double crochet bobble with 2 dc

dc3 bob - double crochet bobble with 3 dc

FPdc5-bob - front post double crochet bobble with 5 dc

dc-cl - double crochet cluster

pop - popcorn stitch with 4 dc

popcorn embellishment (5 dc)

CABLES AND PUFFS

Materials

Scheepjes Stone Washed XL
Color A: Crystal Quartz (854) – 22 balls

Scheepjes River Washed XL
Color B: Ural (977) – 2 balls

J-10 (6.00 mm) Crochet Hook

Tapestry Needle

Stitch Markers - 4

Size
About 40" wide by 52" long (102 cm by 132 cm)

Gauge
13 hdc & 10 hdc-rows = 4" (10 cm)

Pattern Notes

1. The body of the Blanket is worked in rows, and the Border is worked in joined rounds.

2. To avoid gaps along the edges, the rows start with a turning chain of only one stitch (instead of the usual two chains for hdc rows/rounds). This turning chain does count as the first stitch and needs to be worked in at the end of the following row.

Reverse Single Crochet (rsc):
With loop on hook (image 1), working from left to right, *insert hook in next stitch or space to the right (image 2) and pull up a loop, yarn over and draw through both loops on hook (image 3); repeat from * across/around

Image 1 Image 2 Image 3

Front Post Double Crochet Cross Stitch (FPdc-X): Worked over 2 stitches. Skip next st, FPdc in next st, FPdc in skipped st (working in front of stitch just made).

Double Front Post Treble Cross Stitch (FPtr-XX): Worked over 4 stitches. Skip next 2 sts, FPtr around each of next 2 sts, FPtr around each of skipped 2 sts (working in front of stitches just made).

BLANKET

Row 1: (Right Side) Using Color A, ch 120; hdc in 3rd ch from hook (skipped ch count as first hdc) and in each ch across. (119 hdc)

Row 2: Ch 1 (counts as first hdc, now and throughout), turn, (skip first st) [hdc in next hdc] across, with last stitch worked in 2nd ch of skipped ch-2. (119 hdc)

Row 3: (See Special Stitches) Ch 1, turn, hdc in each of next 3 sts, FPdc-X (over next 2 sts), hdc in each of next 2 sts, puff-st in next st, hdc in each of next 2 sts, FPdc-X (over next 2 sts), hdc in each of next 2 sts, *FPtr-XX (over next 4 sts), hdc in each of next 2 sts, FPdc-X (over next 2 sts), hdc in each of next 2 sts, puff-st in next st, hdc in each of next 2 sts, FPdc-X (over next 2 sts), hdc in each of next 2 sts; repeat from * 5 times more, hdc in each of last 2 sts (last stitch worked in turning ch). (60 hdc, 7 puff-sts, 14 FPdc-X & 6 FPtr-XX)

Row 4: Ch 1, turn, hdc in each of next 3 sts, BPhdc in each of next 2 sts, hdc in each of next 2 sts, BPhdc in next st (this is the puff-st), hdc in each of next 2 sts, BPhdc around each of next 2 sts, hdc in each of next 2 sts, *BPhdc in each of next 4 sts, hdc in each of next 2 sts, BPhdc in each of next 2 sts, hdc in each of next 2 sts, BPhdc in next st (this is the puff-st), hdc in each of next 2 sts, BPhdc around each of next 2 sts, hdc in each of next 2 sts; repeat from * 5 times more, hdc in each of next 2 sts. (60 hdc, 59 BPhdc)

Rows 5-116: Repeat Rows 3 & 4. At the end of Row 116, fasten off and weave in all ends.

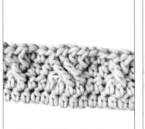

Row 4 - First 7 stitches, showing the BPhdc in each FPdc

Row 4 - BPhdc in puff-st

Row 4 - BPhdc around each FPtr

After Row 4 - with right side facing

BORDER

Designer's Note: The true corner stitch is the top chain stitch of the turning chain. However, I found that the chain stitch was too fragile to hold all the corner stitches, so I've moved the corner to the hdc before the chain stitch to give the corner more stability. To compensate "losing" the turning chain, the first corner has 4 sc stitches to keep stitch count correct.

Round 1: With right side facing, join Color B with standing sc in first hdc, sc in same st, [sc in next st] across to second last st, 3 sc in second last st (corner made – mark center sc), skip turning ch, working in sides of rows, *sc in same row (over turning ch), [2 sc in next row (over last hdc), sc in next row (over turning ch)] across to next corner*, ending with 2 sc in first row; working in unused loops on other side of starting chain, 3 sc in first ch (corner made – mark center sc), [sc in next ch] across to last ch, 3 sc in last ch; repeat from * to * once, ending with 2 sc in last row, 2 sc in same first corner (mark last sc worked as center sc); join with sl st in first sc. (119 sc across short sides, 174 sc across long sides & 4 corner sc-sts)

Round 2: (See Special Stitches) Ch 1, DO NOT TURN, rsc in marked corner st, working from left to right, *[rsc in next st] across to next corner, 2 rsc in marked corner st; repeat from * around, omitting last rsc on final repeat; join with sl st in first rsc. (119 rsc across short sides, 174 rsc across long sides & 4 corner 2-rsc) Fasten off and weave in all ends.

Round 1

Round 1

Round 1

Round 1

Round 2

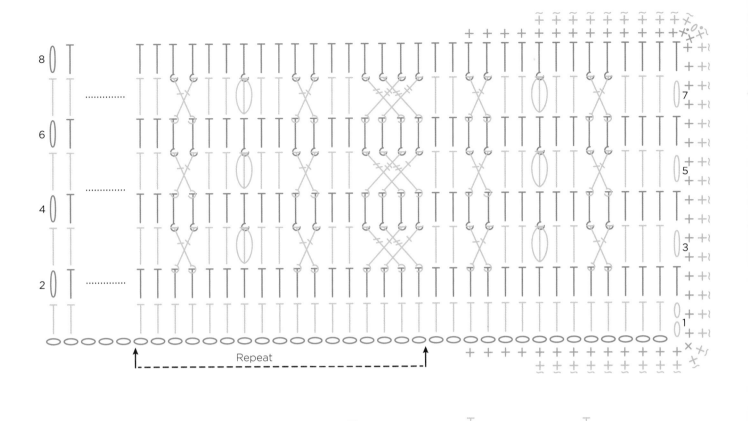

8

7

6

5

4

3

2

1

Repeat

- **sl st** - slip stitch
- **rsc** - reverse sc
- **sc** - single crochet
- **ch** - chain
- **hdc** - half double crochet
- **BPhdc** - back post half double crochet
- **FPdc** - front post double crochet
- **FPtr** - front post treble crochet

ALL THE OCEANS BLUE

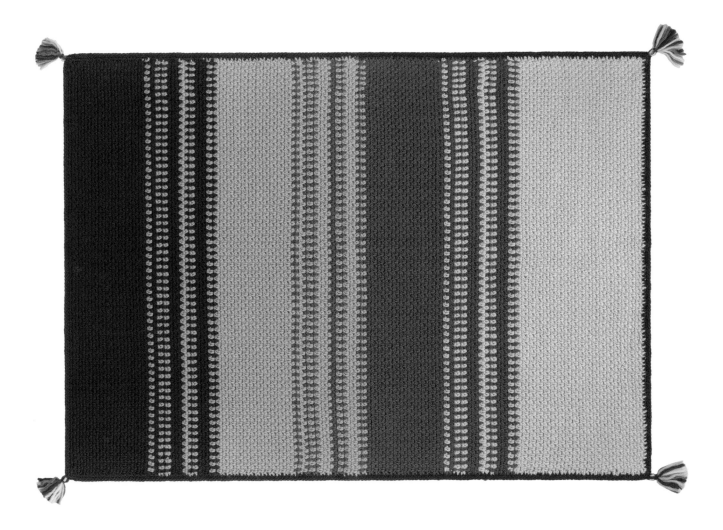

Materials

Scheepjes Namaste
Color A: Warrior (614) - 4 balls
Color B: Scale (625) - 4 balls
Color C: Upward Bow (629) - 4 balls
Color D: Staff (626) - 4 balls

L-11 (8.00 mm) Crochet Hook

Tapestry Needle

Stitch Markers

Size
About 41½" wide by 58" long (105 cm by 147 cm)

Gauge
Using Moss Stitch - 13 sts (sc in next ch-sp, [ch 1, sc in next ch-sp] 6 times) & 12 rows = 4" (10 cm)

Pattern Notes

1 The Blanket is worked in rows of Moss Stitch, also known as Granite Stitch or Linen Stitch.

2 The Border is worked in joined rounds and tassels are added to each corner.

Changing Colors

Note: The new color is joined in the last stitch of the row.

Insert hook in turning chain and pull up a loop (2 loops on hook) (image 1), with new color, yarn over and draw through both loops on hook (last single crochet made) (image 2). Continue the next row with the new color by making 2 chains (image 3) and turning, and working across as usual (image 4).

Image 1

Image 2

Image 3

Image 4

BLANKET

Row 1: (Right Side) Using Color A, ch 118, sc in 4th ch from hook (skipped ch counts as turning ch-sp), [ch 1, skip next ch, sc in next ch] across. (58 sc, 57 ch-1 sps & turning ch-sp)

Row 2: Ch 2 (counts as turning ch-sp), turn, [sc in next ch-1 sp, ch 1, skip next st] across, ending with sc in last turning ch-sp. (58 sc, 57 ch-1 sps & turning ch-sp)

Rows 3-35: Repeat Row 2.

At the end of Row 35, change color to Color C.

Rows 36-160: Follow the color distribution chart, for all three passes (42 rows for each of First & Second passes, and 41 rows for Third pass), changing color at the end of the required number of rows. At the end of Row 160, DO NOT FASTEN OFF (Color D).

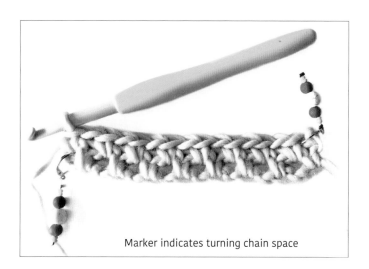

Marker indicates turning chain space

Color Distribution Chart

Number of Rows	First Pass Rows 36-77	Second Pass Rows 78-119	Third PassRows 120-160
1	Color C	B	D
1	Color A	C	B
4	Color C	B	D
1	Color A	C	B
1	Color C	B	D
2	Color A	C	B
4	Color C	B	D
1	Color A	C	B
1	Color C	B	D
1	Color A	C	B
2	Color C	B	D
1	Color A	C	B
22	Color C	B	D (21 rows only)

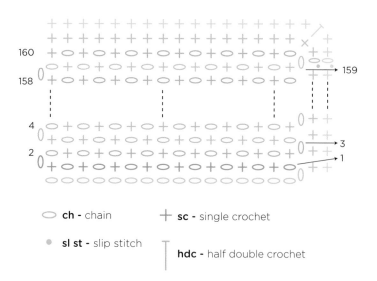

⬯ **ch** - chain   ✛ **sc** - single crochet

● **sl st** - slip stitch   ⊤ **hdc** - half double crochet

BORDER

Round 1: With Color D, ch 1, turn, (right side facing), 3 sc in first sc (**mark center sc**), [sc in next ch-1 sp, sc in next sc] across, working 3 sc in last turning ch (**mark center sc**); *working in sides of rows, sc in each row across to next corner*; working in unused loops on other side of starting ch, 3 sc in first ch (**mark center sc**), [sc in next sp, sc in next ch] across, working 3 sc in last turning ch (**mark center sc**); repeat from * to * once; join with sl st in first sc. (116 sc across short sides, 161 sc across long sides & 4 corner sc-sts)

Round 2: Ch 1, sc in each st around, working (sc, hdc, sc) in each marked corner st; join with sl st in first sc. (118 sc across short sides, 163 sc across long sides & 4 corner hdc-sts) Fasten off and weave in all ends.

FINAL TOUCH

TASSELS

Attach a Tassel to each center hdc in each corner.

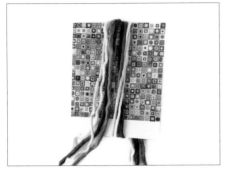

Step 1: Use a piece of card with a 6" (15 cm) width. Cut a 30" (75 cm) strand of each color yarn. Holding the 4 strands together, wind them around the width of the card twice.

Step 2: Cut another 20" (50 cm) strand of Color D. Gently remove strands from card, and tie this strand tightly around the center of the folded loops. Knot it twice to secure.

Step 3: Thread both tails of the Color D strand onto a needle. With right side of Blanket facing, insert the needle from back to front through the corner hdc.

Step 4: Insert the needle under the Color D strand tied around the group.

Step 5: Insert needle again into center hdc, but this time from front to back.

Step 6: Separate the Color D tails, and weave them along either side of the corner.

Step 7: Cut another 20" (50 cm) strand of Color D. Wrap it 3 times tightly around yarn group and tie 3 knots at the back of the tassel.

Step 8: Using a needle thread the tails through the Color D strand tied around group. Cut the strand loops and then trim the tassel to desired length.

Repeat for all four corners.

PAINTING THE WOODS

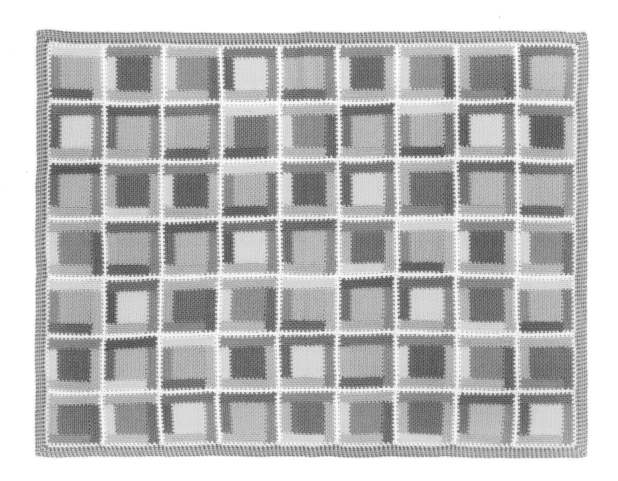

Materials

Scheepjes Merino Soft
Color A: Giotto (613) - 4 balls
Color B: Caravaggio (642) - 4 balls
Color C: Matisse (635) - 4 balls
Color D: Constable (629) - 4 balls
Color E: Dürer (644) - 4 balls
Color F: Monet (639) - 4 balls
Main Color (MC): Raphaël (602) - 4 balls

#7 (4.50 mm) Crochet Hook

Tapestry Needle

Size
About 40" wide by 52" long (102 cm by 132 cm)

Gauge
Each Square: About 5" (12.5 cm) wide by
5¼" long (13 cm) (without Edging).

Pattern Notes

1 Each Square is made up of five colored blocks, all worked together in one piece to form a Motif. There are eleven different color variations for the Motifs.

2 The Squares are joined together using the JAYGO (join as you go) method while working the Edging around each Square.

3 The images used are purely for illustration and do not match any of the Motifs listed.

Join As You Go (JAYGO): Ch 1, remove hook, working on previous Square, insert hook (from right side to wrong side) in stitch or space specified (image A), place loop back on hook and pull loop through stitch or space (image B), ch 1 (image C) and continue working on current Square (image D).

| Image A | Image B | Image C | Image D |

SQUARE (MAKE 63)

Using the table and color charts, work up the required number of Motifs for each color variation. (63 squares in total.)

	#	Center Block 1	Top Block 2	Left Block 3	Bottom Block 4	Right Block 5
Motif 1	10	B	A	D	C	F
Motif 2	9	F	E	D	B	C
Motif 3	5	D	B	F	C	A
Motif 4	9	C	E	B	F	D
Motif 5	3	D	C	F	A	E
Motif 6	5	A	D	C	F	B
Motif 7	10	E	F	D	C	A
Motif 8	5	A	B	E	D	C
Motif 9	5	D	C	F	B	E
Motif 10	1	A	B	F	C	E
Motif 11	1	B	A	E	C	F

COLOR CHART FOR MOTIFS

Motif 1
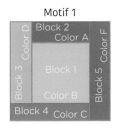
Make 10

Motif 2
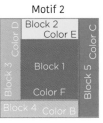
Make 9

Motif 3

Make 5

Motif 4
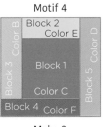
Make 9

Motif 5

Make 3

Motif 6

Make 5

Motif 7
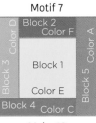
Make 10

Motif 8
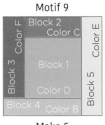
Make 5

Motif 9
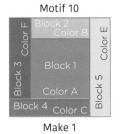
Make 5

Motif 10

Make 1

Motif 11

Make 1

CENTER BLOCK 1

Row 1: (Right Side) Using Block 1 color ch 18; sc in 4th ch from hook, [ch 1, skip next ch, sc in next ch] across. (8 sc, 7 ch-1 sps & 1 ch-3 sp)

Row 2: Ch 2, turn, sc in first ch-1 sp, [ch 1, skip next st, sc in next ch-1 sp] across, with last sc worked in ch-3 sp. (8 sc, 7 ch-1 sps & 1 ch-2 sp)

Row 3: Ch 2, turn, sc in first ch-1 sp, [ch 1, skip next st, sc in next ch-1 sp] across, with last sc worked in ch-2 sp. (8 sc, 7 ch-1 sps & 1 ch-2 sp)

Rows 4-16: (13 rows) Repeat Row 3.
At the end of Row 16, change to next color in last sc.

TOP BLOCK 2

Rows 17-21: Using next color, repeat Row 3.
At the end of Row 21, change to next color in last sc.

LEFT BLOCK 3

Row 1: With right side facing, ch 2, working in the turning chains of each row (across the Top Block and Center Block), sc in first ch-sp, [ch 1, skip next st, sc in next ch-sp] across, ending with, ch 1, skip last row, sc in base of first chain stitch made in foundation chain. (11 sc, 10 ch-1 sps & 1 ch-2 sp)

Row 2: Ch 2, turn, sc in first ch-1 sp, [ch 1, skip next st, sc in next ch-1 sp] across, with last sc worked in ch-2 sp. (11 sc, 10 ch-1 sps & 1 ch-2 sp)

Rows 3-5: Repeat Row 2.
At the end of Row 5, change to next color in last sc.

BOTTOM BLOCK 4

Row 1: With right side facing, ch 2, working in the turning chains of each row **(Left Block)** and the skipped chain spaces of the foundation chain **(Center Block)**, sc in first ch-sp, [ch 1, skip next st, sc in next ch-sp] across, with last sc worked in the ch-3 sp of Center Block. (10 sc, 9 ch-1 sps & 1 ch-2 sp)

Rows 3-5: Repeat Row 2.
At the end of Row 5, change to next color in last sc.

Row 1

RIGHT BLOCK 5

Row 1: With right side facing, ch 2, working in the turning chains of each row **(across Bottom Block, Center Block and Top Block)**, sc in first ch-sp, [ch 1, skip next st, sc in next ch-sp] across, with last sc worked in the last ch-2 sp of Top Block. (13 sc, 12 ch-1 sps & 1 ch-2 sp)

Row 2: Ch 2, turn, sc in first ch-1 sp, [ch 1, skip next st, sc in next ch-1 sp] across, with last sc worked in ch-2 sp. (13 sc, 12 ch-1 sps & 1 ch-2 sp)

Rows 3-5: Repeat Row 2.
At the end of Row 5, fasten off and weave in all ends.

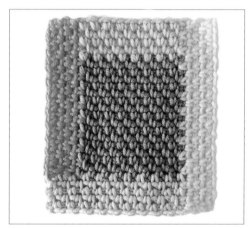

Finished Square

JOINING SQUARES

Lay out the Colored Motifs according to the chart to form a rectangle – 7 squares wide by 9 squares long. Make sure the Squares are all right side facing and have the correct orientation.

After Square 1 (Motif #6), join the Squares together sequentially - join Square 2 (Motif #2) to Square 1, then join Square 3 to Square 2, etc.

1 Motif #6	2 Motif #2	3 Motif #9	4 Motif #4	5 Motif #1	6 Motif #7	7 Motif #9
8 Motif #4	9 Motif #11	10 Motif #7	11 Motif #3	12 Motif #8	13 Motif #1	14 Motif #2
15 Motif #7	16 Motif #9	17 Motif #6	18 Motif #1	19 Motif #2	20 Motif #3	21 Motif #4
22 Motif #1	23 Motif #2	24 Motif #4	25 Motif #7	26 Motif #5	27 Motif #10	28 Motif #7
29 Motif #8	30 Motif #7	31 Motif #9	32 Motif #1	33 Motif #2	34 Motif #4	35 Motif #3
36 Motif #4	37 Motif #3	38 Motif #1	39 Motif #8	40 Motif #7	41 Motif #1	42 Motif #2
43 Motif #8	44 Motif #2	45 Motif #7	46 Motif #9	47 Motif #6	48 Motif #5	49 Motif #4
50 Motif #1	51 Motif #4	52 Motif #8	53 Motif #2	54 Motif #1	55 Motif #7	56 Motif #6
57 Motif #7	58 Motif #6	59 Motif #5	60 Motif #4	61 Motif #3	62 Motif #2	63 Motif #1

EDGING
NO JOINING SQUARE #1 (MOTIF #6)

Round 1: With right side facing, join MC with standing sc in corner ch-2 sp at beginning of the last row worked on Right Block, ch 2, sc in same corner sp (**first corner made**);
First Side: [ch 2, sc in next ch-sp] 11 times, ch 2, skip last ch-sp, (sc, ch 2, sc) in last sc (**corner made**);
Second Side: *[ch 2, sc in next ch-sp] 9 times, ch 2, skip next ch-sp (**last ch-sp of current Block**), sc in next ch-sp (**ch-2 sp of next Block**), ch 2, sc in next ch-sp, ch 2, (sc, ch 2, sc) in corner ch-sp (**corner made**);
Third Side: repeat from * once more;
Fourth Side: [ch 2, sc in next ch-sp] 11 times, ch 2; join with sl st in first sc. (52 sc, 48 ch-2 sps & 4 corner ch-2 sps) Fasten off and weave in all ends.

ONE-SIDED VERTICAL JOINING (SQUARES #2 – #7)

Note: This join is made across the third side of the Square.

Round 1: With right side facing, join MC with standing sc in corner ch-2 sp at beginning of the last row worked on Right Block, ch 2, sc in same corner sp (**first corner made**);
First Side: [ch 2, sc in next ch-sp] 11 times, ch 2, skip last ch-sp, (sc, ch 2, sc) in last sc (**corner made**);
Second Side: [ch 2, sc in next ch-sp] 9 times, ch 2, skip next ch-sp (**last ch-sp of current Block**), sc in next ch-sp (**ch-2 sp of next Block**), ch 2, sc in next ch-sp, ch 2, sc in corner ch-sp, JAYGO in corresponding corner ch-2 sp, sc in same corner ch-sp (**corner made**);

Third Side: [JAYGO in next corresponding ch-sp, sc in next ch-sp] 9 times, JAYGO in next corresponding ch-sp, skip next ch-sp (**last ch-sp of current Block**), sc in next ch-sp (**ch-2 sp of next Block**), JAYGO in next corresponding ch-sp, sc in next corner ch-sp, JAYGO in next corner sp, sc in same corner ch-sp (**corner made**);
Fourth Side: [ch 2, sc in next ch-sp] 11 times, ch 2; join with sl st in first sc. (52 sc, 48 ch-2 sps & 4 corner ch-2 sps) Fasten off and weave in all ends.

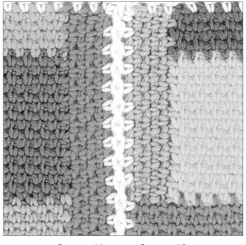

Square #1   Square #2

ONE-SIDED HORIZONTAL JOINING (SQUARES #8, #15, #22, #29, #36, #43, #50 & #57)

Note: This join is made across the second side of the Square.

Round 1: With right side facing, join MC with standing sc in corner ch-2 sp at beginning of the last row worked on Right Block, ch 2, sc in same corner sp (**first corner made**);

First Side: [ch 2, sc in next ch-sp] 11 times, ch 2, skip last ch-sp, sc in corner ch-sp, JAYGO in corresponding corner ch-2 sp, sc in same corner ch-sp (**corner made**);

Second Side: [JAYGO in next corresponding ch-sp, sc in next ch-sp] 9 times, JAYGO in next corresponding ch-sp, skip next ch-sp (last ch-sp of current Block), sc in next ch-sp (ch-2 sp of next Block), JAYGO in next corresponding ch-sp, sc in next corner ch-sp, JAYGO in next corner sp, sc in same corner ch-sp (corner made);

Third Side: [ch 2, sc in next ch-sp] 9 times, ch 2, skip next ch-sp (last ch-sp of current Block), sc in next ch-sp (ch-2 sp of next Block), ch 2, sc in next ch-sp, ch 2, (sc, ch 2, sc) in corner ch-sp (corner made);

Fourth Side: [ch 2, sc in next ch-sp] 11 times, ch 2; join with sl st in first sc. (52 sc, 48 ch-2 sps & 4 corner ch-2 sps) Fasten off and weave in all ends.

TWO SIDED JOINING - REMAINING SQUARES

Note: These joins are made across the second and third sides of the Square.

Round 1: With right side facing, join MC with standing sc in corner ch-2 sp at beginning of the last row worked on Right Block, ch 2, sc in same corner sp (first corner made);
First Side: [ch 2, sc in next ch-sp] 11 times, ch 2, skip last ch-sp, sc in corner ch-sp, JAYGO in corresponding corner ch-2 sp, sc in same corner ch-sp (corner made);
Second Side: [JAYGO in next corresponding ch-sp, sc in next ch-sp] 9 times, JAYGO in next corresponding ch-sp, skip next ch-sp (last ch-sp of current Block), sc in next ch-sp (ch-2 sp of next Block), JAYGO in next corresponding ch-sp, sc in next corner ch-sp, JAYGO in next corner sp, sc in same corner ch-sp (corner made);

Third Side: [JAYGO in next corresponding ch-sp, sc in next ch-sp] 9 times, JAYGO in next corresponding ch-sp, skip next ch-sp (last ch-sp of current Block), sc in next ch-sp (ch-2 sp of next Block), JAYGO in next corresponding ch-sp, sc in next corner ch-sp, JAYGO in next corner sp, sc in same corner ch-sp (corner made);

Fourth Side: [ch 2, sc in next ch-sp] 11 times, ch 2; join with sl st in first sc. (52 sc, 48 ch-2 sps & 4 corner ch-2 sps) Fasten off and weave in all ends.

BORDER

Round 1: With right side of assembled Blanket facing, join Color E with standing sc in any corner ch-2 sp; ch 2, sc in same corner sp (corner made), *ch 1, [sc in next ch-2 sp, ch 1] across to next corner**, (sc, ch 2, sc) in corner ch-2 sp; repeat from * around, ending at ** on final repeat; join with sl st in first sc. (98 sc & 97 ch-1 sps across short sides & 126 sc & 125 ch-1 sps across long sides & 4 corner ch-2 sps) Fasten off and weave in all ends.

Round 2: With right side facing, join Color F with standing sc in any corner ch-2 sp; ch 2, sc in same sp (corner made), *ch 1, [sc in next ch-1 sp, ch 1] across to next corner**, (sc, ch 2, sc) in corner ch-2 sp; repeat from * around, ending at ** on final repeat; join with sl st in first sc. (99 sc & 98 ch-1 sps across short sides & 127 sc & 126 ch-1 sps across long sides & 4 corner ch-2 sps) Fasten off and weave in all ends.

Rounds 3-6: Repeat Round 2, using the following color sequence:
Round 3 – Color B
Round 4 – Color C
Round 5 – Color D
Round 6 – Color A

Round 7: With right side facing, join MC with standing sc in any corner ch-2 sp; ch 2, sc in same sp (corner made), *sc in next st, [sc in next sp, sc in next st] across to corner**, (sc, ch 2, sc) in next corner ch-2 sp; repeat from * around, ending at ** on final repeat; join with sl st in first sc. (207 sc across short sides & 263 sc across long sides & 4 corner ch-2 sps) Fasten off and weave in all ends.

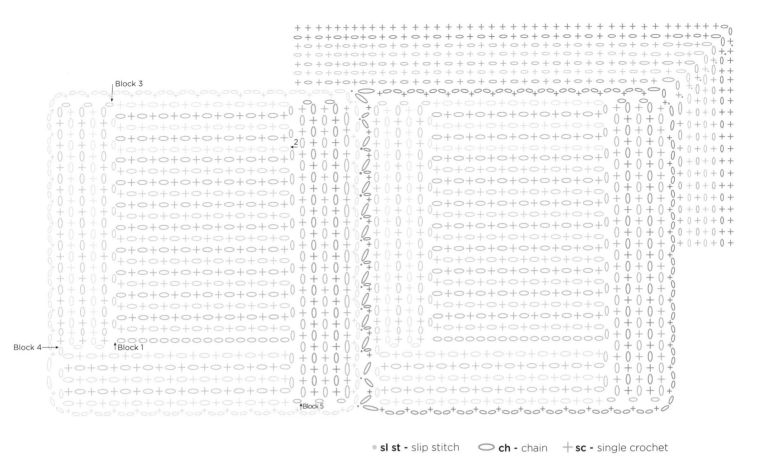

Block 3

2

Block 4

Block 1

Block 5

• **sl st -** slip stitch   ◯ **ch -** chain   + **sc -** single crochet

TWINKLING STAR

Materials

Scheepjes Stone Washed
Color A: Moonstone (801) - 4 balls
Color B: Amazonite (813) - 6 balls
Color C: Blue Apatite (805) - 4 balls
Color D: Brown Agate (822) - 5 balls
Color E: Boulder Opal (804) - 7 balls

G-6 (4.00 mm) Crochet Hook

Tapestry Needle

Stitch Markers

Size
About 51" (130 cm) square.

Gauge
Round 1 to Round 8 (88 sts) = 4 ⅜" (11 cm)

Pattern Notes

1 The blanket is worked in right-side facing, joined rounds.

2 After the Center Circle, corners are added, to make it square.

3 Unless noted otherwise, always skip the stitch behind a Front Post stitch, and skip the stitch in front of a Back Post stitch.

Extended Double Crochet (exdc)

Yarn over, insert hook in stitch or space specified and pull up a loop (3 loops on hook), yarn over, draw through first loop on hook (3 loops remain on hook); [yarn over and draw through 2 loops on hook] twice.

Triple Treble Decrease (trtr2tog)

Yarn over 4 times, insert hook in first stitch or space specified and pull up a loop (6 loops on hook), [yarn over, draw through 2 loops on hook] 4 times (2 loops remain on hook), yarn over 4 times, insert hook in next stitch or space specified and pull up a loop, [yarn over, draw through 2 loops on hook] 4 times more (3 loops on hook); yarn over, draw through remaining 3 loops.

Front Post Treble Decrease (FPtr2tog)

Yarn over twice, insert hook from front to back to front around post of specified stitch and pull up a loop (4 loops on hook), [yarn over, draw through 2 loops on hook] twice (2 loops remain on hook), yarn over twice, insert hook around post of next indicated stitch and pull up a loop, [yarn over, draw through 2 loops on hook] twice (3 loops on hook); yarn over, draw through remaining 3 loops. **Unless noted otherwise, always skip the stitch behind the post stitch.**

Front Post Double Treble Decrease (FPdtr2tog)

Yarn over 3 times, insert hook from front to back to front around post of specified stitch and pull up a loop (5 loops on hook), [yarn over, draw through 2 loops on hook] 3 times (2 loops remain on hook), yarn over 3 times, insert hook around post of next indicated stitch and pull up a loop, [yarn over, draw through 2 loops on hook] 3 times more (3 loops on hook); yarn over, draw through remaining 3 loops. **Unless noted otherwise, always skip the stitch behind the post stitch.**

Front Post Triple Treble Decrease (FPtrtr2tog)

Yarn over 4 times, insert hook from front to back to front around post of specified stitch and pull up a loop (6 loops on hook), [yarn over, draw through 2 loops on hook] 4 times (2 loops remain on hook), yarn over 4 times, insert hook around post of next indicated stitch and pull up a loop, [yarn over, draw through 2 loops on hook] 4 times more (3 loops on hook); yarn over, draw through remaining 3 loops. **Unless noted otherwise, always skip the stitch behind the post stitch.**

Double Crochet Bobble (with 3 dc) (dc3-bob)

Yarn over, insert hook in stitch or space specified and pull up a loop (3 loops on hook), yarn over, draw through 2 loops on hook (2 loops remain on hook); [yarn over, insert hook in same stich and pull up a loop, yarn over, draw through 2 loops on hook] twice more (4 loops on hook); yarn over, draw through remaining 4 loops.

Double Crochet Bobble (with 4 dc) (dc4-bob)

Yarn over, insert hook in stitch or space specified and pull up a loop (3 loops on hook), yarn over, draw through 2 loops on hook (2 loops remain on hook); [yarn over, insert hook in same stich and pull up a loop, yarn over, draw through 2 loops on hook] 3 times more (5 loops on hook); yarn over, draw through remaining 5 loops.

Double Crochet Bobble (with 5 dc) (dc5-bob)

Yarn over, insert hook in stitch or space specified and pull up a loop (3 loops on hook), yarn over, draw through 2 loops on hook (2 loops remain on hook); [yarn over, insert hook in same stich and pull up a loop, yarn over, draw through 2 loops on hook] 4 times more (6 loops on hook); yarn over, draw through remaining 6 loops.

Treble Bobble (with 2 tr) (tr2-bob)

Yarn over twice, insert hook in stitch or space specified and pull up a loop (4 loops on hook), [yarn over, draw through 2 loops on hook] twice, (2 loops remain on hook); yarn over twice, insert hook in same stich and pull up a loop, [yarn over, draw through 2 loops on hook] twice (3 loops on hook); yarn over, draw through remaining 3 loops.

Treble Bobble (with 3 tr) (tr3-bob)

Yarn over twice, insert hook in stitch or space specified and pull up a loop (4 loops on hook), [yarn over, draw through 2 loops on hook] twice, (2 loops remain on hook); *yarn over twice, insert hook in same stich and pull up a loop, [yarn over, draw through 2 loops on hook] twice; repeat from * once more (4 loops on hook); yarn over, draw through remaining 4 loops.

Treble Bobble (with 4 tr) (tr4-bob)

Yarn over twice, insert hook in stitch or space specified and pull up a loop (4 loops on hook), [yarn over, draw through 2 loops on hook] twice, (2 loops remain on hook); *yarn over twice, insert hook in same stich and pull up a loop, [yarn over, draw through 2 loops on hook] twice; repeat from * twice more (5 loops on hook); yarn over, draw through remaining 5 loops.

Double Treble Bobble (with 3 dtr) (dtr3-bob)

Yarn over 3 times, insert hook in stitch or space specified and pull up a loop (5 loops on hook), [yarn over, draw through 2 loops on hook] 3 times, (2 loops remain on hook); *yarn over 3 times, insert hook in same stich and pull up a loop, [yarn over, draw through 2 loops on hook] 3 times; repeat from * once more (4 loops on hook); yarn over, draw through remaining 4 loops.

BLANKET

CENTER CIRCLE

Note: All rounds start with right side facing.

Round 1: (Right Side) With Color A, make a magic ring; ch 2 (counts as first hdc, now and throughout), 7 hdc in ring; join with sl st in first hdc (2nd ch of beg ch-2). (8 hdc) DO NOT FASTEN OFF.

Round 2: Ch 2, hdc in same st as joining, [2 hdc in next st] around; join with sl st in first hdc. (16 hdc) Fasten off and weave in all ends.

Note: Do NOT skip the stitch behind FPtr.

Round 3: With right side facing, join Color B with standing sc in any st, *sc in next st, FPtr in corresponding st on Rnd 1, sc in next st; repeat from * around; join with sl st in first sc. (16 sc & 8 FPtr) Fasten off and weave in all ends.

Notes:
1. Do NOT skip the stitch behind FPdc.
2. The center sc of each 3-sc group is worked in the FPtr.

Round 4: Join Color A with standing sc in any FPtr, sc in next st, *FPdc around corresponding st on Rnd 2, sc in each of next 3 sts; repeat from * around, omitting last 2 sc on final repeat; join with sl st in first sc. (24 sc & 8 FPdc) Fasten off and weave in all ends.

Notes:
1. The slip stitches are worked in the FPdc.
2. The bobbles are worked in the sc-sts, which were worked in the FPtr (Rnd 3).

Round 5: Join Color C with sl st in any FPdc, *ch3, skip next st, dc5-bob in next st, ch 3, skip next st, sl st in next st; repeat from * around, working last sl st on final repeat in the first sl st (to join). (8 sl sts, 8 bobbles & 16 ch-3 sps) Fasten off and weave in all ends.

Notes:
1. The FPtr2tog uses the Color B FPtr-sts on Rnd 3. The first leg of the decrease is around the FPtr under the previous bobble and the second leg is around the FPtr under the next bobble.
2. On the last FPtr2tog, the second leg is made behind the first leg of first FPtr2tog.

Round 6: Join Color B with standing FPhdc around any bobble, *3 sc in next ch-3 sp, FPtr2tog (using corresponding FPtr-sts on Rnd 3), 3 sc in next ch-3 sp, FPhdc around next bobble; repeat from * around, omitting last FPhdc on final repeat; join with sl st in first FPhdc. (48 sc, 8 FPhdc & 8 FPtr2tog) Fasten off and weave in all ends.

Round 3

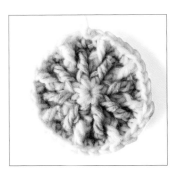

Round 4

Round 5

Round 5

Round 6

Round 6

Round 6

Round 7: Join Color A with standing FPhdc around any FPtr2tog, *ch 7, skip next 7 sts (3-sc, FPhdc & 3-sc), FPhdc around next FPtr2tog; repeat from * around, omitting last FPhdc on final repeat; join with sl st in first FPhdc. (8 FPhdc & 8 ch-7 loops) DO NOT FASTEN OFF.

Round 8: Ch 1, *(sc, 2 hdc) in next ch-7 lp, dc in sc before FPhdc on Rnd 6, dc in same ch-7 lp, FPtr around bobble on Rnd 5, dc in same ch-7 lp, dc in sc after FPhdc on Rnd 6, (2 hdc, sc) in same ch-7 lp, skip next st; repeat from * around; join with sl st in first sc. (16 sc, 32 hdc, 32 dc & 8 FPtr) Fasten off and weave in all ends.

Round 9: Working in BLO, join Color D with standing FPhdc around any FPtr, *sc in each of next 5 sts, FPdc4-bob around post of FPhdc on Rnd 7, sc in each of next 5 sts, FPhdc around next FPtr; repeat from * around, omitting last FPhdc on final repeat; join with sl st in first FPhdc. (8 FPhdc, 80 sc & 8 bobbles) Fasten off and weave in all ends.

Note: The sc-sts are worked in the FPhdc of Rnd 9.

Round 10: Join Color B with standing hdc in 3rd st before any FPhdc, hdc in next st, *ch 1, skip next st, sc in next st, ch 1, skip next st, hdc in each of next 2 sts, ch 1, skip next 2 sts, FPtr around bobble, ch 1, skip next 2 sts**, hdc in each of next 2 sts; repeat from * around, ending at ** on final repeat; join with sl st in first hdc. (32 hdc, 8 sc, 8 FPtr & 32 ch-1 sps) Fasten off and weave in all ends.

Round 11: Join Color E with standing hdc in any FPtr, hdc in same st, *exdc (over ch-1) in 2nd skipped st on Rnd 9 (before 1st hdc of 2-hdc group), hdc in each of next 2 sts, exdc (over ch-1) in next skipped st on Rnd 9 (after last hdc of 2-hdc group), 2 hdc in next st, exdc (over ch-1) in next skipped st on Rnd 9 (before 1st hdc of 2-hdc group), hdc in each of next 2 sts, exdc (over ch-1) in next skipped st on Rnd 9 (after last hdc of 2-hdc group)**, 2 hdc in next FPtr; repeat from * around, ending at ** on final repeat; join with sl st in first hdc. (64 hdc & 32 exdc) Fasten off and weave in all ends.

Note: The last FPdtr of the round is worked behind the first FPdtr made.

Round 12: Working in BLO, join Color B with standing sc in first hdc of any 2-hdc group worked in FPtr on Rnd 10, sc in each of next 3 sts, FPdtr around FPtr (below on right) on Rnd 10, (skip st behind FPdtr), sc in each of next 5 sts, FPdtr around next FPtr on Rnd 10, (do NOT skip st behind FPdtr), sc in each of next 6 sts, *FPdtr around same FPtr (below on right) on Rnd 10, (skip st behind FPdtr), sc in each of next 5 sts, FPdtr around next FPtr on Rnd 10, (do NOT skip st behind FPdtr), sc in each of next 6 sts; repeat from * around, omitting last 4 sc on final repeat; join with sl st in first sc. (88 sc & 16 FPdtr) Fasten off and weave in all ends.

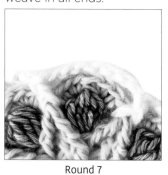
Round 7

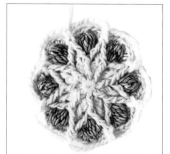
Round 7

Round 8

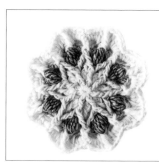
Round 8

Round 9

Round 9

Round 10

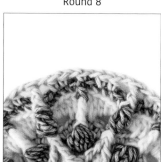
Round 10

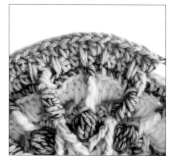
Round 11

Round 11

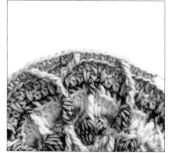
Round 12

Round 12

Round 13: Working in BLO, join Color C with standing sc in any FPdtr to the right of a Rnd 9 bobble, sc in each of next 9 sts, *puff-st in FLO of 2nd hdc (of corresponding 2-hdc group on Rnd 11), skip next st, sc in each of next 12 sts; repeat from * around, omitting last 10 sc on final repeat; join with sl st in first sc. (96 sc & 8 puff-sts) Fasten off and weave in all ends.

Round 14: Working in BLO, join Color E with standing FPdc around any puff-st, hdc in each of next 12 sts, FPdc around next puff-st; repeat from * around; omitting last FPdc on final repeat; join with sl st in first FPdc. (96 hdc & 8 FPdc) Fasten off and weave in all ends.

Note: Last sc of each sc-13 group is in the FPdc.

Round 15: Working in BLO, join Color B with standing sc in any FPdc, *FPdtr2tog (using FPdtr from Rnd 12, on right of corresponding puff-st, and then next FPdtr on left of puff-st), sc in each of next 13 sts; repeat from * around, omitting last sc on final repeat; join with sl st in first sc. (104 sc & 8 FPdtr2tog) Fasten off and weave in all ends.

Round 16: Join Color D with standing FPdc around any FPdtr2tog, *hdc in each of next 4 sts, 2 hdc in next st, hdc in each of next 3 sts, 2 hdc in next st, hdc in each of next 4 sts, FPdc around next FPdtr2tog; repeat from * around, omitting last FPdc on final repeat; join with sl st in first FPdc. (120 hdc & 8 FPdc) Fasten off and weave in all ends.

Hint: Mark any 12th hdc of 15-hdc group (for Round 20).

Round 17: Join Color A with standing puff-st in any FPdc, ch 1, skip next st, *[puff-st in next st, ch 1, skip next st, hdc in each of next 3 sts, ch 1, skip next st] twice, [puff-st in next st, ch 1, skip next st] twice; repeat from * around, omitting last puff-st on final repeat; join with sl st in first puff-st. (32 puff-sts, 48 hdc & 48 ch-1 sps) Fasten off and weave in all ends.

Round 18: Join Color C with standing puff-st in ch-1 sp between first 2 puff-sts of any 3-puff-st group, *ch 1, puff-st in next ch-1 sp, ch 1, hdc next ch-1 sp, hdc in each of next 3 sts, hdc in next ch-1 sp, ch 1, FPhdc around next puff-st, ch 1, hdc in next ch-1 sp, hdc in each of next 3 sts, hdc in next ch-1 sp, ch 1, puff-st in next ch-1 sp; repeat from * around, omitting last puff-st on final repeat; join with sl st in first puff-st. (16 puff-sts, 8 FPhdc, 80 hdc & 40 ch-1 sps) Fasten off and weave in all ends.

Round 19: Join Color A with standing puff-st in ch-1 sp between any 2 puff-st group, *ch1, skip next st, hdc in next ch-1 sp, hdc in each of next 5 sts, hdc in next ch-1 sp, ch 1, skip next st (FPhdc), hdc in next ch-1 sp, hdc in each of next 5 sts, hdc in next ch-1 sp, ch 1, skip next st, puff-st in next ch-1 sp; repeat from * around, omitting last puff-st on final repeat; join with sl st in first puff-st. (8 puff-sts, 112 hdc & 24 ch-1 sps) Fasten off and weave in all ends.

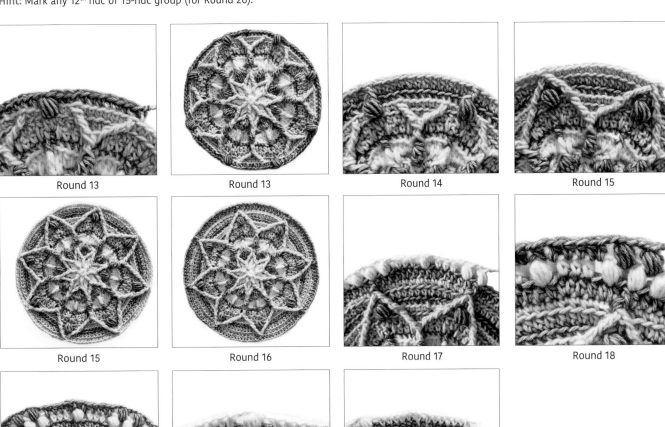

Round 13

Round 13

Round 14

Round 15

Round 15

Round 16

Round 17

Round 18

Round 18

Round 19

Round 19

Note: When ascending, work stitches to the left of the stitches already worked in the same space. When descending, rotate piece and work stitches before (or to left) of stitches already in the same space.

Round 20: Join Color B with standing FPsc around 4th st before FPdc on Rnd 16 (or marked st), *ch 2, sc in corresponding ch-1 sp on Rnd 17 (before first puff-st of 3-puff-st group), ch 2, sc in corresponding ch-1 sp on Rnd 18 (before first puff-st of 2-puff-st group), ch 2, FPsc around puff-st (Rnd 19), ch 2, sc in ch-1 sp on Rnd 18 (after 2nd puff-st), ch 2, sc in ch-1 sp on Rnd 17 (after 3rd puff-st), ch 2, FPsc around 3rd st after FPdc on Rnd 16, ch 2, skip next st, FPsc around next st on Rnd 16 (6th after FPdc), ch 3, FPsc around puff-st (Rnd 17), ch 3, FPsc around 6th st before next FPdc (Rnd 16), ch 2, FPsc around 4th st before same FPdc on Rnd 16; repeat from * around, omitting last FPsc on final repeat; join with sl st in first FPsc. (32 sc, 48 FPsc, 64 ch-2 sps & 16 ch-3 sps) Fasten off and weave in all ends.

Round 21: Working in Round 19, join Color B with standing sc in any ch-1 sp above the single puff-st from Rnd 17, *BPtr around next FPsc (from Rnd 20), sc in each of next 7 sts, 2 sc in next ch-1 sp, BPsc around next FPsc (from Rnd 20), sc in next ch-1 sp, sc in each of next 7 sts, sc in next ch-1 sp; repeat from * around, omitting last sc on final repeat; join with sl st in first sc. (144 sc, 8 BPtr & 8 BPsc) Fasten off and weave in all ends.

Note: The 2-hdc are worked in the BPsc.

Round 22: Working in BLO, join Color E with standing hdc in any BPsc, hdc in same st, *hdc in each of next 19 sts, 2 hdc in next st; repeat from * around, omitting last 2 sts; join with sl st in first hdc. (168 hdc) Fasten off and weave in all ends.

Round 23: Working in BLO, join Color D with standing hdc in any hdc worked in BPtr from Rnd 21, *tr4-bob in FLO of corresponding BPtr from Rnd 21, hdc in each of next 21 sts; repeat from * around, omitting last hdc on final repeat; join with sl st in first hdc. (168 hdc & 8 bobbles) Fasten off and weave in all ends.

Round 24: Working in BLO, join Color E with standing FPhdc around any bobble, * hdc in each of next 21 sts, FPhdc around next bobble; repeat from * around, omitting last FPhdc on final repeat; join with sl st in first FPhdc. (168 hdc & 8 FPhdc) Fasten off and weave in all ends.

Note: Bobbles are worked in FLO of corresponding hdc-sts on Rnd 23.

Round 25: Working in BLO, join Color D with standing hdc in any FPhdc, hdc in each of next 7 sts, *tr4-bob in 7th st after bobble on Rnd 23, hdc in each of next 7 sts, tr4-bob in 8th st before next bobble on Rnd 23, hdc in each of next 15 sts; repeat from * around, omitting last 8 hdc on final repeat; join with sl st in first hdc. (176 hdc & 16 bobbles) Fasten off and weave in all ends.

Note: The bobbles on Rnd 23 already have FPhdc from Rnd 24.

Round 26: Working in BLO, join Color B with standing FPhdc around any bobble (Rnd 25) to right of bobble on Rnd 23, *skip next (hidden) st, hdc in each of next 5 sts, FPdtr around next bobble on Rnd 23, hdc in each of next 4 sts, FPdtr around same bobble, hdc in each of next 5 sts, FPhdc around next bobble (Rnd 25), hdc in each of next 7 sts, FPhdc around next bobble (Rnd 25); repeat from * around, omitting last FPhdc on final repeat; join with sl st in first FPhdc. (168 hdc, 16 FPhdc & 16 FPdtr) Fasten off and weave in all ends.

Ascending stitches

Descending stitches

Round 20

Round 20

Round 21

Round 25

Round 25

Round 26

Round 26

Round 27: Working in BLO, join Color C with standing hdc in any FPhdc before first FPdtr, hdc in each of next 5 sts, *FPhdc around next FPdtr, FPdtr around corresponding FPhdc on Rnd 24, hdc in each of next 4 sts, FPdtr around same FPhdc on Rnd 24, FPhdc around next FPdtr, hdc in each of next 19 sts; repeat from * around, omitting last 6 hdc on final repeat; join with sl st in first hdc. (184 hdc, 16 FPhdc & 16 FPdtr) Fasten off and weave in all ends.

Note: Do not skip the stitch behind FPhdc. (The stitches behind the FPdtr are skipped.)

Round 28: Working in BLO, join Color A with standing hdc in first FPhdc before first FPdtr, *FPhdc around next FPdtr, hdc in each of next 2 sts, dtr3-bob in corresponding FPhdc from Rnd 24, hdc in each of next 2 sts, FPhdc around next FPdtr, hdc in next st, skip next st, hdc in each of next 5 sts, FPdtr around corresponding bobble on Rnd 25, hdc in each of next 7 sts, FPdtr around corresponding bobble on Rnd 25, hdc in each of next 5 sts; repeat from * around, omitting last hdc on final repeat; join with sl st in first hdc. (176 hdc, 16 FPhdc, 16 FPdtr & 8 bobbles) Fasten off and weave in all ends.

Round 29: Working in BLO, join Color D with standing sc in any FPhdc before bobble, sc in each of next 2 sts, *FPsc around next bobble, sc in each of next 26 sts; repeat from * around, omitting last 3 sc on final repeat; join with sl st in first sc. (208 sc & 8 FPsc) Fasten off and weave in all ends.

Note: The 2-hdc are worked in the FPsc.

Round 30: Working in BLO, join Color E with standing hdc in any FPsc, hdc in same st, *hdc in each of next 26 sts, 2 hdc in next st; repeat from * around, omitting last 2 hdc on final repeat; join with sl st in first hdc. (224 hdc) Fasten off and weave in all ends.

Round 31: Working in BLO, join Color C with standing sc in first hdc of any 2-hdc group, sc in each of next 14 sts, *2 sc in next st, sc in each of next 27 sts; repeat from * around, omitting last 15 sc; join with sl st in first sc. (232 sc) Fasten off and weave in all ends.

Round 32: Join Color B with standing tr3-bob in any st, *ch4, skip next 3 sts, tr3-bob in next st; repeat from * around, omitting last bobble on final repeat; join with sl st in first bobble. (58 bobbles & 58 ch-4 sps) Fasten off and weave in all ends

Note: Work the tr3-bob in front of the ch-4 sp.

Round 33: Join Color C with standing FPsc around any bobble, *2 sc in next ch-4 sp, tr3-bob in 2nd (center) skipped sc on Rnd 31, 2 sc in same ch-4 sp, FPsc around next bobble; repeat from * around, omitting last FPsc on final repeat; join with sl st in first FPsc. (232 sc, 58 FPsc & 58 bobbles) Fasten off and weave in all ends

Round 34: Working in BLO, join Color A with standing sc in any FPsc, sc in each of next 2 sts, *FPsc around next bobble, sc in each of next 5 sts; repeat from * around, omitting last 3 sc on final repeat; join with sl st in first sc. (290 sc & 58 FPsc) Fasten off and weave in all ends.

Round 35: Working in BLO, join Color E with standing dc in any st, dc in every st around; join with sl st in first dc. (348 dc) Fasten off and weave in all ends.

Round 36: Join Color D with standing BPhdc in any st, BPhdc in every st around; join with sl st in first BPhdc. (348 BPhdc) DO NOT FASTEN OFF.

Round 37: Ch 1, sc in same st as joining, sc in every st around; join with sl st in first sc. (348 sc) Fasten off and weave in all ends.

Round 27

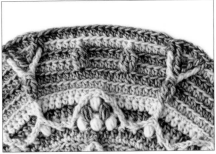

Round 27

Round 28

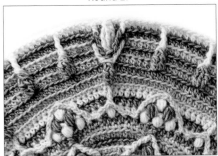

Round 28

Round 29

Round 32

Round 33

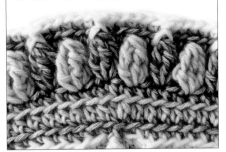

Round 34

Round 36

ADDING CORNERS

Find the first corner by marking a stitch on Round 37 which aligns to a star point - the single puff-stitch on top of a pyramid - and the center stitch of the 7 stitches between the two FPdtr-stitches on Round 28.

 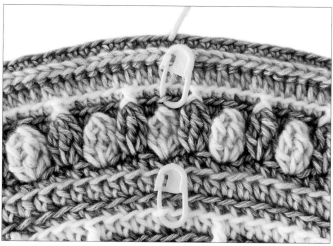

From this stitch, place another marker in each 87th stitch. There are 4 markers with 86 open stitches between them.

CORNER ROWS

Note: Both rows start with right side facing.

Row 1: Join Color B with sl st in 5th st before marked st, ch 1, skip next 4 sts, ([tr, ch 1] 7 times) in marked st, skip next 4 sts, sl st in next st. (7 tr, 8 ch-1 sps & 2 sl sts) Fasten off and weave in all ends.

Row 2: Join Color C with sl st in 4th st to right of Row 1's first st sl on Round 37, working in Row 1, tr4-bob in first ch-1 sp, ch 2, skip next st, [tr in next ch-1 sp, ch 2, skip next st] twice,

tr4-bob in next ch-1 sp, ch 3, skip next st, tr4-bob in next ch-1 sp, ch 2, skip next st, [tr in next ch-1 sp, ch 2, skip next st] twice, tr4-bob in last ch-1 sp, skip next 3 sts on Round 37, sl st in next st. (4 tr, 4 bobbles, 6 ch-2 sps & 1 ch-3 sp) Fasten off and weave in all ends.

Repeat Rows 1 & 2 on each of the remaining three corners. Work continues in square rounds.

Row 1

Row 2

SQUARE ROUNDS

Note: The FPdtr are worked around the tr-sts on Row 1.

Round 38: Join Color B with standing sc in 2nd st before Row 2's first sl st on Round 37, working in Row 2, *FPsc around first bobble, [sc in next ch-2 sp, FPdtr around corresponding tr, sc in same ch-2 sp, FPsc around next st] 3 times, 2 sc in next ch-3 sp, FPdtr around corresponding tr, 2 sc in same ch-3 sp, [FPsc around next st, sc in next ch-2 sp, FPdtr in corresponding tr, sc in same ch-2 sp] 3 times, FPsc around last bobble, working in Round 37, skip next st after sl st, sc in each of next 66 sts; repeat from * around, omitting last sc on final repeat; join with sl st in first sc. (328 sc, 32 FPsc & 28 FPdtr) Fasten off and weave in all ends.

Notes:

① The puff-sts are worked in the FPdtr-sts on Rnd 38. The stitches between them are skipped.

② As the puff-st already has a chain-st (to secure), there are actually 3-chain sts between puffs. To keep consistency, a chain-3 sp (instead of chain-2) is made after the hdc stitches.

Round 39: Join Color A with standing puff-st in 3rd st before first FPsc of any corner, *ch 2, skip next 4 sts, [puff-st in next FPDtr, ch 2] 3 times, (puff-st, ch 2, puff-st) in next FPdtr (new corner made), [ch 2, puff-st in next FPdtr] 3 times, ch 2, skip next 3 sts, puff-st next st (3rd st after last FPsc), [ch 2, skip next 3 sts, puff-st in next st] twice, ch 2, skip next 3 sts, hdc in each of next 3 sts, sc in each of next 32 sts, hdc in next 3 sts, ch 3, skip next 3 sts, puff-st in next st, [ch 2, skip next 3 sts, puff-st in next st] twice; rep from * around, omitting last puff-st on final repeat; join with sl st in first puff-st. (33 sc, 6 hdc, 14 puff-sts, 13 ch-2 sps & 1 ch-3 sp across each side & 4 corner ch-2 sps) Fasten off and weave in all ends.

Note: The corner tr is worked in front of the ch-2 sp, into the dtr on Rnd 38, which already has 2 puff-sts. Insert the stitch between the puff-sts.

Round 40: Join Color B with standing FPhdc around third puff-st before any corner, *hdc in next ch-2 sp, dtr in skipped st on Rnd 37 (before first sl st on Row 2), hdc in same ch-2 sp, FPsc around next puff-st, [sc in next ch-2 sp, tr in center skipped st (FPsc) on Rnd 38, sc in same ch-2 sp, FPsc around next puff-st] 3 times, sc in next corner ch-2 sp, tr in corresponding dtr on Rnd 38 (corner st made), sc in same corner ch-2 sp, FPsc around next puff-st, [sc in next ch-2 sp, tr in center skipped st on Rnd 38, sc in same ch-2 sp, FPsc around next puff-st] 3 times, hdc in next ch-2 sp, dtr in skipped st on Rnd 37 (after last sl st on Row 2), hdc in same ch-2 sp, [FPhdc around next puff-st, hdc in next ch-2 sp, tr in center skipped st on Rnd 38, hdc in same ch-2 sp] 3 times, hdc in each of next 3 sts, sc in each of next 5 sts, [ch 1, skip next st, sc in next 6 sts] 3 times, ch 1, skip next st, sc in each of next 5 sts, hdc in each of next 3 sts, [hdc in next ch-2 sp, tr in center skipped st on Rnd 37, hdc in same ch-2 sp, FPhdc around next puff-st] 3 times; repeat from * around, omitting last FPhdc on final repeat; join with sl st in first FPhdc. (42 sc, 22 hdc, 12 tr, 2 dtr, 6 FPhdc, 8 FPsc & 4 ch-1 sps across each side & 4 corner tr-sts) Fasten off and weave in all ends.

Note: The puff-sts are worked in the dtr on previous round.

Round 41: Join Color E with standing tr in any corner st, (tr, ch 2, 2 tr) in same st (corner made), *ch 1, skip next st, tr in next st, [ch 1, skip next st, dc in next st] 6 times, ch 1, skip next st, puff-st in next st, [ch 1, skip next st, hdc in next st] 5 times, ch 1, skip next st, sc in each of next 10 sts, sc in next ch-1 sp, [sc in each of next 6 sts, sc in next ch-1 sp] 3 times, sc in each of next 10 sts, [ch 1, skip next st, hdc in next st] 5 times, ch 1, skip next st, puff-st in next st, [ch 1, skip next st, dc in next st] 6 times, ch 1, skip next st, tr in next st, ch 1, skip next st, (2 tr, ch 2, 2 tr) in next corner st; repeat from * around, omitting last corner on final repeat; join with sl st in first tr. (6 tr, 12 dc, 10 hdc, 42 sc, 2 puff-sts & 28 ch-1 sps across each side & 4 corner ch-2 sps) Fasten off and weave in all ends.

Round 39

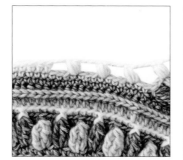

Round 39

Round 40

Round 40

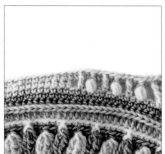

Round 40

Round 40

Round 41

Round 41

Round 42: Join Color D with standing tr3-bob in any corner ch-2 sp, ch 3, tr3-bob in same corner ch-2 sp, *ch 2, skip next 2 sts, [tr in next ch-1 sp, FPtr around next st] 9 times, dc in next ch-1 sp, [FPdc around next st, dc in next ch-1 sp] 4 times, hdc in each of next 11 sts, sc in each of next 20 sts, hdc in each of next 11 sts, dc in next ch-1 sp, [FPdc around next st, dc in next ch-1 sp] 4 times, [FPtr around next st, tr in next ch-1 sp] 9 times, ch 2, skip next 2 sts, (tr3-bob, ch 3, tr3-bob) in corner ch-2 sp; repeat from * around, omitting last corner on final repeat; join with sl st in first bobble. (18 tr, 18 FPtr, 10 dc, 8 FPdc, 22 hdc, 20 sc & 2 bobbles across each side & 4 corner ch-3 sps) Fasten off and weave in all ends.

Note: The dtr-sts are worked in front of the ch-2 sp, into the skipped tr-sts on Rnd 41.

Round 43: Join Color A with standing hdc in any corner ch-3 sp, (hdc, ch 2, 2 hdc) in same ch-3 sp, *FPhdc around next bobble, dtr in each of skipped 2 sts on Rnd 41, hdc in each of next 96 sts, dtr in each of skipped 2 sts on Rnd 41, FPhdc around next bobble, (2 hdc, ch-2, 2 hdc) in next corner ch-3 sp; repeat from * around, omitting last corner on final repeat; join with sl st in first hdc. (100 hdc, 2 FPhdc & 4 dtr across each side & 4 corner ch-2 sps) Fasten off and weave in all ends.

Notes:

① The FPtr are worked in the stitches of Rnd 42 – either around the corner bobble or around the tr and dc stitches directly below the previous stitch worked. (The FPtr are NOT worked in the post stitches below.)

② The trtr2tog are worked in the skipped stitches on Round 39. The first leg is worked in the skipped stitch to the right, and the second leg in the next skipped stitch to the left. From the second trtr2tog, the first leg is worked in the same stitch as the previous second leg.

Round 44: Working in BLO, join Color C with standing hdc in any corner ch-2 sp, ch 2, hdc in same sp, *hdc in each of next 2 sts, FPtr around corresponding bobble on Rnd 42, FPhdc around each of next 2 sts, skip next st, hdc in each of next 2 sts, [FPtr around corresponding tr on Rnd 42, hdc in next st] 6 times, FPtr2tog (using next 2 corresponding tr on Rnd 42), skip 3 sts (behind post st), hdc in next st, FPtr around corresponding dc on Rnd 42] 5 times, sc in each of next 14 sts, trtr2tog (see Note 2 - skip st behind trtr2tog), [sc in each of next 6 sts, trtr2tog (skip st behind trtr2tog)] twice, sc in each of next 13 sts, [FPtr around corresponding dc on Rnd 42, hdc in next st] 5 times, FPtr2tog (using next 2 corresponding tr on Rnd 42), skip next 3 sts, [hdc in next st, FPtr around

corresponding tr on Rnd 42] 6 times, hdc in next st, FPhdc around each of next 2 sts, FPtr around corresponding bobble on Rnd 42, hdc in each of next 2 sts, (hdc, ch 2, hdc) in corner ch-2 sp; repeat from * around, omitting last corner on final repeat; join with sl st in first hdc. (39 sc, 32 hdc, 4 FPhdc, 24 FPtr, 2 FPtr2tog & 3 trtr2tog across each side & 4 corner ch-2 sps) Fasten off and weave in all ends.

Note: The dc4-bob is worked in both loops.

Round 45: Working in BLO, join Color B with standing dtr in any corner ch-3 sp on Rnd 42 (between the center 2 hdc of Rnd 43 already there), *(dc, ch 2, dc) in corner ch-2 sp, dtr in same corner ch-3 sp on Rnd 42 (between the center 2 hdc), dc in each of next 2 sts, ch 1, skip next st, dc4-bob in next st, ch 1, skip next st, dc in each of next 14 sts, ch 1, skip next st, dc4-bob between the legs of FPtr2tog, ch 1, skip next st, dc in each of next 9 sts, hdc in each of next 4 sts, sc in each of next 10 sts, [dc4-bob between the legs of trtr2tog, sc in each of next 6 sts] 3 times, sc in each of next 3 sts, hdc in each of next 4 sts, dc in each of next 9 sts, ch 1, skip next st, dc4-bob between the legs of FPtr2tog, ch 1, skip next st, dc in each of next 13 sts, ch 1, skip next st, dc4-bob in next st, ch 1, skip next st, dc in each of next 2 sts, dtr in corresponding corner ch-3 sp on Rnd 42 (between the center 2 hdc); repeat from * around, omitting last dtr on final repeat; join with sl st in first dtr. (31 sc, 8 hdc, 51 dc, 2 dtr, 7 bobbles & 8 ch-1 sps across each side & 4 corner ch-2 sps) Fasten off and weave in all ends.

Round 46: Working in BLO, join Color E with standing dc in any corner ch-2 sp, (dc, ch 2, 2 dc) in same sp, *dc in each of next 4 sts, dc in next ch-1 sp, FPdc around next dc4-bob, dc in next ch-1 sp, dc in each of next 14 sts, dc in next ch-1 sp, FPdc around next dc4-bob, dc in next ch-1 sp, dc in each of next 23 sts, [FPdc around next dc4-bob, dc in each of next 6 sts] 3 times, dc in each of next 16 sts, dc in next ch-1 sp, FPdc around next dc4-bob, dc in next ch-1 sp, dc in each of next 13 sts, dc in next ch-1 sp, FPdc around next dc4-bob, dc in next ch-1 sp, dc in each of last 4 sts, (2 dc, ch 2, 2 dc) in next corner ch-2 sp; repeat from * around, omitting last corner on final repeat; join with sl st in first dc. (104 dc & 7 FPdc across each side & 4 corner ch-2 sps) Fasten off and weave in all ends.

Round 47: Join Color D with standing dc in any corner ch-2 sp, (dc, ch 2, 2 dc) in same sp, *BPdc in each of next 111 sts, (2 dc, ch 2, 2 dc) in next corner ch-2 sp; repeat from * around, omitting last corner on final repeat; join with sl st in first dc. (4 dc & 111 BPdc across each side & 4 corner ch-2 sps) Fasten off and weave in all ends.

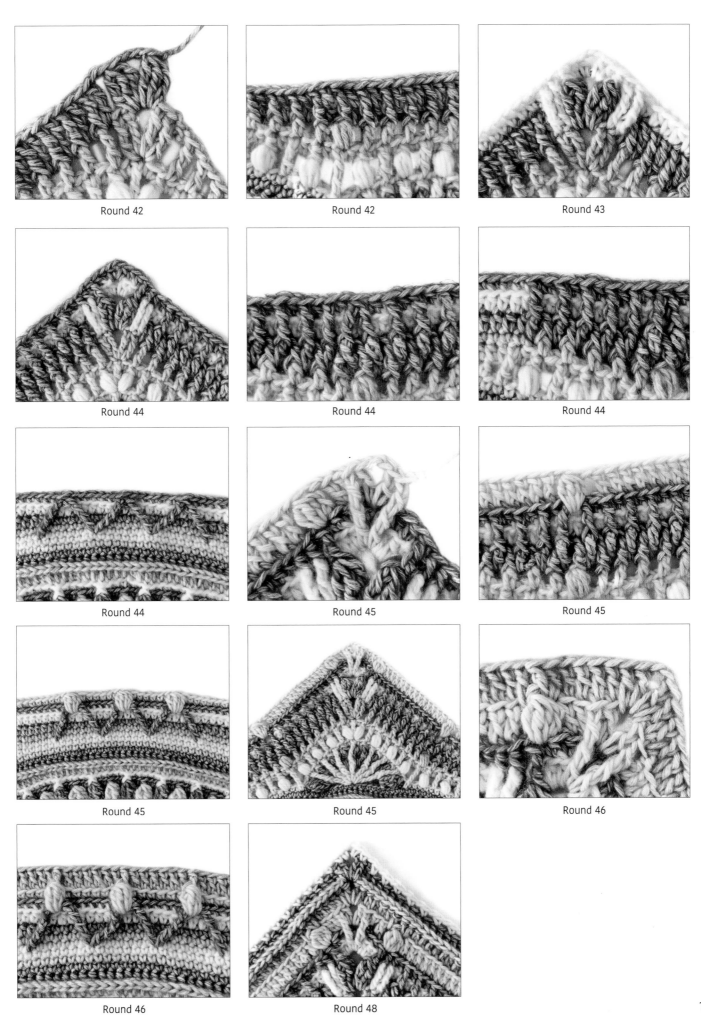

Round 42

Round 42

Round 43

Round 44

Round 44

Round 44

Round 44

Round 45

Round 45

Round 45

Round 45

Round 46

Round 46

Round 48

Round 48: Join Color A with standing sc in any corner ch-2 sp, ch 2, sc in same sp, *sc in next st, [ch 1, skip next st, sc in next st] across to next corner, (sc, ch 2, sc) in next corner ch-2 sp; repeat from * around, omitting last corner on final repeat; join with sl st in first sc. (60 sc & 57 ch-1 sps across each side & 4 corner ch-2 sps) Fasten off and weave in all ends.

Round 49 - 56: Repeat Round 48, with the following color changes (each Round has 4 corner ch-2 sps):
Color C - (61 sc & 58 ch-1 sps across each side)
Color B - (62 sc & 59 ch-1 sps across each side)
Color E - (63 sc & 60 ch-1 sps across each side)
Color A - (64 sc & 61 ch-1 sps across each side)
Color D - (65 sc & 62 ch-1 sps across each side)
Color B - (66 sc & 63 ch-1 sps across each side)
Color C - (67 sc & 64 ch-1 sps across each side)
Color A - (68 sc & 65 ch-1 sps across each side)

Round 57: Join Color E with standing dc in any corner ch-2 sp, (dc, ch 2, 2 dc) in same sp, *dc in each of next 2 sts, [dc in next ch-1 sp, dc in next st] across to next corner, dc in last st, (2 dc, ch 2, 2 dc) in next corner ch-2 sp; repeat from * around, omitting last corner on final repeat; join with sl st in first dc. (137 dc across each side & 4 corner ch-2 sps)
Fasten off and weave in all ends.

Round 58: Join Color D with standing dc in any corner ch-2 sp, (dc, ch 2, 2 dc) in same sp, *BPdc around each st across to next corner, (2 dc, ch 2, 2 dc) in next corner ch-2 sp; repeat from * around, omitting last corner on final repeat; join with sl st in first dc. (4 dc & 137 BPdc across each side & 4 corner ch-2 sps) Fasten off and weave in all ends.

Round 59: Join Color A with standing hdc in any corner ch-2 sp, (hdc, ch 2, 2 hdc) in same sp, *hdc in each st across to next corner, (2 hdc, ch 2, 2 hdc) in next corner ch-2 sp; repeat from * around, omitting last corner on final repeat; join with sl st in first hdc. (145 hdc across each side & 4 corner ch-2 sps) Fasten off and weave in all ends.

Round 60: Working in BLO, join Color C with standing sc in any corner ch-2 sp, ch 2, sc in same sp, *sc in each of next 2 sts, FPtr around corresponding first corner st on Rnd 58, [sc in next st] across to last 3 sts before corner, FPtr around corresponding last corner st on Rnd 58, sc in each of last 2 sts, (sc, ch 2, sc) in corner ch-2 sp; repeat from * around, omitting last corner on final repeat; join with sl st in first sc. (145 sc & 2 FPtr across each side & 4 corner ch-2 sps) Fasten off and weave in all ends.

Note: The dc4-bob is worked in both loops.

Round 61: Working in BLO, join Color B with standing dc in any corner ch-2 sp, (dc, ch 2, 2 dc) in same sp, *skip next (hidden) st, dc in each of next 2 sts, FPdc4-bob around post of next FPtr, skip st behind dc4-bob, dc in each of next 21 sts, [ch 1, skip next st, dc in each of next 5 sts] 17 times, dc in each of next 16 sts, FP4dc-bob around post of next FPtr, skip st behind dc4-bob, dc in each of next 3 sts, (2 dc, ch 2, 2 dc) in next corner ch-2 sp; repeat from * around, omitting last corner on final repeat; join with sl st in first dc. (131 dc, 2 bobbles & 17 ch-1 sps across each side & 4 corner ch-2 sps) Fasten off and weave in all ends.

Note: The tr is worked in both loops of corresponding skipped st on Rnd 60, in front of the ch-1 sp.

Round 62: Working in BLO, join Color C with standing sc in any corner ch-2 sp, ch 2, sc in same sp, *sc in each of next 4 sts, FPsc around dc4-bob, sc in each of next 21 sts, [tr in skipped st on Rnd 60, sc in each of next 5 sts] 17 times, sc in each of next 16 sts, FPsc around next dc4-bob, sc in each of next 5 sts, (sc, ch 2, sc) in next corner ch-2 sp; repeat from * around, omitting last corner on final repeat; join with sl st in first sc. (133 sc, 17 tr & 2 FPsc across each side & 4 corner ch-2 sps) Fasten off and weave in all ends.

Note: The puff-sts are worked in both loops of the FPsc.

Round 63: Working in BLO, join Color E with standing dc in any corner ch-2 sp, (dc, ch 2, 2 dc) in same sp, *dc in each of next 3 sts, ch 1, skip next 2 sts, (puff-st, ch 2, puff-st) in next st, ch 1, skip next 2 sts, dc in each of next 18 sts, ch 1, FPtr4-bob around post of next tr, ch 1, skip 3 sts (behind bobble), [dc in each of next 9 sts (5th dc is in tr), ch 1, FPtr4-bob around post of next tr, ch 1, skip 3 sts (behind bobble)] 8 times, dc in each of next 18 sts, ch 1, skip next 2 sts, (puff-st, ch 2, puff-st) in next st, ch 1, skip next 2 sts, dc in each of next 4 sts, (2 dc, ch 2, 2 dc) in next corner ch-2 sp; repeat from * around, omitting last corner on final repeat; join with sl st in first dc. (119 dc, 9 bobbles, 4 puff-sts, 2 ch-2 sps & 22 ch-1 sps across each side & 4 corner ch-2 sps) Fasten off and weave in all ends.

Round 57

Round 62

Round 62

Round 63

Round 63

Note: The tr-sts on either side of the (puff-st, ch 2, puff-st) are worked in front of the ch-1 sps, in both loops of the skipped sts before and after the FPsc on Rnd 62.

Round 64: Working in BLO, join Color C with standing sc in any corner ch-2 sp, ch 2, sc in same sp, *sc in each of next 5 sts, tr in first skipped st on Rnd 62, FPsc around next puff-st, 2 sc in next ch-2 sp, FPsc around next puff-st, tr in last skipped st on Rnd 62, sc in each of next 18 sts, sc in next ch-1 sp, FPsc around next tr4-bob, sc in next ch-1 sp, [sc in each of next 4 sts, FPtr around corresponding tr on Rnd 62, sc in each of next 4 sts, sc in next ch-1 sp, FPsc around next tr4-bob, sc in next ch-1 sp] 8 times, sc in each of next 18 sts, tr in first skipped st on Rnd 62, FPsc around next puff-st, 2 sc in next ch-2 sp, FPsc around next puff-st, tr in last skipped st on Rnd 62, sc in each of next 6 sts, (sc, ch 2, sc) in corner ch-2 sp; repeat from * around, omitting last corner on final repeat; join with sl st in first sc. (135 sc, 4 tr, 13 FPsc & 8 FPtr across each side & 4 corner ch-2 sps) Fasten off and weave in all ends.

Note: The puff-sts are worked in both loops.

Round 65: Working in BLO, join Color B with standing dc in any corner ch-2 sp, (dc, ch 2, 2 dc) in same sp, *dc in each of next 3 sts, FPtrtr around corner sc on Rnd 62, dc in each of next 4 sts, dc3-bob in ch-2 sp on Rnd 63 (working over the 2-sc already there), dc in each of next 2 sts, ch 1, skip next 2 sts, (puff-st, ch 2, puff-st) in next st, ch 1, skip next 2 sts, dc in each of next 19 sts, ch 1, FPtr4-bob around post of next FPtr, ch 1, skip 3 sts (behind bobble), [dc in each of next 9 sts (5th dc in FPsc), ch 1, FPtr4-bob around post of next FPtr, ch 1, skip 3 sts (behind bobble)] 7 times, dc in each of next 19 sts, ch 1, skip next 2 sts, (puff-st, ch 2, puff-st) in next st, ch 1, skip next 2 sts, dc in each of next 2 sts, dc3-bob in ch-2 sp on Rnd 63 (working over the 2-sc already there) , dc in each of next 5 sts, FPtrtr around corner sc on Rnd 62, dc in each of next 3 sts, (2 dc, ch 2, 2 dc) in next corner ch-2 sp;

repeat from * around, omitting last corner on final repeat; join with sl st in first dc. (124 dc, 2 dc-bobbles, 8 tr-bobbles, 2 FPtrtr, 4 puff-sts, 2 ch-2 sps & 20 ch-1 sps across each side & 4 corner ch-2 sps) Fasten off and weave in all ends.

Note: The tr-sts on either side of the (puff-st, ch 2, puff-st) are worked in front of the ch-1 sps, in both loops of the skipped sts before and after the FPsc on Rnd 64.

Round 66: Working in BLO, join Color C with standing sc in any corner ch-2 sp, ch 2, sc in same sp, *sc in each of next 5 sts, FPsc around next st (FPtrtr), sc in each of next 4 sts, FPsc around next st (dc3-bob), sc in each of next 2 sts, tr in first skipped st on Rnd 64, FPsc around next puff-st, sc in next ch-2 sp, FPsc around next puff-st, tr in last skipped st on Rnd 64, sc in each of next 19 sts, sc in next ch-1 sp, FPsc around next st (tr4-bob), sc in next ch-1 sp, [sc in each of next 9 sts, sc in next ch-1 sp, FPsc around next st (tr4-bob), sc in next ch-1 sp] 8 times, sc in each of next 19 sts, tr in first skipped st on Rnd 64, FPsc around next puff-st, sc in next ch-2 sp, FPsc around next puff-st, tr in last skipped st on Rnd 64, sc in each of next 2 sts, FPsc around next st (dc3-bob), sc in each of next 4 sts, FPsc around next st (FPtrtr), sc in each of next 5 sts, (sc, ch 2, sc) in corner ch-2 sp; repeat from * around, omitting last corner on final repeat; join with sl st in first sc. (146 sc, 4 tr & 16 FPsc across each side & 4 corner ch-2 sps) Fasten off and weave in all ends.

Note: The puff-sts are worked in both loops.

Round 67: Working in BLO, join Color A with standing hdc in any corner ch-2 sp, (hdc, ch 2, 2 hdc) in same sp, *hdc in each of next 6 sts, puff-st in next st (FPsc), hdc in each of next 150 sts, puff-st in next st (FPsc), hdc in each of next 6 sts, (2 hdc, ch 2, 2 hdc) in next corner ch-2 sp; repeat from * around, omitting last corner on final repeat; join with sl st in first hdc. (166 hdc & 2 puff-sts across each side & 4 corner ch-2 sps) Fasten off and weave in all ends.

Round 64

Round 65

Round 65

Round 66

Round 67

Round 68: Working in BLO, join Color E with standing dc in any corner ch-2 sp, (dc, ch 2, 2 dc) in same sp, *dc in each of next 8 sts, FPdc around next puff-st, dc in each of next 150 sts, FPdc around next puff-st, dc in each of next 8 sts, (2 dc, ch 2, 2 dc) in next corner ch-2 sp; repeat from * around, omitting last corner on final repeat; join with sl st in first dc. (170 dc & 2 FPdc across each side & 4 corner ch-2 sps) Fasten off and weave in all ends.

Round 69: Join Color D with standing dc in any corner ch-2 sp, (dc, ch 2, 2 dc) in same sp, *BPdc around each of next 172 sts, (2 dc, ch 2, 2 dc) in next corner ch-2 sp; repeat from * around, omitting last corner on final repeat; join with sl st in first dc. (4 dc & 172 BPdc across each side & 4 corner ch-2 sps) Fasten off and weave in all ends.

Round 70: Join Color B with standing sc in any corner ch-2 sp, ch 2, sc in same sp, *sc in next st, [ch 1, skip next st, sc in next st] across to last st before next corner, ch 1, skip last st, (sc, ch 2, sc) in corner ch-2 sp; repeat from * around, omitting last corner on final repeat; join with sl st in first sc. (90 sc & 88 ch-1 sps across each side & 4 corner ch-2 sps) Fasten off and weave in all ends.

Round 71 - 78: Repeat Round 70, with the following color changes (each Round has 4 corner ch-2 sps):
Color A - (91 sc & 89 ch-1 sps across each side)
Color E - (92 sc & 90 ch-1 sps across each side)
Color C - (93 sc & 91 ch-1 sps across each side)
Color B - (94 sc & 92 ch-1 sps across each side)
Color A - (95 sc & 93 ch-1 sps across each side)
Color E - (96 sc & 94 ch-1 sps across each side)
Color D - (97 sc & 95 ch-1 sps across each side)
Color B - (98 sc & 96 ch-1 sps across each side)

Round 79: Join Color E with standing dc in any corner ch-2 sp, (dc, ch 2, 2 dc) in same sp, *dc in each of next 2 sts, [dc in next ch-1 sp, dc in next st] across to corner, (2 dc, ch 2, 2 dc) in next corner ch-2 sp; repeat from * around, omitting last corner on final repeat; join with sl st in first dc. (198 dc across each side & 4 corner ch-2 sps) Fasten off and weave in all ends.

Round 80: Join Color D with standing dc in any corner ch-2 sp, (dc, ch 2, 2 dc) in same sp, *BPdc around each of next 198 sts, (2 dc, ch 2, 2 dc) in next corner ch-2 sp; repeat from * around, omitting last corner on final repeat; join with sl st in first dc. (4 dc & 198 BPdc across each side & 4 corner ch-2 sps) Fasten off and weave in all ends.

Round 81: Join Color B with standing hdc in any corner ch-2 sp, (hdc, ch 2, 2 hdc) in same sp, *hdc in each st across to corner, (2 hdc, ch 2, 2 hdc) in next corner ch-2 sp; repeat from * around, omitting last corner on final repeat; join with sl st in first hdc. (206 hdc across each side & 4 corner ch-2 sps) Fasten off and weave in all ends.

Round 82: Join Color A with standing dc in any corner ch-2 sp, (dc, ch 2, 2 dc) in same sp, *ch 1, skip next 2 sts, [dc in each of next 2 sts, ch 1, skip next st] 3 times, puff-st in next st, [ch 3, skip next 3 sts, puff-st in next st] 46 times, ch 1, skip next st, [dc in each of next 2 sts, ch 1, skip next st] 3 times, (2 dc, ch 2, 2 dc) in next corner ch-2 sp; repeat from * around, omitting last corner on final repeat; join with sl st in first dc. (16 dc, 47 puff-sts, 46 ch-3 sps & 8 ch-1 sps across each side & 4 corner ch-2 sps) Fasten off and weave in all ends.

Note: The puff-sts are worked in the second (center) skipped st on Rnd 81, in front of the ch-3 sp.

Round 83: Join Color E with standing sc in any corner ch-2 sp, ch 2, sc in same sp, *sc in each of next 2 sts, [ch 1, skip next ch-1 sp, sc in each of next 2 sts] 3 times, ch 3, [puff-st in skipped st on Rnd 81, ch 3] 46 times, sc in each of next 2 sts, [ch 1, skip next ch-1 sp, sc in each of next 2 sts] 3 times, (sc, ch 2, sc) in corner ch-2 sp; repeat from * around, omitting last corner on final repeat; join with sl st in first sc. (18 sc, 46 puff-sts, 47 ch-3 sps & 6 ch-1 sps across each side & 4 corner ch-2 sps) Fasten off and weave in all ends.

Note: The FPdtr2tog are worked in skipped sts on Rnd 81. (Remember to skip the stitch behind the post stitch.)

Round 84: Join Color B with standing sc in any corner ch-2 sp, ch 2, sc in same sp, *sc in each of next 3 sts, sc in next ch-1 sp, sc in next st, FPdtr2tog (using 2nd skipped st (of 2-skipped sts) and next single skipped st on Rnd 81), sc in next ch-1 sp, sc in next st, FPdtr2tog (using same skipped st as last leg of previous FPdtr2tog and next skipped st on Rnd 81), sc in next ch-1 sp, sc in each of next 2 sts, sc in next ch-1 sp on Rnd 82 (working over ch-3 on Rnd 83), sc in same ch-3 sp (Rnd 83), [sc over both ch-3 sps (Rnds 82 & 83), sc in center of ch-3 sp of Rnd 82, sc over both ch-3 sps (Rnds 82 & 83), sc in center of ch-3 sp of Rnd 83] 46 times, sc in next ch-1 sp on Rnd 82 (working over ch-3 on Rnd 83), sc in each of next 2 sts, sc in next ch-1 sp, sc in next st, FPdtr2tog (using 1st and 2nd skipped sts on Rnd 81), sc in next ch-1 sp, sc in next st, FPdtr2tog (using same 2nd skipped st and next skipped st on Rnd 81), sc in next ch-1 sp, sc in each of next 3 sts, (sc, ch 2, sc) in next corner ch-2 sp; repeat from * around, omitting last corner on final repeat; join with sl st in first sc.
(209 sc & 4 FPdtr2tog across each side & 4 corner ch-2 sps) Fasten off and weave in all ends

Round 85: Join Color C with standing sc in any corner ch-2 sp, ch 2, sc in same sp, *sc in each st across to next corner, (sc, ch 2, sc) in next corner ch-2 sp; repeat from * around, omitting last corner on final repeat; join with sl st in first sc. (215 sc across each side & 4 corner ch-2 sps) Fasten off and weave in all ends.

Round 80

Round 82

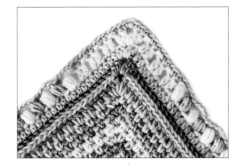

Round 83

Round 84

Round 84

Round 84

Round 86: Working in BLO, join Color E with standing hdc in any corner ch-2 sp, (hdc, ch 2, 2 hdc) in same sp, *hdc in each of next 6 sts, ch 1, dc4-bob around FPdtr2tog (Rnd 84), skip next 2 sts (behind bobble), hdc in each of next 2 sts, dc4-bob around FPdtr2tog (Rnd 84), ch 1, skip next 2 sts (behind bobble), hdc in each of next 192 sts, ch 1, dc4-bob around FPdtr2tog (Rnd 84), skip next 2 sts (behind bobble), hdc in each of next 2 sts, dc4-bob around FPdtr2tog (Rnd 84), ch 1, skip next 2 sts (behind bobble), hdc in each of next 5 sts, (2 hdc, ch 2, 2 hdc) in next corner ch-2 sp; repeat from * around, omitting last corner on final repeat; join with sl st in first hdc. (211 hdc, 4 bobbles & 4 ch-1 sps across each side & 4 corner ch-2 sps) DO NOT FASTEN OFF.

Round 87: Ch 3 (counts as first dc, now and throughout), working in BLO, dc in next st, *(2 dc, ch 2, 2 dc) in next corner ch-2 sp, skip next st, dc in each of next 7 sts, dc in next ch-1 sp, FPdc around next dc4-bob, dc in each of next 2 sts, FPdc around next dc4-bob, dc in next ch-1 sp, [dc in each of next 11 sts, ch 1, skip next st] 15 times, dc in each of next 12 sts, dc in next ch-1 sp, FPdc around next dc4-bob, dc in each of next 2 sts, FPdc around next dc4-bob, dc in next ch-1 sp, dc in each of next 7 sts; repeat from * around, omitting last 2 dc on final repeat; join with sl st in first dc (3rd ch of beg ch-3). (199 dc, 15 ch-1 sps & 4 FPdc across each side & 4 corner ch-2 sps) Fasten off and weave in all ends.

Notes:

1 The FPsc-sts are worked in the FPdc-st from previous round.

2 The bobbles are worked in both loops, and the alternate bobbles are worked behind the ch-1 sps into the skipped stitches on Round 86.

3 Mark the front loop of the 3rd (center) sc on each of the two 5-sc groups (for optional bobble embellishments).

Round 88: Working in BLO, join Color B with standing sc in any corner ch-2 sp, ch 2, sc in same sp, *sc in each of next 2 sts, FPtr around skipped hdc on Rnd 86, sc in next st, FPdtr around 1st sc on Rnd 85, sc in each of next 5 sts, FPsc around next st, sc in each of next 2 sts, FPsc around next st, sc in next st, ch 12, skip next 11 sts, dc5-bob in skipped st on Rnd 86, [ch 7, skip next 5 sts, dc5-bob in next st, ch 7 skip next 5 sts, dc5-bob in next skipped st (Rnd 86)] 14 times, ch 12, skip next 12 sts, sc in next st, FPsc in next st, sc in each of next 2 sts, FPsc in next st, sc in each of next 5 sts, FPdtr around last sc on Rnd 85, sc in next st, FPtr around hdc on Rnd 86, sc in each of next 2 sts, (sc, ch 2, sc) in next corner ch-2 sp; repeat from * around, omitting last corner on final repeat; join with sl st in first sc. (24 sc, 4 FPsc, 2 FPtr, 2 FPdtr, 29 bobbles, 28 ch-7 sps & 2 ch-12 sps across each side & 4 corner ch-2 sps) Fasten off and weave in all ends.

Round 86

Round 87

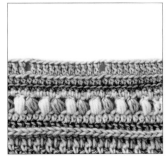

Round 87

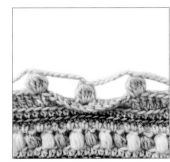

Round 88

Note: The dc-sts are worked in front of the ch-12 & ch-7 loops.

Round 89: Working in BLO, join Color E with standing hdc in any corner ch-2 sp, (hdc, ch 2, 2 hdc) in same sp, *hdc in each of next 16 sts (last st is in sc before ch-12), dc in each of next 11 skipped sts (Rnd 87), FPdc around next dc5-bob (through ch-1 sp, pulling bobble to front), [dc in each of next skipped 5 sts (Rnd 87), ch 1, skip next st (dc5-bob), dc in each of next skipped 5 sts (Rnd 87), FPdc around next dc5-bob (through ch-1 sp, pulling bobble to front)] 14 times, dc in each of next skipped 12 sts (Rnd 87), hdc in each of next 16 sts (first st is in first sc after ch-12), (2 hdc, ch 2, 2 hdc) in next corner ch-2 sp; repeat from * around, omitting last corner on final repeat; join with sl st in first hdc. (35 hdc, 63 dc, 15 FPdc & 14 ch-1 sps across each side & 4 corner ch-2 sps) DO NOT FASTEN OFF.

Round 90: Ch 2 (counts as first hdc, now and throughout), working in BLO, hdc in next st, *(2 hdc, ch 2, 2 hdc) in next corner ch-2 sp, hdc in each of next 35 sts, FPdc around next skipped dc5-bob (through ch-1 sp, pulling bobble to front), [hdc in each of next 11 sts, FPdc around next skipped dc5-bob (through ch-1 sp, pulling bobble to front)] 13 times, hdc in each of next skipped 36 sts; repeat from * around, omitting last 2 sts on final repeat;

join with sl st in first hdc. (217 hdc & 14 FPdc across each side & 4 corner ch-2 sps) Fasten off and weave in all ends.

Round 91: Working in BLO, join Color C with standing sc in any corner ch-2 sp, ch 2, sc in same sp, *skip next st, sc in each of next 3 sts, FPdtr around 1st sc on Rnd 88, sc in each of next 4 sts, FPtrtr around 4th dc on Rnd 87 (between the FPtr & FPdtr of Rnd 88), sc in each of next 8 sts, FPtrtr2tog (using the 2 FPdc sts on Rnd 87), sc in each of 196 sts, FPtrtr2tog (using the 2 FPdc sts on Rnd 87), sc in each of next 8 sts, FPtrtr around 4th last dc on Rnd 87 (between the FPdtr & FPtr of Rnd 88), sc in each of next 4 sts, FPdtr around last sc on Rnd 88, sc in each of next 2 sts, (sc, ch 2, sc) in next corner ch-2 sp; repeat from * around, omitting last corner on final repeat; join with sl st in first sc. (227 sc, 2 FPdtr, 2 FPtrtr & 2 FPtrtr2tog across each side & 4 corner ch-2 sps) Fasten off and weave in all ends.

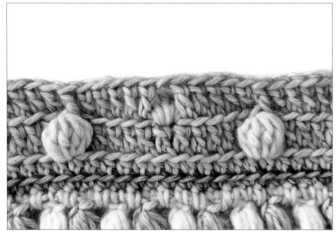
Round 89

Round 90

CHAIN LOOPS (OPTIONAL)

Working in Rnd 88, join Color A with standing FPsc around first dc5-bob, [ch 6, FPsc around next dc5-bob] 28 times. Fasten off and weave in all ends.
Repeat across each side. (29 FPsc & 28 ch-6 sps across each side)

BOBBLE EMBELLISHMENTS (OPTIONAL)

Using Color A, make a standing dc5-bob in both loops of any marked st on Rnd 88. Fasten off and cut yarn. Thread each tail to the back of the blanket and tie them together in a knot, to secure. Weave in ends. Repeat until 8 bobbles are made. (2 bobbles across each side)

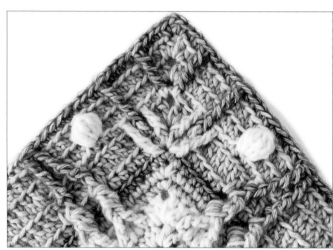

Note: The puff-sts are worked in both loops.

Round 92: Working in BLO, join Color B with standing hdc in any corner ch-2 sp, (hdc, ch 2, 2 hdc) in same sp, *hdc in each of next 3 sts, ch 1, skip next st, puff-st in next st (FPdtr), ch 1, skip next st, hdc in each of next 2 sts, ch 1, skip next st, puff-st in next st (FPtrtr), ch 1, skip next st, hdc in each of next 6 sts, ch 1, skip next st, puff-st in next st (FPtrtr2tog), ch 1, skip next st, hdc in each of next 194 sts, ch 1, skip next st, puff-st in next st (FPtrtr2tog), ch 1, skip next st, hdc in each of next 6 sts, ch 1, skip next st, puff-st in next st (FPtrtr), ch 1, skip next st, hdc in each of next 2 sts, ch 1, skip next st, puff-st in next st (FPdtr), ch 1, skip next st, hdc in each of next 2 sts, (2 hdc, ch 2, 2 hdc) in next corner ch-2 sp; repeat from * around, omitting last corner on final repeat; join with sl st in first hdc. (219 hdc, 6 puff-sts & 12 ch-1 sps across each side & 4 corner ch-2 sps) Fasten off and weave in all ends.

Round 93: Working in BLO, join Color E with standing dc in any corner ch-2 sp, (dc, ch 2, 2 dc) in same sp, *skip next st, dc in each of next 4 sts, dc in next ch-1 sp, FPdc around next puff-st, dc in next ch-1 sp, dc in each of next 2 sts, dc in next ch-1 sp, FPdc around next puff-st, dc in next ch-1 sp, dc in each of next 6 sts, dc in next ch-1 sp, FPdc around next puff-st, dc in next ch-1 sp, dc in each of next 194 sts, dc in next ch-1 sp, FPdc around next puff-st, dc in next ch-1 sp, dc in each of next 6 sts, dc in next ch-1 sp, FPdc around next puff-st, dc in next ch-1 sp, dc in each of next 2 sts, dc in next ch-1 sp, FPdc around next puff-st, dc in next ch-1 sp, dc in each of next 4 sts, (2 dc, ch 2, 2 dc) in next corner ch-2 sp; repeat from * around, omitting last corner on final repeat; join with sl st in first dc. (234 dc & 6 FPdc across each side & 4 corner ch-2 sps) Fasten off and weave in all ends.

Round 94: Join Color D with standing dc in any corner ch-2 sp, (dc, ch 2, 2 dc) in same sp, *BPdc around every st across to next corner, (2 dc, ch 2, 2 dc) in next corner ch-2 sp; repeat from * around, omitting last corner on final repeat; join with sl st in first dc. (4 dc & 240 BPdc across each side & 4 corner ch-2 sps) Fasten off and weave in all ends.

BORDER

Round 1: Join Color B with standing tr2-bob in any corner ch-2 sp, [ch 3, tr2-bob] 4 times in same sp, ♥ch 1, skip next 5 sts, sc in next st, ch 3, skip next 2 sts, sc in next st, skip next 3 sts, (tr2-bob, [ch 3, tr2-bob] twice) in next st, *skip next 3 sts, sc in next st, ch 3, skip next 2 sts, sc in next st, skip next 3 sts, (tr2-bob, [ch 3, tr2-bob] twice) in next st; repeat from * 19 times more, skip next 3 sts, sc in next st, ch 3, skip next 2 sts, sc in next st, ch 1, skip last 4 sts, (tr2-bob, [ch 3, tr2-bob] 4 times) in corner ch-2 sp; repeat from ♥ around, omitting last corner on final repeat; join with sl st in first dc. (44 sc, 21 3-bobble groups & 2 ch-1 sps across each side & 4 corner 5-bobble groups) Fasten off and weave in all ends.

Round 2: Join Color A with standing puff-st in first ch-3 sp of any corner, ch 2, puff-st in same sp, ♥[ch 2, (puff-st, ch 2, puff-st) in next ch-3 sp] 3 times, ch 2, sc in next ch-3 sp (between sc-sts), *[ch 2, (puff-st, ch 2, puff-st) in next ch-3 sp (of puff-st group)] twice, ch 2, sc in next ch-3 sp; repeat from * 20 times more, ch 2, (puff-st, ch 2, puff-st) in next ch-3 sp (of corner puff-st group); repeat from ♥ around, omitting 2 puff-sts on final repeat; join with sl st in first puff-st. (22 sc, 21 4-bobble groups & 44 ch-2 sps across each side & 4 corner 8-bobble groups) Fasten off and weave in all ends.

Note: Work the tr-sts in front of ch-2 sps into the ch-sps on Rnd 1.

Round 3: Join Color D with standing FPsc around first puff-st of any corner group, ♥sc in next ch-2 sp, tr in ch-3 sp on Rnd 1, sc in same ch-2 sp, FPsc around next puff-st, [3 sc in next ch-2 sp, FPsc around next puff-st, sc in next ch-2 sp, tr in ch-3 sp on Rnd 1, sc in same ch-2 sp, FPsc around next puff-st] 3 times, sc in next ch-2 sp, FPsc around next sc, *sc in next ch-2 sp, FPsc around next puff-st, sc in next ch-2 sp, tr in ch-3 sp on Rnd 1, sc in same ch-2 sp, FPsc around next puff-st, 3 sc in next ch-2 sp, FPsc around next puff-st, sc in next ch-2 sp, tr in ch-3 sp on Rnd 1, sc in same ch-2 sp, FPsc around next puff-st, sc in next ch-2 sp, FPsc around next sc; repeat from * 20 times more, sc in next ch-2 sp, FPsc around next first puff-st of next corner; repeat from ♥ around, omitting last FPsc on final repeat; join with sl st in first FPsc. (191 sc, 106 FPsc & 42 tr across each side & in each corner, 17 sc, 8 FPsc & 4 tr) Fasten off and weave in all ends.

Round 4: Working in BLO, join Color C with standing sc in first FPsc on any corner, ♥sc in each of next 5 sts, FPdtr around second tr2-bob on Rnd 1, [sc in each of next 7 sts, FPdtr around next tr2-bob on Rnd 1] twice, sc in each of next 6 sts, FPdtr2tog (around last corner 2tr-bob and first 2tr-bob of next bobble-group on Rnd 1), skip next 3 sts (sc, FPsc & sc - behind FPdtr2tog), sc in each of next 6 sts, FPdtr around next tr2-bob (Rnd 1), sc in each of next 6 sts, *FPdtr2tog (around last 2tr-bob and first 2tr-bob of next bobble-group on Rnd 1), skip next 3 sts, sc in each of next 6 sts, FPdtr around next tr2-bob (Rnd 1), sc in each of next 6 sts; repeat from * 19 times more, FPdtr2tog (around last 2tr-bob and first 2tr-bob of next corner bobble-group on Rnd 1), skip next 3 sts, sc in each of next 6 sts; repeat from ♥ around, omitting last sc on final repeat; join with sl st in first sc. (252 sc, 21 FPdtr & 22 FPdtr2tog across each side & in each corner, 26 sc & 3FPdtr) Fasten off and weave in all ends.

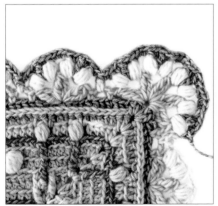

Round 3

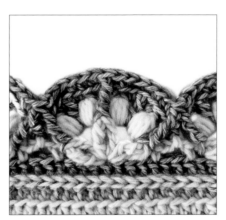

Round 4

Round 4

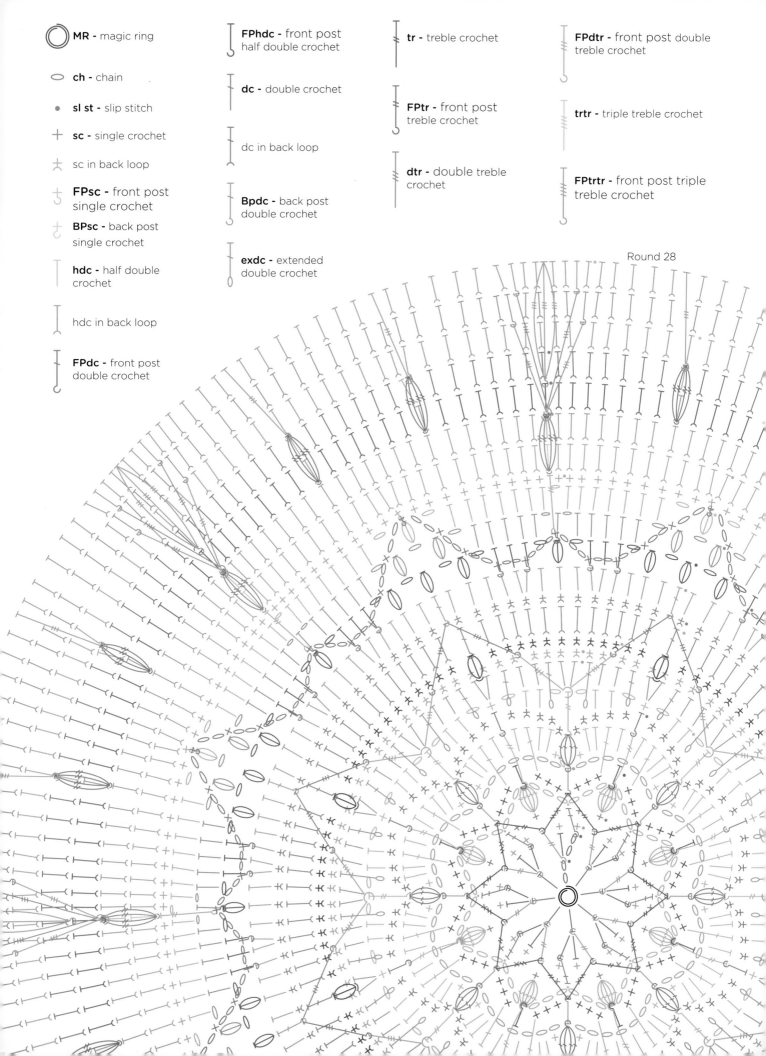

MR - magic ring

ch - chain

sl st - slip stitch

sc - single crochet

sc in back loop

FPsc - front post single crochet

BPsc - back post single crochet

hdc - half double crochet

hdc in back loop

FPdc - front post double crochet

FPhdc - front post half double crochet

dc - double crochet

dc in back loop

Bpdc - back post double crochet

exdc - extended double crochet

tr - treble crochet

FPtr - front post treble crochet

dtr - double treble crochet

FPdtr - front post double treble crochet

trtr - triple treble crochet

FPtrtr - front post triple treble crochet

Round 28

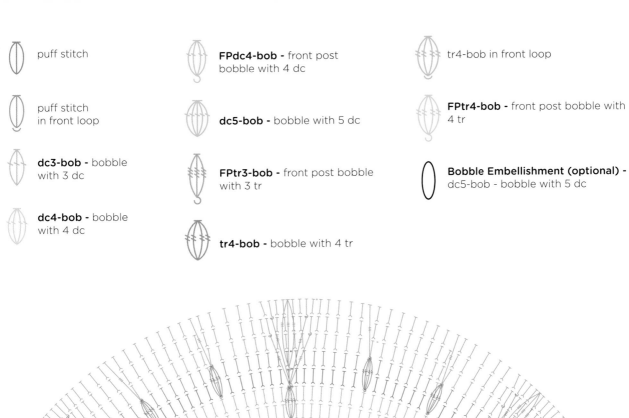

puff stitch

puff stitch in front loop

dc3-bob - bobble with 3 dc

dc4-bob - bobble with 4 dc

FPdc4-bob - front post bobble with 4 dc

dc5-bob - bobble with 5 dc

FPtr3-bob - front post bobble with 3 tr

tr4-bob - bobble with 4 tr

tr4-bob in front loop

FPtr4-bob - front post bobble with 4 tr

Bobble Embellishment (optional) - dc5-bob - bobble with 5 dc

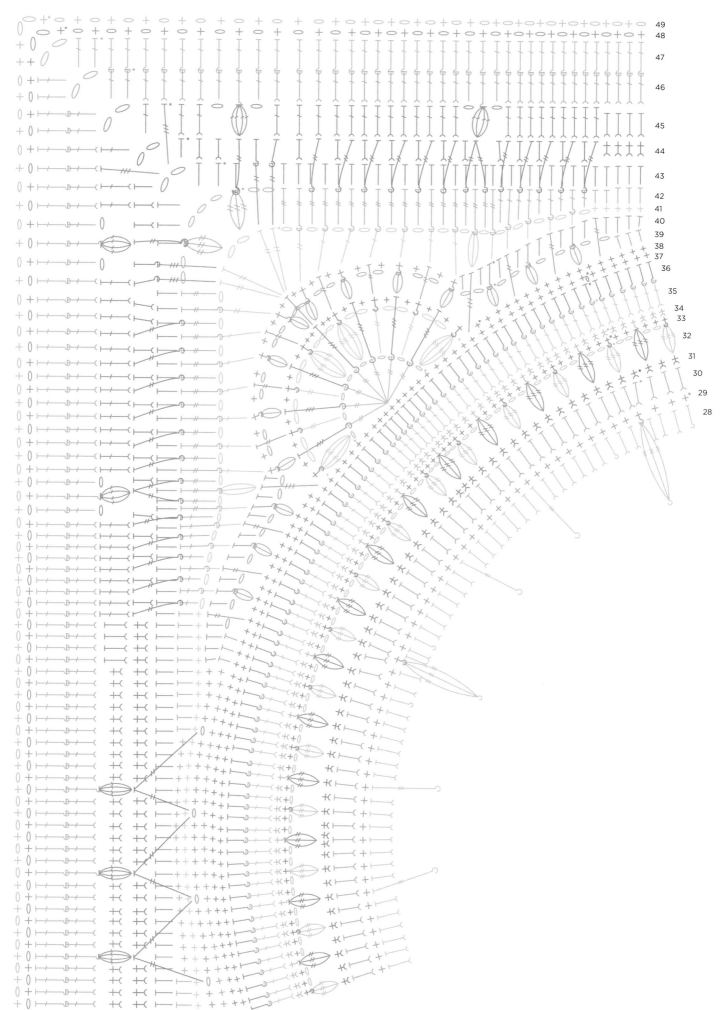

49
48
47
46
45
44
43
42
41
40
39
38
37
36
35
34
33
32
31
30
29
28

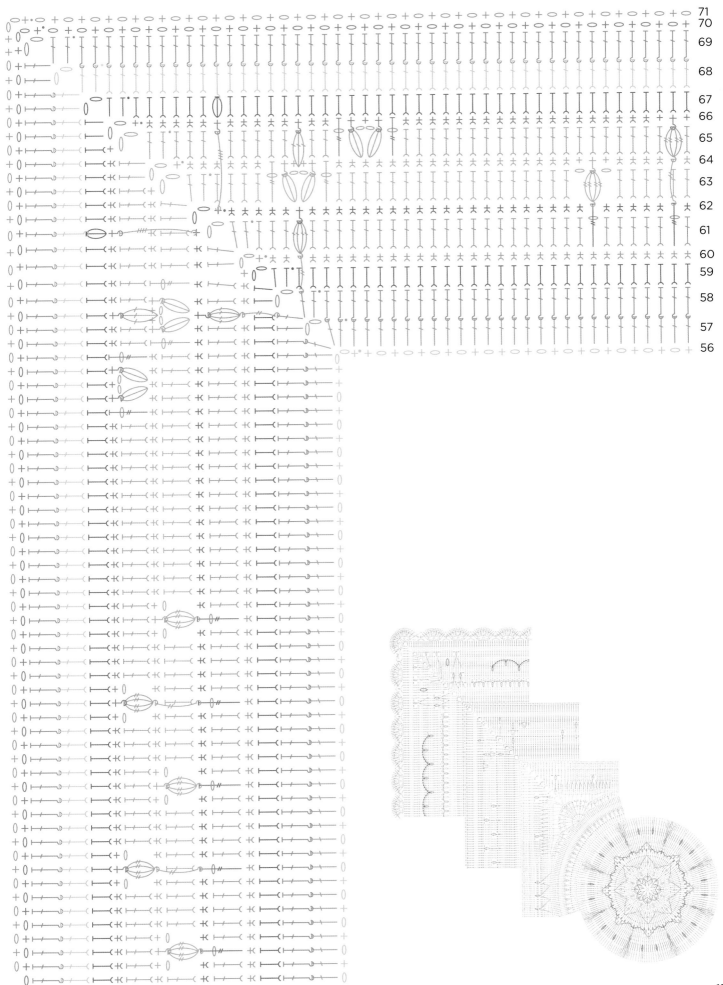

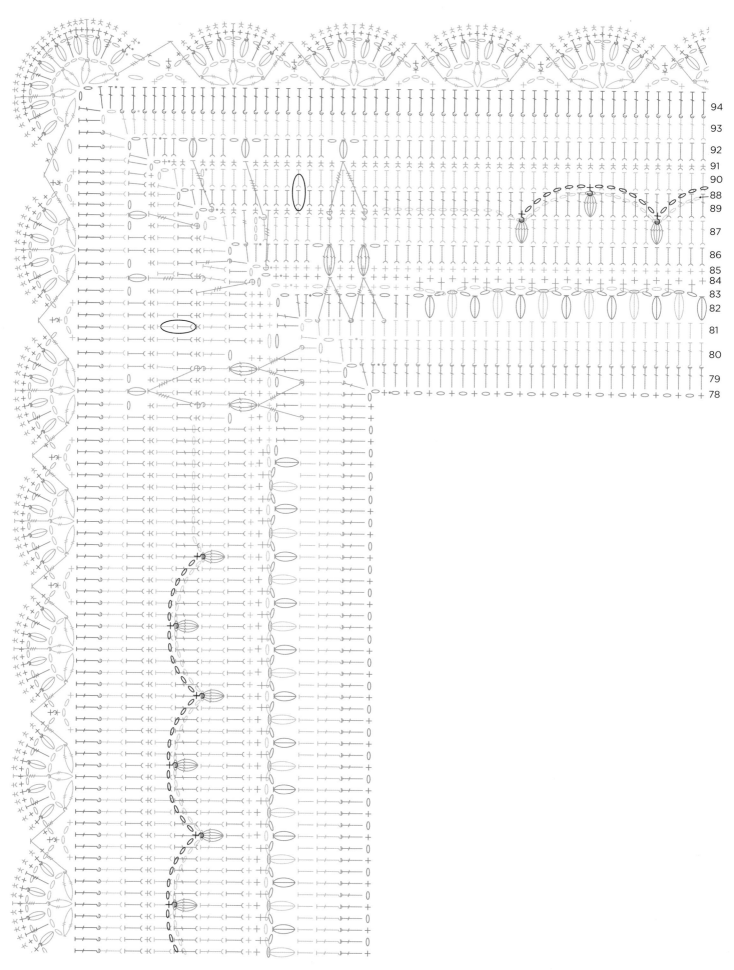

DAIGO-JI GARDEN

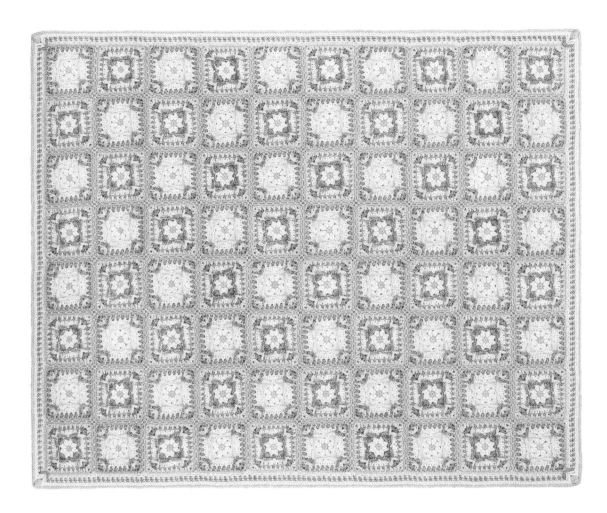

Materials

Scheepjes Stone Washed
Color A: Lemon Quartz (812) - 6 balls
Color B: Moon Stone (801) - 5 balls
Color C: Corundum Ruby (808) - 5 balls
Color D: Rose Quartz (820) - 5 balls

G-6 (4.00 mm) Crochet Hook - for Motifs and Border
#7 (4.50 mm) Crochet Hook - for joining Motifs

Tapestry Needle

Stitch Markers

Size

About 35½" wide by 44½" long (90 cm by 113 cm)

Gauge

Each Motif: About 4" (10 cm) square.

Pattern Notes

❶ Motifs are worked in right-side facing joined rounds. They are joined by crocheting together, on the wrong side.

❷ On the Border, when the stitches differ between the Short and Long sides, the long side numbers will be after the slash. For example: dc in each of next 3/5 sts, means that on the short side, three stitches are worked; and on the long side, five stitches are worked. Similarly, [dc in next st] 6/8 times, means that the instructions within the brackets are repeated 6 times across short sides and 8 times across long sides.

Double Crochet Bobble (with 3 dc) (dc3-bob)

Yarn over, insert hook in stitch or space specified and pull up a loop (3 loops on hook), yarn over, draw through 2 loops on hook (2 loops remain on hook); [yarn over, insert hook in same stich and pull up a loop, yarn over, draw through 2 loops on hook] twice more (4 loops on hook); yarn over, draw through remaining 4 loops.

Treble Bobble (with 3 tr) (tr3-bob)

Yarn over twice, insert hook in stitch or space specified and pull up a loop (4 loops on hook), [yarn over, draw through 2 loops on hook] twice (2 loops remain on hook); *yarn over twice, insert hook in same stich and pull up a loop, [yarn over, draw through 2 loops on hook] twice; repeat from * once more (4 loops on hook); yarn over, draw through remaining 4 loops.

Long Single Crochet (long-sc)

Work a single crochet in the stitch or space of the specifed row or round, pulling up the loop to the height of current row's stitches before drawing through both loops on hook.

Long (or spike) stitches are worked in one or more rows/rounds below the current row into the stitches or spaces specified, creating a vertical "spike".

BLANKET

MOTIFS (MAKE 80 – 40 EACH WITH ALTERNATING COLOR C & COLOR D)

Round 1: (Right Side) Using Color A, make a magic ring; ch 1, 8 hdc in ring; join with sl st in first hdc. (8 hdc) Fasten off and weave in all ends.

Round 2: With right side facing, join Color B with standing dc3-bob between any 2 sts, [ch 2, dc3-bob between next 2 sts] around, ending with ch 2; join with sl st in first bobble. (8 bobble & 8 ch-2 sps) Fasten off and weave in all ends.

Round 3: With right side facing, join Color C/D with standing sc in any ch-2 sp, 2 sc in same sp, *(hdc, dc, 3 tr, dc, hdc) in next ch-2 sp**, 3 sc in next ch-2 sp; repeat from * around, ending at ** on final repeat; join with sl st in first sc. (12 sc, 8 hdc, 8 dc & 12 tr) Fasten off and weave in all ends.

Round 4: With right side facing, join Color B with standing sc in center sc of any 3-sc group, *ch 1, skip next st, BPsc in each of next 7 sts, ch 1, skip next st**, sc in next (center) st; repeat from * around, ending at ** on final repeat; join with sl st in first sc. (28 BPsc, 4 sc & 8 ch-1 sps) DO NOT FASTEN OFF.

Round 5: Ch 2, hdc in same st as joining, *hdc in next ch-1 sp, hdc in each of next 3 sts, (hdc, ch 2, hdc) in next st (corner made), hdc in each of next 3 sts, hdc in next ch-1 sp**, hdc in next st; repeat from * around, ending at ** on final repeat; join with sl st in first hdc. (44 hdc & 4 corner ch-2 sps) Fasten off and weave in all ends.

Round 6: With right side facing, working in BLO, join Color D/C with standing sc in st before any corner ch-2 sp, *ch 3, sl st (through both loops) in center tr (of 3-tr group) on Rnd 3, ch 3, skip next ch-2 sp, sc in next st, [ch 1, skip next st, sc in next st] 5 times; repeat from * around, omitting last sc on final repeat; join with sl st in first sc. (24 sc, 20 ch-1 sps & 8 ch-3 lps) Fasten off and weave in all ends.

Round 7: With right side facing, join Color C/D with standing hdc in any corner ch-2 sp on Rnd 5, (hdc, ch 2, 2 hdc) in same sp (corner made), *[ch 1, skip next st, hdc in skipped st on previous round (working in front of ch-1 sps)], 5 times, ch 1, skip next st**, (2 hdc, ch 2, 2 hdc) in next corner ch-2 sp on Rnd 5; repeat from * around, ending at ** on final repeat; join with sl st in first hdc. (36 hdc, 24 ch-1 sps & 4 corner ch-2 sps) Fasten off and weave in all ends.

Round 3

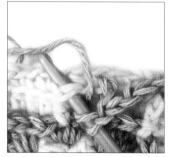
Round 6

Round 7

Round 7

Round 8: With right side facing, join Color D/C with standing hdc in any corner ch-2 sp, ch 2, hdc in same sp, *hdc in next st, ch 1, skip next st, hdc in next ch-1 sp, ch 1, hdc in corresponding skipped sc on Rnd 6 (working in front of ch-1 sps)] 4 times, ch 1, skip next st, hdc in next ch-1 sp, ch 1, skip next st, hdc in next st**, (hdc, ch 2, hdc) in next corner ch-2 sp; repeat from * around, ending at ** on final repeat; join with sl st in first hdc. (40 hdc, 28 ch-1 sps & 4 corner ch-2 sps) Fasten off and weave in all ends.

Round 9: With right side facing, join Color A with standing sc in any corner ch-2 sp, (hdc, sc) in same sp, *skip next (hidden) st, [sc in next st, long-sc in corresponding skipped st on Rnd 7] 7 times, sc in each of next 2 sts**, (sc, hdc, sc) in next corner ch-2 sp; repeat from * around, ending at ** on final repeat; join with sl st in first sc. (44 sc, 28 long-sc & 4 corner hdc-sts) Fasten off and weave in all ends.

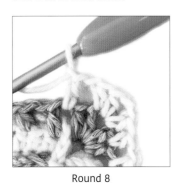
Round 8

Round 8

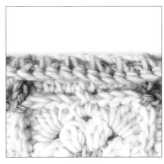
Round 9

Round 9

JOINING MOTIFS

HORIZONTAL JOIN

Alternating Colors C & D, lay out the motifs (with right side facing) in an 8 by 10 grid.

Using Color A and larger hook, working from right to left across chart, hold 2 Motifs (one from each row) with wrong sides facing (right sides together), working through both thicknesses, starting with a standing sc in corner hdc, *ch 1, skip next st, sc in next st (image 1), [ch 2, skip next 2 sts, sc in next st] 5 times, ch 1, skip next st, sc in next (corner) hdc (image 2)**, ch 1 (connecting ch), holding next 2 Motifs together, sc in first corner hdc (image 3); repeat from * across row ending at ** on final repeat

Repeat Horizontal Join until all Motifs are connected horizontally.

Image 1

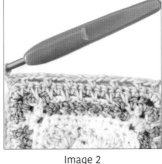
Image 2

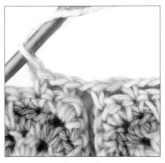
Image 3

VERTICAL JOIN

Working from top to bottom across chart, follow the Horizontal Join method, with the connecting chain going over the horizontal connecting chain.

Repeat until all Motifs are connected vertically.

BORDER

Round 1: With right side of Blanket facing, using smaller hook, working in back loops only, join Color B with standing sc in any corner hdc, ch 2, sc in same st (corner made), *sc in each of next 19 sts, hdc in join (see photo below), [sc in each of next 20 sts, hdc in join] 6/8 times, sc in each of next 19 sts**, (sc, ch 2, sc) in next corner hdc; repeat from * around, ending at ** on final repeat; join with sl st in first sc. (160 sc & 7 hdc across short sides, 200 sc & 9 hdc across long sides & 4 corner ch-2 sps) Fasten off and weave in all ends.

Round 2: With right side facing, join Color D with standing sc in any corner ch-2 sp, ch 2, sc in same sp, *ch 1, skip next st, [sc in next st, ch 1, skip next st] across to next corner**, (sc, ch 2, sc) in next corner ch-2 sp; repeat from * around, ending at ** on final repeat; join with sl st in first sc. (85 sc & 84 ch-1 sps across short sides, 106 sc & 105 ch-1 sps across long sides & 4 corner ch-2 sps) Fasten off and weave in all ends.

Round 3: With right side facing, join Color C with standing sc in 2ⁿᵈ ch-1 sp before any corner, *ch 1, FPtr around corner hdc (on last round of Motif), ch 1, skip next 3 sts (sc, ch-1 sp & last sc before corner), (sc, ch 2, sc) in corner ch-2 sp, ch 1, FPtr around same hdc (on last round of Motif), ch 1, skip next 3 sts (sc, ch-1 & sc), sc in next ch-1 sp, [ch 1, skip next st, sc in next ch-1 sp] across to last 3 sts; repeat from * around, omitting last sc on final repeat; join with sl st in first sc. (84 sc, 85 ch-1 sps & 2 FPtr across short sides, 105 sc, 106 ch-1 sps & 2 FPtr across long sides & 4 corner ch-2 sps) Fasten off and weave in all ends.

Round 4: With right side facing, join Color D with standing sc in any corner ch-2 sp, ch 2, sc in same sp, *ch 1, tr in corner hdc (on last round of Motif), ch 1, skip next 3 st (sc, ch-1 sp & FPtr), sc in next ch-1 sp, ch 1, skip next st, sc in next ch-1 sp] across to last 3 sts, ch 1, tr in corner hdc (on last round of Motif), ch 1, skip next 3 st (sc, ch-1 sp & FPtr)**, (sc, ch 2, sc) in next corner ch-2 sp; repeat from * around, ending at ** on final repeat; join with sl st in first sc. (85 sc, 86 ch-1 sps & 2 tr across short sides, 106 sc, 107 ch-1 sps & 2 tr across long sides & 4 corner ch-2 sps) Fasten off and weave in all ends.

Round 5: With right side facing, join Color B with standing sc in any corner ch-2 sp, ch 2, sc in same sp, *sc in next st, tr in corner ch-2 sp on Rnd 1, skip next ch-1 sp, sc in next tr, [sc in next st, sc in next ch-1 sp] across to last ch-1 sp, tr in corner ch-2 sp on Rnd 1, skip last ch-sp, sc in last st** (sc, ch 2, sc) in next corner ch-2 sp; repeat from * around, ending at ** on final repeat; join with sl st in first sc. (173 sc & 2 tr across short sides, 215 sc & 2 tr across long sides & 4 corner ch-2 sps) Fasten off and weave in all ends.

Round 6: With right side facing, working in BLO, join Color A with standing sc in any corner ch-2 sp, tr3-bob in corner ch-2 sp on Rnd 3, sc in same current corner sp, *[sc in next st] across to corner, (sc, tr3-bob in corner ch-2 sp on Rnd 3, sc) in next corner ch-2 sp; repeat from * around, ending at ** on final repeat; join with sl st in first sc. (177 sc across short sides, 219 sc across long sides & 4 corner bobbles) Fasten off and weave in all ends.

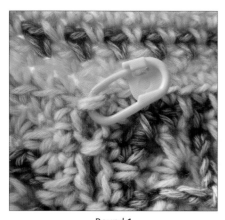

Round 1
Marker showing hdc worked in the loops behind the joining st.

Round 4

Round 6

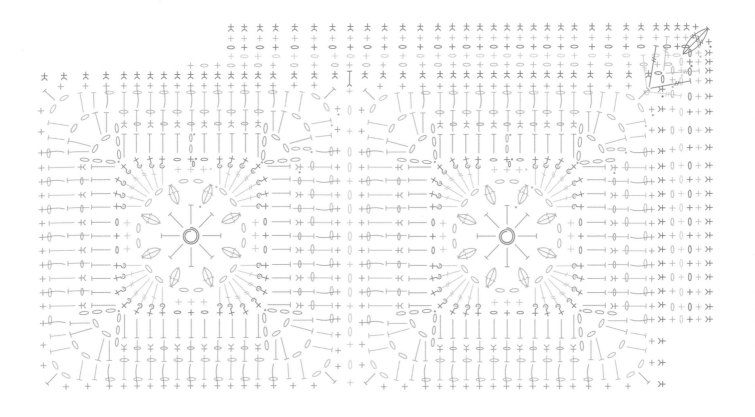

 MR - magic ring

ch - chain

sl st - slip stitch

sc - single crochet

sc in back loop

BPsc - front post single crochet

long sc

hdc - half double crochet

hdc in back loop

dc - double crochet

tr - treble crochet

FPtr - front post treble crochet

3-dc bobble

3-tr bobble